CONQUESTS, CATASTROPHE AND RECOVERY

John Gillingham is Emeritus Professor of History at the London School of Economics and Political Science and a Fellow of the British Academy. His books include *Richard I*, *The English in the Twelfth Century: Imperialism, National Identity and Political Values*, *The Angevin Empire* and *The War of the Roses: Peace and Conflict in Fifteenth-Century England*.

JOHN GILLINGHAM

Conquests, Catastrophe and Recovery

Britain and Ireland 1066–1485

VINTAGE BOOKS
London

Published by Vintage 2014

2 4 6 8 10 9 7 5 3 1

Copyright © John Gillingham 2014

John Gillingham has asserted his right under the Copyright, Designs
and Patents Act 1988 to be identified as the author of this work

First published in Great Britain in 2014 by
Vintage
Random House, 20 Vauxhall Bridge Road,
London SW1V 2SA

www.vintage-books.co.uk

Addresses for companies within The Random House Group Limited
can be found at: www.randomhouse.co.uk/offices.htm

The Random House Group Limited Reg. No. 954009

A CIP catalogue record for this book
is available from the British Library

ISBN 9780099563242

The Random House Group Limited supports the Forest Stewardship
Council® (FSC®), the leading international forest-certification
organisation. Our books carrying the FSC label are printed on FSC®-
certified paper. FSC is the only forest-certification scheme supported by
the leading environmental organisations, including Greenpeace.
Our paper procurement policy can be found at:
www.randomhouse.co.uk/environment

Printed and bound by Clays Ltd, St Ives plc

For Brenda, Emma and Kate

Contents

List of Illustrations

Every effort has been made to trace and contact all holders of copyright in illustrations. If there are any inadvertent omissions, the publishers will be pleased to correct these at the earliest opportunity.

PREFACE

This book has been many years in the making, and during that time I have incurred very considerable obligations. I am indebted to all those who embarked on the plan to write what was then a newly inclusive approach to the history of Britain and Ireland back in 2004, and especially to Jonathan Clark and James Campbell. Over an even longer period I am indebted to generations of BA History students at the LSE and to those who have contributed to seminars at the Institute of Historical Research in London.

I have benefitted a great deal from the fact that Bruce Campbell, David Carpenter, John Hudson, Jinty Nelson and Susan Reynolds have all read and commented on parts of the text.

If the text as a whole does not show just how long it has been in the making, much of the credit for this is due to David Milner's copy-editing and, especially, to Frances Jessop's crucial help in the final sprint to the tape.

As work on this book came to an end, I learned of the

death of Stephen Pratt, the school teacher who sixty years ago now inspired in me and others a love of history. He will not be forgotten.

INTRODUCTION

These centuries witnessed some of the most famous and dramatic events in the recorded history of Britain and Ireland: the Black Death, the Norman Conquest of England, the murder of Thomas Becket. Measured in the simple terms of loss of life, the Black Death was unquestionably the greatest catastrophe in British and Irish history. In English history, 1066 – from the point of the view of the English ruling elite its worst crisis so far – is the one universally remembered date, so well known that banks advise customers not to choose it as their PIN number. No other occurrence produced so spectacular an upheaval or left so enduring a legacy in the national memory. But other violent developments of these centuries, though less well known to the English, remain deeply embedded in the memories of those whose lands were invaded by the English: Ireland's year of destiny in 1169, the conquest of Wales, the Scottish War of Independence.

Yet other momentous developments of this period have slipped from memory. One of the greatest changes, the dying out of slavery in Britain and Ireland, took place during the twelfth century. It has, however, been forgotten partly because at the time it went very largely unrecorded, and partly because it was followed by serfdom, a condition which in the eyes of many subsequent historians was almost as bad; indeed some historians conflated the two. They were, however, quite distinct. While serfs could in effect be sold, it was as a package which included their families and the ground on which they were tenants; slaves, by contrast, could be separated from their families and bought and sold as individual items. Slaves, moreover, unlike serfs, were often acquired as part of the plunder seized during the raids which made up the terrifying bread and butter routine of war in almost all early human history. The dying out of this form of total war is another of these unnoticed changes in British and Irish history.

To consider more than 400 years of the history of Britain and Ireland in a single short book is quite a tall order. The intention is easily stated: to lay out the ways in which by the end of the period the inhabitants of these islands lived and thought within economic, social, cultural and political contexts quite different from those that had prevailed c.1050. But the attempt to pour several gallons into a pint pot will mean that a great deal is left out. Most readers will have their own views as to the most reprehensible of omissions and misguided of interpretations. In addition to the impossibility of striking a satisfying balance between overlapping types of history – economic, social, religious, cultural and political – there are three major problem areas: the first social, the second chronological, the third national.

First, there will not be enough on ordinary people, and especially not enough on women. As long ago as 1905 the Board of Education regretted that history taught in English schools was 'too much confined to . . . narratives of the doings of great kings and nobles' with the result that there was not enough on 'the life of the people as a whole'.[1] But historians have to make the best they can of the evidence they have. The writings which have survived the centuries best record the doings of men of power, locally as well as nationally, and only very rarely those of the poor, the weak and of women. The reigns of kings do have the advantage of providing a chronological framework which is helpful because it is relatively widely known. I take this to be unproblematic so long as we do not forget the less familiar chronologies of non-political change, often no less radical for being gradual and not always recognised at the time.

In the hope of being able to compose a history which includes lots of people doing the kinds of things that lots of people did, one response has been to rely less on written sources and prioritise instead the rapidly increasing volume of archaeological evidence, itself being subject to increasingly sophisticated scientific analysis. This approach undoubtedly allows us to see past societies in a new light.[*] And is useful for dispelling misconceptions such as the notion that medieval people were much shorter than those of the post-medieval centuries. But much as archaeology can tell us about the physical culture of the past, both the material environment and the medical health of individuals, only words and pictures, above all words, can tell us about thoughts, ideas and emotions. Since one of the fundamental trends of this period is the growing volume, century by century, of surviving written evidence, archaeology becomes less prominent as time flows by.

The surviving words make plain that while much depended

---

[*] For a fine example see Robin Fleming, *Britain after Rome*, London, 2010.

upon matters such as social status and stage of life cycle as well as sheer individuality there were basic inequalities between men and women throughout this period. Very occasionally this turned to women's advantage. The fact that wives were generally seen as being under the control of their husbands sometimes led to them being absolved of responsibility for crimes committed in their presence on the grounds that as wives they could not contradict their husbands. But sometimes words have been used in ways which made women seem less important than in fact they were. The Latin word *homines* and the Old English *manna*, for example, should be translated as 'people', but both are still often translated as 'men'. Indeed as early as the thirteenth century the famous passages in Magna Carta about the rights of the *liber homo* were understood as referring to the rights of the 'free man'. Of course this reflects the fact that the word 'man' has often been taken to include 'woman', but it has also had the subliminal effect of writing women out of history.

Second, overall I have allotted more space to the twelfth and thirteenth centuries than to the fourteenth and fifteenth. In part this imbalance results from the decision to write a history based as far as possible on the words of contemporaries while also making it 'front-loaded' in the sense of giving more weight to early surviving expressions of ideas than to later ones. But it also reflects the widely held view – one I share – that the twelfth century was the 'golden age' of history writing in medieval England.

Third, for many there will be too much on England and not enough on Ireland, Scotland and Wales. Undeniably most previous histories of Britain, and of Britain and Ireland, have been very Anglocentric. This too is in part a reflection of the volume of the surviving evidence, very much greater for

England than for the other three countries. This is particularly the case if we look for a central government, and for the records which it generated and stored; ever since the tenth century England has been an unusually centralised and bureaucratic polity, and in the medieval period was much more so than either France or Germany. But Anglocentric modern histories have also reflected an assumption of English superiority, a belief that the greater the English influence over the three countries of the 'Celtic fringe' the better for all concerned. Aspects of this belief have been influential for a very long time. It was, after all, David Hume, a Scot as well as a great historian, who described the English as 'a civilised nation . . . who have happily established the most perfect and accurate system of liberty that was ever found compatible with government'.[2] I have tried to avoid making this assumption, but it may be that I have failed. And I have undoubtedly felt the weight of that greater bulk of English evidence, in terms of both medieval sources and modern historical writing. In addition I have consciously borne in mind the fact that recent estimates suggest that mid period, c.1300, the population of England was well over four million, perhaps twice as many as the combined populations of Ireland, Scotland and Wales.

Historians are inclined to believe that the more closely the institutions of the past approach those of modern times, the better they were and the more rational the people who lived and worked within them. Medievalists, for example, find it hard not to applaud as they trace the emergence and development of professions such as the law and teaching, both at school and university. There is no historian who can successfully plead not guilty to the charge of writing present-centred history. Indeed since the interests and concerns of her or his own day can lead to the posing of hitherto unasked questions there is something to be said in favour of it. In the eighteenth century Europeans began to write histories about the progress of civilisation and constitutional development. In consequence perceptions of the course of English history took root which remained persuasive for at least 200 years, and which to a large extent still find believers.

In one of the most influential models of developmental thought, Adam Smith maintained that after the hunting and pastoral stages of human development and before the commercial society of his own day came the agricultural stage characterised by what he called 'feudal government'. In the nineteenth century the English constitutional state came to be understood as the outcome of an alliance between the ruling prince and the 'people' against the 'feudal aristocracy'. When such interpretations become so entrenched as to be regarded as basic truths about the past, they have achieved the status of myth. And, as was observed by the authors of 1066 and All That, 'The truth is, of course, that the importance of Myths cannot be exaggerated (bad luck).'[3] For decades now, many historians have questioned the usefulness of the word 'feudal' since it has had, and continues to have, a very wide range of meanings. In general usage it is a term of opprobrium, meaning 'oppressive' or 'primitive', conjuring up images of powerful lords and poor peasants. Historians in the nineteenth and twentieth centuries tried to give it a more precise and technical meaning, but since their more precise definitions depended upon their own varying national or philosophical tradition, these definitions were often confusingly different. Not surprisingly during the last fifty years many historians have called for the abandonment of the term. But even in the twenty-first century it remains in use. Since in English history the concept is often associated with the Norman Conquest, and since the impact of that worst crisis remains highly con-troversial, I have devoted what may seem to be an inordinate amount of space to the myth that the Normans introduced a feudal system.

The most powerful myth remains the developmental notion that the modern was preceded by a period which was necessarily pre-modern and therefore less developed, less sophisticated, indeed 'positively medieval' in the usual sense of that phrase. The English version of this has long placed the beginning of the 'early modern' period in 1485, a date whose potency is reinforced by its chronological closeness to 1492, and so to the myth that Columbus by sailing to the Americas disproved the old idea that the earth was flat. In fact learned people had for centuries known that it was, in Bede's words (written in the early eighth century), 'not round like a shield, but round like a ball'. Britain and Ireland throughout most of the many centuries before the establishment of the Greenwich meridian were felt to lie on the periphery of the known world. Seen in terms of these global perspectives these two islands witnessed little change during this period but, as already indicated, in other respects fundamental changes occurred, and in what follows I try to explore them.

Part I:
Material Cultures

When Duke William of Normandy invaded England in 1066, he intended to conquer a kingdom whose wealth was the envy of its neighbours – Scandinavian, Welsh and Scots, as well as Norman. According to his sycophantic chaplain, William of Poitiers, when Duke William returned to Normandy in 1067, he brought back 'vast quantities of gold and silver, for in its wealth of precious metals this kingdom is much richer than Gaul. Wonderfully rich in grain, it is fabulously rich in gold. It should surely be called the granary of Ceres because of its abundance of corn, and the treasury of Arabia because of its richness in gold.'[1] If the wealth of eleventh-century England fascinated ambitious contemporaries, so too a record of that wealth, in the shape of Domesday Book, has mesmerised modern historians. No other part of early medieval Europe lies as seductively open as that part of the kingdom covered by Domesday Book, the extraordinary document compiled in

1086 on William the Conqueror's orders.* In the words of the
Anglo-Saxon Chronicle:

> he sent his men over all England into every shire and
> had them find out how many hundred hides there were
> in the shire and what land and cattle the king himself
> had in the country, and what dues he ought to have
> annually from the shire. Also he had a record made of
> how much land the archbishops had, and his bishops
> and his abbots and his earls and – though I am going on
> at too great a length about it – what and how much
> every landholder in England had in land and cattle and
> how much money it was worth. So closely did he have
> it investigated that there was not a single hide or virgate
> of land, nor indeed – it is shameful to relate it, though it
> did not seem shameful to him to do – a single ox or cow
> or pig left out and not put down in his record.[2]

Domesday Book stands as a monumental signpost at the
beginning of a series of documents that tell us much about
English society, economy and government. For Ireland,
Scotland and Wales there is neither a Domesday Book nor
anything to match the subsequent richness of English administrative records. This skewed survival of evidence makes it hard
to know whether a historian is exaggerating or minimising
real differences between England and the other three countries.
But crucially important differences there were.

---

* The rulers of the Carolingian Empire had carried out a much more extensive survey
in 843, but only a tiny fragment of it survives.

The physical environment

Geology meant that England contained a much higher proportion of good fertile soil, as opposed to mountain, bog and moor, than Ireland, Wales and Scotland. Climate too was kinder to England. Both during the Medieval Warm Period (from *c.*1050 to *c.*1300), and in the cooler times which followed, it was generally sunnier and warmer in the south than in the north, and drier in the east than in the west. According to William of Malmesbury (writing in the 1120s), conditions in the Vale of Gloucester were so benign that even lazy cultivators were tempted to do a little work because nature repaid them a hundred times over.[3] Almost everywhere in Britain a mixed farming regime prevailed, but in the north and west there was greater dependence on oats, barley and animal husbandry. In the south and east a higher proportion of the land surface was under the plough, and a wider variety of crops, including wheat and legumes, could be successfully grown. Domesday Book records vineyards planted as far north as Ely. Cattle, including draught oxen, were raised everywhere, but in the south and east, sheep were also of vital economic importance, particularly from the eleventh century onwards. The size and long coastlines of Britain and Ireland mean that no place was more than two days' journey from the sea, and hence from the commercial opportunities offered by maritime trade. None the less the south and east of England enjoyed the particular advantage of standing at the northern end of the rich and highly urbanised corridor which stretched down through the Low Countries and the Rhineland as far as northern Italy. Good communications across the Channel and North Sea made for important cultural contacts as well as for profitable trade, and not just trade in luxury products, but sometimes as items in mixed cargoes in foodstuffs as basic as cabbages, onions and leeks.[4]

Throughout Britain and Ireland dependence upon the power of draught animals, oxen and horses, meant that grassland was as vital to the rural economy as arable. Cattle and sheep provided meat, milk, leather, wool, tallow for candles and manure for fields, as well as vellum and parchment for writing. Except for horses and pigs most male farm animals were castrated so that they put on weight. Castrated bullocks – oxen – could pull the heaviest carts; castrated rams – wethers – produced the heaviest fleeces; castrated cockerels – capons – were fattened for the table. Old horses were butchered for dog food, and occasionally also – despite the disapproval of the church – for human consumption. In regions where there was plenty of natural pasture, as in parts of Scotland, Wales, Ireland and northern England, herdsmen practised transhumance, moving to and fro with their livestock and their families between winter and summer pastures – a form of management often indicated by place names with elements such as 'shiel' or 'scale' or (in Welsh) 'hafod'.

In the north and west there was less scope for taking wool to market and in consequence cattle, providing milk, meat and traction, were far more important than sheep. The Irish word for farmer, *bóaire*, means 'lord of cows'. Taken together with archaeological evidence of anything between two thirds and 90 per cent of animal bones from settlement sites being of cattle (and sheep rarely more than 20 per cent), this implies an economy of dairying, and the regular slaughter of male calves. Hence nearly all early Irish manuscripts are calfskin, as opposed to the sheepskin parchment more common elsewhere. Thus the contrasts pointed to – and doubtless exaggerated – by Gerald de Barri, the earliest author (*c.*1190) to describe the economy and society of Ireland and Wales. Ireland, he wrote, was 'more grass than grain' and 'its pastures more productive than its ploughed fields'. As for the Welsh, they 'are used to plenty of meat but not so much to bread . . . They live off their herds, oats, milk, cheese and butter.'[5] Since wheat was used to make white bread (regarded as superior), and, when malted, also produced a high-class ale, the absence of wheat from Gerald's list of Welsh foodstuffs is significant. The Welsh themselves may have shared the view of the Scottish academic John Major, who claimed, in his *Description of Britain* (1521), to prefer bread made with oats to bread made with wheat.[6] Ale, in any case, was generally made from barley or oats; and the evidence suggests that the further north you were, the cheaper the ale. Almost – but not quite – everywhere woodland was an indispensable part of the landscape, providing grazing, timber for building, and fuel for heating and cooking. In a few treeless localities building stone was more accessible than timber (Shetland), and there were others in which peat (Ireland and the far north of Britain) and coal (north-eastern England) were used instead of firewood. Domesday Book measured the extent of woodland in terms of the number of pigs it could support. Unlike other domesticated animals, pigs were kept exclusively as providers of meat; as the only animals whose flesh was regularly preserved (bacon and ham), they had a particular value.

Common to the whole of Britain and Ireland was the fact that rivers were much more important then than now. The use of shallow-draught cargo ships meant that rivers were navigable for trade far above present-day limits. York, for example, remained, as in Viking times, one of the great ports of eastern England. A guide to navigation from English waters to the eastern end of the Mediterranean, composed by the twelfth-century chronicler Roger of Howden, began with the voyage down the Ouse from York.[7] Part of Henry of Huntingdon's glowing assessment of the wealth of Britain in the 1120s was his observation that its cities 'are sited in delightful positions and glitter on the banks of fruitful and very beautiful rivers'.[8] Rivers provided power for watermills. River valleys supplied well-watered meadow land which could be mown to produce hay to feed draught animals through the winter. Rivers were also a source of fish, relatively easily harvested by means of fish traps or weirs – indeed the presence of bypass channels suggests that in some places there were worries about overfishing.[9] Such was the conflict of interests between river traders and fish-harvesters that Magna Carta was to order the removal of fish-weirs throughout England, specifically on the Thames and Medway, an order largely unenforced. Fish such as pike, bream and roach were even more easily harvested in inland fish farms. Artificial fish ponds were constructed in large numbers, especially during the twelfth and thirteenth centuries. Because ecclesiastical sites are unusually well documented, we can see, for instance, that by c.1300 Byland Abbey in Yorkshire had dammed nearby valleys and constructed fish ponds covering an area of one hundred acres. Wetlands such as the Fens also represented an important way of exploiting inland water. Hugh Candidus, a monk of Peterborough, an abbey on an island in the Fens, listed products of the wetlands and their reed beds: wildfowl, fish, straw, hay and thatch, all vital.[10]

Far more than they do today, fish, including shellfish, provided food for all. This may be linked with the church placing greater emphasis on the avoidance of meat. Throughout the year Wednesdays, Fridays and Saturdays were meant to be fish days. A model bishop such as Hugh of Lincoln (d.1200) ate no meat at all. The archaeologically recovered evidence of fish bones – inevitably skewed since not all skeletal remains survive well (lampreys, for example, do not) – suggests that whereas fish caught in rivers and estuaries, especially eels, had previously been the most commonly eaten, from the eleventh century onwards sea fish became much more important, hake caught in western waters, and cod, haddock and herring in eastern waters. Since no place was more than two days' journey by packhorse from sea, fresh marine fish was available everywhere, but at a price, and most sea fish was doubtless either dried, as in the form of stockfish (primarily wind-dried cod), smoked or salted. Coastal marshlands were a source of sea salt. Herring, which in the eleventh century was still upper-class fare, moved to being by far the cheapest salted fish in the later Middle Ages when massive herring shoals off East Anglia brought prosperity to Great Yarmouth.[11] By the late fifteenth century a Venetian visitor was surprised by what he saw as the English preference for sea fish despite the abundance of freshwater fish.[12]

Three zones

The developments of this period suggest not so much a division of Britain into two economic zones (highland and lowland) as a division of Britain and Ireland into three. The first zone lay in the rich kingdom that William conquered. Domesday Book records the existence of 112 towns and another thirty-nine places where markets were held. In about forty of those towns coins were minted. In the eyes of a would-be ruler, among England's assets was a system of national taxation. All the towns and markets lay south and east of a line drawn from York to Exeter via Chester and Gloucester.

In Britain north and west of this line only Durham could be considered a town – defined here as a permanent concentration of at least a few hundred people, many following a variety of non-agricultural occupations. There were also a few Viking port-towns on river estuaries in Ireland: Waterford, Wexford, Cork, Limerick and, above all, Dublin, where indeed coins had been minted *c.*1000. But when William conquered England, it looks as though there were no towns in Scotland and Wales, and there were certainly no Scottish or Welsh rulers minting their own coin.

In the twelfth and thirteenth centuries a tide of economic and commercial expansion swept into northern England, Wales, Ireland and Scotland, transforming many regions. By 1300 there were some seventy-five towns in Wales, more than fifty in Ireland, and about sixty burghs in Scotland. As a result of the English conquest of Wales and invasion of Ireland, coin issued by the kings of England circulated in both those countries; in the 1130s the kings of Scots began to mint coin of their own. This was zone two. But in zone three it looks as though material conditions remained much as in the Iron Age. In parts of the far west of Ireland, towns and markets were conspicuous by their absence. In late medieval Scotland there were still no burghs north and west of a line from Cromarty to Kintyre. According to the thirteenth-century *Chronicle of the Kings of Man and the Isles*, the inhabitants of the Isle of Lewis lived 'mostly by hunting and fishing for the land is mountainous and rocky, almost all of it unfit for tillage'.[13]

Since most of this section will be about developments in zones one and two, it is worth staying for a moment in the third zone. The *Orkneyinga Saga* describes the hands-on economy of one of the lords of Orkney, Svein Asleifarson of Gairsay:

In the spring he was busy, with a great deal of seed to sow which he saw to carefully himself. That done, he would go off plundering in the Hebrides and Ireland on what he called the 'spring trip'. He returned home just after midsummer, staying until the fields had been reaped and the grain safely in. Then he was away raiding again until after the end of the first month of winter. This he called the 'autumn trip'.[14]

In territories such as these, the resources of lords were measured in numbers of men, not in money income or extent of land. Thus to his list of Highlanders arrested by the Scottish king in 1428, Walter Bower added the number of their followers; Alexander Macruarie of Gamoran, for example, was 'chief of a thousand'.[15] The fourteenth-century Scottish historian John Fordun contrasted the inhabitants of the second and third zones:

The people of the Lowlands speak English; those who live in the Highlands and Outer isles speak Gaelic. The lowlanders are home-loving, civilised, trustworthy, tolerant and polite, dress decently and are affable and pious. The islanders and highlanders are a wild untamed people, primitive and proud, given to plunder and the easy life, clever and quick to learn, handsome in appearance but slovenly in dress.[16]

None the less when the Italian Aeneas Sylvius Piccolomini travelled south from Scotland in 1435, it was not until he reached Newcastle that he felt he was once again in a civilised country.[17]

A similarly condescending view was taken of Gaelic

societies in Ireland. When Raymond of Perelhos (in the Pyrenees) went on a pilgrimage to St Patrick's Purgatory (in Loch Derg in Donegal) in 1397, he described a warrior society of impoverished herders, living in close contact with their cattle and horses. They didn't eat bread or drink wine; instead they ate beef and, while the lords drank milk or beef tea, the common people made do with water. In dress they seemed to take no account of social status or decency. They all wore a tunic down to the knee, but no shoes, no hose, no breeches. In consequence both men and women showed 'all they had and with as little shame as showing their faces'.[18] The English colonisation of Ireland in the twelfth and thirteenth centuries had resulted in the establishment of towns and villages and an expansion of cereal cultivation; the Irish resurgence of the fourteenth and fifteenth centuries (see p. 136) meant less cultivation of the soil and a return to dairying and cattle-rustling. Whether this represents a decline in civilisation is another matter. Modern scholars, without necessarily sharing Raymond's shocked attitude, value his sketch of a material culture. 'Irish chiefs in the later Middle Ages lived in a society where cattle-raiding had the same honourable status accorded to duelling in the eighteenth century.'[19] According to Raymond, King O'Neill (the Irish chief he met) considered Irish customs to be the best in the world.

Domesday Book

Immediately after Christmas 1085 William I 'had great thought and very deep conversation with his council about this land'.[20] The outcomes of that 'great thought' were Domesday Book and a number of related documents known as Domesday satellites. Together they name and give detailed information about more than 13,400 places in England. By the twelfth century the book was already part of the mythical history of England, called by a name – 'Domesday' – that linked it with the Last Judgement. Historians have often been tempted to use Domesday Book as though it were an economic survey of England, with just a few gaps leaving well-known unknowns (London, Winchester and the far north) for which allowance can readily be made. But this it was not. The king wanted to know how rich the lords of manors were, because this was information he could exploit (see p. 172). He was interested in the rents, whether in money or services, that tenants paid to lords of manors, but not in the other resources and products of those tenants. We know that 4,000 herrings were owed to William de Warenne from the Sussex fishing village of Brighton, but we do not know the size of the catch. The only livestock belonging to the tenants that interested the king were those draught animals that performed ploughing services for their lords. Domesday records altogether 81,184 plough teams (at eight oxen per team), but takes no account of the plough animals that belonged to tenants who owed only a money rent. Domesday tells us how many hides there were in each manor, but this represents the size of its tax liability, not its size on the ground (though the two were often in some way related). Domesday Book gives monetary values for most of the lands it lists, and adding up all its valuations of manors, we reach a total of about £73,000. But this figure has to be used with extreme caution. Domesday values appear to represent only that part of the annual income of lords which their tenants owed in money, i.e. certainly not market value, not even full rental value – since when actual rents, taking into account rents paid in kind and labour services, were recorded, they are for sums greater than Domesday valuations. The sum of £73,000 was nothing like an estimate of GDP. An entirely unquantifiable part of economic output went unrecorded.

None the less these records provide us with remarkable glimpses of the economy and administration of eleventh-century England, both 'now' (i.e. 1086) and on the eve of the Conquest. In Oakley, Bucks, for example, 'Ælfgyth the maid had half a hide which Godric the sheriff granted her as long as he was sheriff, on condition of her teaching his daughter gold embroidery work. This land Robert FitzWalter holds now.' Ælfgyth's special skill made her an unusual tenant. Domesday Book shows that over 70 per cent of rural tenants were either farmers (*villani* in Domesday Latin) typically holding fifteen to forty acres each, or cottagers, smallholders who characteristically held five acres or less. Although the former should have been able to support themselves and their families from the produce of their farms and gardens, the latter would certainly have depended upon wages to supplement what they grew themselves. Several early twelfth-century estate surveys indicate that *villani* owed heavy labour services, sometimes as much as three days' work a week on their lord's farm. To meet this obligation they almost certainly had slaves of their own or employed waged servants, some doubtless being cottagers.

The end of slavery

In the eleventh century slavery was still basic to British and Irish society. Slaves made up about 10 per cent of the population recorded in Domesday Book. Thousands of entries contain items like this one for Cuxham in Oxfordshire: 'In demesne there are 2 ploughs and 4 slaves.' At times of famine, the threat of starvation led to parents selling children into slavery. For some offences enslavement was the punishment laid down in law. War too was a major source of slaves. 'Five times,' wrote Symeon of Durham, 'King Malcolm [III] of Scotland raided Northumbria, devastating the land and carrying the wretched inhabitants off into slavery.'[21] Decades later it was still being alleged that every Scottish household had its English slave. There was evidently no taboo against the practice of Christian enslaving fellow Christian in Britain. It had long been seen as charitable, in pagan times as well as Christian, for slave owners to manumit (liberate) all or some of their slaves, but there was no campaign against slavery as such. Indeed Domesday Book demonstrates that particularly large numbers of slaves were owned by ecclesiastical landowners, especially in the west of England. According to William of Malmesbury, there had long been a flourishing slave export trade run by the men of Bristol. 'They buy up people from all over England and export them to Ireland; they sell slave women after they have made them pregnant. You would have groaned to see files of wretched young people of both sexes roped together, being sold and prostituted on a daily basis.'[22] In Ireland the unit of value was a *cumal*, a female slave.[23] In the absence of gang or plantation slavery, it seems likely that females made the best slaves, even though economic historians have found it difficult to measure the domestic work they did: cleaning, washing, mending, childcare, as well as providing sex on demand.

By contrast slavery was already a thing of the past in northern France by 1066. The disappearance of slavery from western Europe north of the Alps and Pyrenees went unremarked in any surviving contemporary sources; as an invisible process it can be dated only very approximately to the ninth to eleventh centuries. The last mention of a slave market at Rouen was *c*.1030. One consequence of slavery's demise was that the Norman Conquest was the first conquest in the history of Britain and

Ireland that did not result in more slaves being taken to market. For a while many of the new French lords retained the slave workforces they took over from their English predecessors, but it is clear from the Domesday Book entry for Essex which, uniquely, records slave numbers for both 1066 and 1086, that slavery was on the way out. Although slavery itself was not legislated against, churchmen such as Archbishop Lanfranc of Canterbury and Bishop Wulfstan of Worcester successfully put pressure on William the Conqueror to halt the export of slaves.[24] Initially he had been reluctant to do so since as king he shared in the trade's profits; Domesday Book records the toll to be paid for each slave sold at Lewes market in Sussex. A church council held at Westminster in 1102 prohibited 'that shameful trade in which people used to be sold like brute beasts'.[25] This was the last church council in England at which a desire to prohibit the slave trade was recorded. Slaves continued to be manumitted, and the decline of the slave trade increased the difficulty and cost of acquiring replacements. In any case it is likely that other forms of labour became a more attractive proposition at a time of rising population and increasing labour supply. Some owners freed slaves and provided them with a few acres of land, presumably in most cases in return for a money rent or onerous labour services. Lawrence of Durham, writing in the early 1130s, noted slavery's passing in England:

> After England was ruled by Norman lords then the English no longer suffered from outsiders that which they had suffered at their own hands. In this respect they found that foreigners treated them better than they had themselves. Meanwhile in Scotland and Ireland, where the natives are still the lords, the old custom of slavery continues, though on a lesser scale now.[26]

Lawrence could have added Wales to the list of lands where 'the old custom' still prevailed. In the 1150s John of Salisbury criticised the Welsh for carrying on 'a regular slave trade'.[27] The continuance of slavery and the slave raid in the rest of Britain and Ireland reinforced the view of a number of influential twelfth-century English authors that their northern and western neighbours were cruel and barbarous (see p. 293–6). But outside England, too, rulers who wanted to be regarded as modern came under pressure to end or set limits to enslavement. To all appearances slavery had died out throughout Britain and Ireland by *c*.1200, though – as on the Continent – it was a process which in Ireland and Wales went entirely unrecorded.

True, the end of slavery still left many people with cause to lament their relative lack of freedom. Yet however servile the conditions of their lives, at least they were not slaves. Families could no longer be broken up, individuals taken to market and sold separately. Nor was it lawful for their lord to kill or wound them – in contrast to the view of the author of the early twelfth-century *Leges Henrici Primi*, who held that a master who killed his slave was guilty of a sin, but not a crime.[28]

Serfdom

The great variety of terms of tenure meant there were many degrees of economic freedom and unfreedom. Tenant farmers who owed heavy labour services had only limited free time to work in their own fields. Tenants who could give, sell or leave their lands without their lord's licence were privileged; most were tied to their holdings, entitled to leave only with permission – and on payment of a fee known as chevage. The English cottagers and farmers of Domesday Book were evidently less free than that 14 per cent of the recorded population who were called precisely 'free'. In England *c.*1200 judges stepped in to create a new distinction in law between free and unfree. It had long been part of the morality of kingship that kings should protect freemen from oppression, but the massive expansion of royal justice resulting from the development of the common law (see p. 210) opened the door to the possibility that the 'lord king' would constantly be called upon to intervene on the side of rustics against lords. To prevent this happening, the judges formulated a set of rules whose effect was to disbar the more disadvantaged tenants from access to the public courts. From now on those who had the right to have their disputes heard in the royal courts were regarded as being free; those who did not were 'servile' and were called serfs or *villani* (now better translated as 'villeins'). Their disputes, whether with each other or with their landlords, could only be heard in their landlord's court, the court of the manor. But when personal status was itself the issue, only the king's courts could decide whether an individual was free or a villein.

Technically not only the villein's land, but also his house and chattels belonged to his lord; in practice the lord's need for services meant that, in return for payments to him, manorial custom allowed both family succession to a tenancy and inheritance of the chattels. But the children of serfs were born into serfdom and all serfs, even the wealthier ones (see p. 51), knew that they enjoyed less freedom than many of their neighbours. The stigma was highlighted by having to pay manorial fines such as 'merchet' when a daughter married, and 'leyrwite' if she had sex before marriage. Similarly harsh terms applied in Scotland to tenants known as 'bondsmen', as also to those known in Welsh as *taeog* and in Irish as *betaghs*. Yet however servile the conditions of their lives at least they were not slaves.

Population 1: growth and marriage

We can only guess at the population of Britain and Ireland in this period. Historians have often turned to Domesday Book in the hope of estimating the population of England in 1086. It records the existence of 283,240 people, and it is generally assumed that almost all of them, with the exception of many of the slaves, were heads of household. Depending on whether we opt for an average household size of three and a half or – as most demographers prefer – of five, we might be tempted to think of a population in the order of 1 million to 1.5 million. Unfortunately the fact that in 1086 the king and his advisers were not interested in people whose labours did not directly contribute to the incomes of manorial lords, manorial subtenants for example, means that it is very likely that there were more households than 283,240, but there is no way of estimating how many more. Thus Domesday Book can yield a population minimum of a million or so, but the actual number could have been over 2.5 million, though 1.5 million is more likely (see graph p. 42).

It is possible to make an evidence-based estimate of the size of the English population in 1377. The 4*d*. poll-tax of 1377 was levied on all lay people over the age of fourteen, except for the very poor and those who lived in the exempt counties of Cheshire and Durham. The returns reveal a total recorded taxed population of 1,355,201. Depending on assumptions about the age structure of the population and allowances for those exempted, we can reach an estimated population of between 2 million and 3 million. What is as certain as anything can be is that the population of England, and indeed of the whole of Britain and Ireland, had been much bigger in 1300 than it was in 1377. The cumulative effect of the plagues of 1348–9, 1361–2 and 1368–9 may well have reduced their populations by over half. Hence estimates for England in 1300 range from 4 million to 6.5 million. What the populations of Ireland, Scotland and Wales were at this date is anybody's guess. Current best guesses suggest a combined population of not much over 2 million.

These estimates, plus a great deal of evidence for particular English manors in the twelfth and thirteenth centuries, do at least make it clear that overall these were centuries of rising population. There were, of course, occasional setbacks, often as a result of bad weather. In his long account of 1258, for example, the St Albans chronicler Matthew Paris returned time and again to the subject of the calamitous weather, oscillating between freezing cold and torrential rain from the start of the year until mid August. In his opinion it was a year unlike any other; some have linked the extraordinary weather with the massive eruption of Mount Rinjani in 1257, probably the greatest volcanic eruption of the last 10,000 years. Whatever the cause, the consequences for the poor of the wet weather of this and the previous summers were all too evident. 'Swollen and rotting in groups of five or six, the dead lay abandoned in pigsties, on dunghills, and in the muddy streets.' Eventually the corpses were gathered up and buried in mass graves, but not before, in Matthew's estimate, 15,000 had died in London alone. Had it not been for imports from Germany and Holland, England, he believed, would have gone under.[29] But despite such episodes the underlying trend remained upward. If mortality rates were as high as forty per 1,000 per year, as has been suggested for tenants of the Bishop of Winchester in the 1240s, then birth rates could have been as high as fifty per 1,000.

For all its limitations, Domesday Book can be made to reveal important things about relative population densities. In 1086 the Sussex coast, Kent, Essex, East Anglia, parts of the Thames Valley and of Lincolnshire (Lindsey and Kesteven) were the most densely populated regions of England; north and west of the Trent were the least populated. Where opportunities for more than one son could be created by opening up hitherto uncultivated land, most farmers practised impartible inheritance, usually primogeniture (inheritance by the eldest son), but sometimes ultimogeniture (inheritance by the youngest). By contrast, a characteristic feature of East Anglia and Kent, densely settled regions in which there was less room to clear land and carve out new holdings, was that all male children inherited equally. The 1377 poll-tax returns show that three centuries after Domesday the north and west were still the most thinly populated parts, but that the area of relatively dense population now took in a wider area of south and east Britain, including the Midlands and Holland (south-east Lincolnshire) – this last the result of draining the fens.

Since a woman's age at first marriage was a significant variable for determining growth or decline of population, the fact that in the two centuries after 1086 population densities in much of the rest of central England seem to have been 'catching up' with East Anglian levels of density may suggest different marriage patterns in different regions, with East Anglia already moving away from a pattern of early marriage towards what has become known as 'the European marriage pattern', i.e. one in which the men 'normally' married in their mid twenties, women in their early twenties, and quite a few never marrying. In all societies, getting married seems to have meant setting up, or being set up in, a household. On these grounds we might expect an early marriage pattern to be characteristic of regions where there was more room to clear and cultivate more land. Both custom and canon law allowed people to marry in their early teens (see p. 242), but there is no direct evidence for medieval Irish, Scottish and Welsh marriage patterns and none for England before the later thirteenth century. Study of Halesowen, a West Midlands manor for which good records survive from 1270 onwards, shows that the children of richer tenant farmers were more likely to marry during the lifetime of their parents than the children of the poorer. One option open throughout the twelfth and thirteenth centuries to many English men and women who saw few prospects at home was migration to Wales, Scotland and, after 1169, to Ireland. In this period the westward and northward movement of settlers has been termed a 'second tidal wave of Anglo-Saxon colonisation'.[30]

Towns and markets

Many English towns suffered badly as a direct result of the Norman Conquest, with streets and houses demolished to make way for castles; the archaeological record suggests that it took several decades for some to recover. On the other hand by 1100 Norman lords had already founded about twenty new towns and during the course of the next hundred years the trend towards urbanisation, visible in England since the tenth century, clearly accelerated. With the population rising, most new towns developed 'naturally' as villages grew in size. By 1200 there were 600–700 places where markets were held by ancient right or royal licence; in the next hundred years

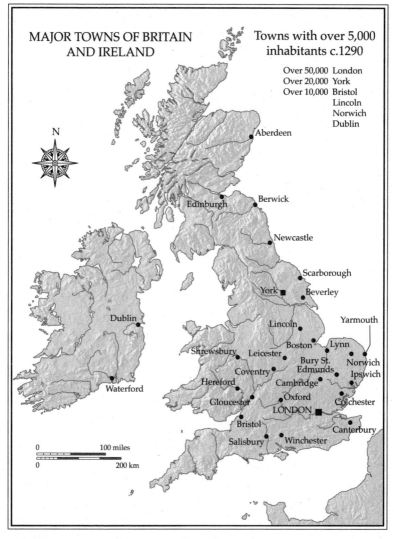

MAJOR TOWNS OF BRITAIN
AND IRELAND

Towns with over 5,000
inhabitants c.1290

Over 50,000 London
Over 20,000 York
Over 10,000 Bristol
Lincoln
Norwich
Dublin

N

Aberdeen

Edinburgh   Berwick

Newcastle

Scarborough

York   Beverley

Dublin

Lincoln   Yarmouth

Boston   Lynn
Shrewsbury   Leicester
Coventry   Bury St.   Norwich
Hereford   Edmunds   Ipswich
Cambridge

Waterford

Gloucester   Oxford   Colchester
LONDON

Bristol   Canterbury

Salisbury   Winchester

0   100 miles
0   200 km

1. Map based on material in B. M. S. Campbell, 'Benchmarking medieval economic development:
England, Wales, Scotland and Ireland c.1290' *Economic History Review*, 61 (2008), pp. 896–945.

another 1,100 market charters were granted, a reflection of what has been called 'the market mania of the thirteenth century'.[31] By 1300 everyone in England lived close enough to a market to be able to walk there and back during the hours of daylight. As the king travelled about the realm, his clerk of the market held court, checking local weights and measures. Most market settlements remained villages. But in places where booths and shops were busy several days a week, sometimes even on Sundays, i.e. not just on market day, some of the inhabitants were able to specialise as artisans, craftsmen or shopkeepers, making and selling goods in exchange for the agricultural production of the countryside or raw materials from forest, quarries and mines. Most such new towns remained small, with a population of only a few hundred, and many residents combined a craft or trade with farming. Yet however small, by 1300 there were more than 500 towns in England, at least four times as many as in 1086.

Analysis of three large and well-established towns, Norwich, Winchester and York, indicates that by 1300 nearly half of their inhabitants were involved in manufacturing, working in textiles (woollen cloth or linen), leather and metal; about 40 per cent were in retail trade, and about 10 per cent in service occupations such as transport, clerical work, law and medicine. Almost everywhere, in village and town, women were prominent in brewing and selling ale, and in selling poultry, fish and dairy produce; in larger towns prostitution was an option, though the authorities tried to restrict it to a suburb (Southwark in the case of London). The larger self-governing towns generated a mass of regulations which were supposed to prevent profiteering in basic foodstuffs and control the activities of artisans by bringing them within 'craft guilds' such as those of weavers, bakers, fishmongers and saddlers.

Reality, no doubt, was more flexible and informal than the regulations suggest.

By 1300 there had been major developments in municipal self-government. Towns had long been marked off legally and administratively from the countryside around them, but they belonged to lords, from the lord king downwards, and the men who presided over town courts and collected revenues were the lords' agents; they remained so unless and until he granted his townsmen 'liberties and free customs'. From the twelfth century onwards records of such grants survive in increasing numbers, mostly in the form of borough charters. Typically these granted the burgesses the right to sell, sublet, mortgage or bequeath their tenements (burgages); freed them from having to pay servile dues or perform labour services, and from paying toll both at the borough's weekly market, and at other markets owned by the same lord. Where the lord was the king this was an extremely valuable privilege since he was lord of most of the oldest and biggest towns in England.

The vocabulary of borough charters reflects the influence of the economically more advanced towns of northern France, the Low Countries and the Rhineland (where the word 'burgess' was first used to mean a full member of an urban community with laws and customs of its own). The law came to recognise the custom that a man able to live in a borough as a burgess for a year and a day would thenceforth be regarded as a freeman. Hence the proverb: 'Town air makes you free.' By granting these freedoms to his tenants, the lord gave up some profitable rights, but did so in the expectation that the town would flourish, bringing in a higher overall income. A lord could guarantee himself a useful annual sum with virtually no effort on his part by leasing to the burgesses the right to administer the town and collect the revenues. By 1130 both London and Lincoln had bought these rights from the king. In this way municipal self-government began to get going. From 1191 London was administered by a mayor and aldermen (who headed the wards); Winchester had a mayor by 1200, Exeter by 1205. By 1300 some fifty English towns were administered by mayor and council. The growing importance of self-governing towns in the nation's life is indicated by the fact that, beginning in 1265, some of them were required to send representatives to Parliament.

The most dramatic sign of urban growth was the number of towns set up on new sites. In England between 1066 and 1330 more than 150 planned towns were established, among them Arundel, Boston, Chelmsford, Devizes, Egremont, Hull, King's Lynn, Liverpool, Maidenhead, Newcastle upon Tyne, Okehampton, Portsmouth, Reigate, Salisbury, Truro, Uxbridge, Watford, Yarmouth (Isle of Wight) and South Zeal (Devon). Kings had founded towns in England before 1066, and continued to do so afterwards. Portsmouth, for example, was founded by Richard I, and Liverpool by John. In the twelfth and thirteenth centuries, however, most were founded by wealthy landowners. Founding new towns involved considerable capital outlay, the laying out of houses, streets and market, often the provision of an amenity such as a church. The grant of borough status, offering burgages at low rent, usually 12d. a year, was intended to attract settlers. The kings and aristocrats of this period were very far from being contemptuous of commerce. The Clare family, for example, as earls of Hertford and Gloucester came to possess more than twenty boroughs. In the mid-twelfth century the Knights Templar founded a new town in Hertfordshire. Ambitiously they named it Baghdad (now Baldock), and diverted the road leading north from London (now the A1) to bring it into their new marketplace. By 1185 a list of occupations in Baghdad includes blacksmith, ironmonger, tailor, shoemaker, tanner, mason, cook, carpenter, mercer, weaver, saddler, goldsmith, merchant and vintner. Throughout these centuries a good deal of effort went into improving the network of communications, in particular bridge-building. Most of the bridges in place in 1750 were already there by 1300. Not all new towns prospered. The prospects for those founded later in the thirteenth century, such as South Zeal, when the country was already well provided with markets, were far from good. They attracted so few settlers that they remained in effect villages. Unlike towns in Wales and Scotland, English towns were not authorised to compel the inhabitants of the surrounding countryside to use their markets. None the less these 'failed towns' are a measure of the prevailing climate of commercial optimism.

In Wales, Scotland and Ireland, the role of town founders was even more prominent than in England. The Norman lords who invaded south Wales from the 1070s onwards founded towns to provide for the needs of their castle garrisons at such places as Brecon, Chepstow, Kidwelly, Monmouth, Cardiff and Pembroke. Such new towns needed walls of their own, behind which English burgesses worked and traded in relative safety. Edward I's conquest of north Wales led to the foundation of a dozen fortified boroughs such as Aberystwyth, Flint, Rhuddlan, Conwy, Caernarfon, Denbigh, Holt, Ruthin and Beaumaris. Most of the seventy or so towns in Wales c.1300 were very small; probably only Cardiff, Carmarthen and Haverford contained over 1,000 inhabitants. None the less they had a major economic impact on a landscape that until the eleventh century, with the possible exception of Caerwent, had known no towns at all. The lion's share of the profits of

economic expansion went to 'the English burgesses of the
English boroughs of Wales', as they called themselves.
According to Gerald de Barri, the Welsh neither 'engage in
trade or industry' nor 'live in towns, villages or castles'.[32] Given
the fact that the invaders had grabbed the lowland regions
most suitable to commercial and industrial development, it is
hardly surprising that it was not until the thirteenth century
that native Welsh princes began to promote towns of their
own such as Welshpool (Powys), and Llanfaes (Anglesey).

In Ireland too, although the Ostmen (former Viking) towns
of Dublin, Waterford, Wexford, Cork and Limerick were
almost certainly growing in size before 1169, and some Gaelic
centres such as Kells and Kildare showed signs of urban
development, there is no doubt that the great surge after that
date was the work of invaders and settlers. By 1275 New Ross,
founded at the beginning of the century by William Marshal,
had become the principal wool- and grain-exporting port of
Ireland, outstripping Waterford and Wexford. Civic pride is
revealed in the poem on the building of New Ross's town wall
in the 1260s, welcoming all foreigners wishing to buy and sell
there. Those coming by sea would have been guided by the
lighthouse at Hook, also built at Marshal's initiative. By 1300
English colonists had founded at least fifty new towns as the
focal points in a new landscape of villages, mills and bridges in
southern and eastern Ireland. By contrast there were very few
towns west and north of a line drawn from Cork to Galway
and across to Carlingford. The towns were inhabited by the
Gaelic-Irish as well as by the English, though the number of
'Irishtowns' in the larger towns implies a degree of segregation,
even, in the cases of Limerick and Kilkenny, enclosed within
walls of their own.

In Scotland, by contrast, it was the native rulers themselves,

The lighthouse at Hook (Co. Wexford). The modern lantern still stands where it did in the thirteenth century, on top of the great tower built *c.*1200 at William Marshal's initiative as a beacon for ships intending to sail up the River Barrow to his town of New Ross.

in particular the anglicised David I who ruled a southern Scottish principality from 1113 and was king from 1124 to 1153, who made the running in the urbanisation of the country. He actively promoted old centres such as Berwick, Roxburgh, Edinburgh, Stirling, Dunfermline, Perth and Aberdeen, all on the east coast or the rivers running down to it, granting them monopolies of local trade and burghal status. His extension of royal authority northwards into Moray was reinforced by the creation of burghs at Forres and Elgin. Scottish burghal custom was based on the customs of Newcastle upon Tyne, and many of those drawn to settle in the new towns were English. According to William of Newburgh, writing in the 1190s, 'the towns and boroughs of the kingdom of Scotland are inhabited by the English'.[33] David's example was followed by his successors, by the bishops at St Andrews and Glasgow and then by other lords. By 1300 there were over fifty Scottish burghs, more than thirty of them royal foundations.

Throughout Britain and Ireland it was generally the older towns that were the richest, whether they went back to the tenth century such as Dublin, Bristol and Norwich or to Roman times, such as York, Winchester, Lincoln, Canterbury, Colchester and, of course, the richest of them all, London. According to a tax assessment made in 1334, London was five times richer than the next town, Bristol. (Significantly for the geographical distribution of wealth the next five were all eastern towns: York, Newcastle upon Tyne, Boston, Yarmouth and Lincoln.) With a population of about 80,000 c.1300, London was much smaller than Paris, but by European standards it was the only genuinely big town in Britain and Ireland. By the early 1190s Richard of Devizes, himself a Winchester man, was advising people to stay clear of London:

> Whatever evil or malicious thing can be found anywhere in the world can also be found in that city. Actors, jesters, smooth-skinned lads, Moors, flatterers, pretty boys, effeminates, pederasts, singing and dancing girls, quacks, belly-dancers, sorcerers, extortioners, night-wanderers, magicians, mimes, beggars, buffoons.[34]

When the Londoner William FitzStephen composed a panegyric in the 1170s in praise of his fellow citizens, 'known everywhere', as he put it, 'for the elegance of their manners, dress and cuisine', he counted 139 churches (thirteen major ones and 126 parish churches) within the city and its suburbs. He was also proud of the cookshops, fast-food places where 'halfpenny pies' could be bought, or pies baked for customers who brought their own meat.[35] It was now that London's position at the centre of the river and road network established by the Romans was reinforced by the building of a stone bridge – one of the great engineering achievements of the age. To allow large ships upstream, it incorporated a drawbridge which remained operational until 1476. Two miles to the west, and already joined to the city by a continuous line of development, lay the Palace of Westminster. Hence many nobles possessed, in addition to their country houses, a residence in London or Westminster or Southwark. The Archbishop of Canterbury built himself a palace in Lambeth. London and Westminster were seen in combination, one the commercial, the other the political capital of the nation. Inevitably there were tensions between the two, most dramatically expressed when in 1215 London opened its gates to the rebels against King John, forcing the latter to accept Magna Carta; to reward them the charter came to include a requirement (clause 35) that London's weights and measures should be standard throughout the realm and a confirmation of 'the liberties and free customs of cities, boroughs, towns and ports' (clause 13).

Age of silver

Throughout Latin Christendom people counted in units of pennies (Latin *denarii*), shillings (12*d*. to the shilling), marks (13*s*. 4*d*. to the mark) and pounds (20*s*. to the pound; Latin *libra*). But from 1066 until 1279, with the exception of a few coins struck during Henry I's and Henry III's reigns, the only coin minted in England was the silver penny. Indeed everywhere north of the Pyrenees the prevailing monetary system was based on silver, a metal which, while precious, was none the less sufficiently widely available to make extended circulation possible. Gold, scarcer and more highly valued, was occasionally used for large transactions, but at this date gold coins were minted only in the Byzantine and Islamic world, and very few found their way into Britain. The silver penny was a high-value coin, the equivalent for many of a day's wage at a time when 2d. could buy a whole sheep. For so indispensable and valuable a coin, it strikes the modern eye as absurdly small and light, about the same size as a 5p piece today (2014), and a good deal lighter. Despite the flexibility of local credit systems, there was clearly a pressing need for coins of a smaller denomination since finds prove that even coins as small as these were cut into halves and quarters – so tiny that many must have escaped even archaeologists' eyes.

The Norman Conquest came at a time when the European stock of silver was dwindling as the silver mines of Goslar (Saxony) gradually ran out. There were silver-bearing lead ores in the Pennines and Devon, but they yielded nothing like enough to provide a home-grown supply. None the less as a conqueror who insisted that he was Edward the Confessor's heir, William maintained the existing English monetary system. Like their English and Danish predecessors, the Norman kings were remarkably successful in ensuring that their coins, and only their coins, bearing their images and names on one side (the obverse) of each coin, circulated throughout the kingdom – in stark contrast to the situation in kingdoms on the Continent where dukes, counts and towns often had currencies of their own. Traders who brought foreign coins into England were required to hand them over to be reminted. The archaeological evidence of coin finds in England shows that astonishingly few escaped the melting pot. Moneyers were licensed to strike the king's coin where needed, principally at London, Lincoln, York, Stamford and

Thetford in the east, and at Winchester and Canterbury in the south. Silver being a soft metal, coins lost value as they became worn through being passed from hand to hand; every few years from the late tenth to the mid twelfth century they were called in and reminted. Before 1066 these recoinages resulted in pennies of fluctuating weight and fineness with a great variety of patterns and royal images.

Despite the declining silver supply the Norman kings maintained a high silver content (93–4 per cent fine), and from William II's accession (1087) a standardised weight set at 1.38 grams. This was, and was intended to be, a strong coinage. When Henry I's soldiers complained in 1124 that they were being paid in debased coin, the king had many of the moneyers castrated. All this resulted in a highly valued and stable currency; the term sterling probably derives from the Old English word *ster* meaning strong. Writing in the 1130s, Henry of Huntingdon associated the fineness of sterling with silver imported from Germany paid for by a flourishing export trade (see p. 44). In the later twelfth century imitation sterling coins were manufactured in continental mints. Until the Italians began to mint in gold, western Europe became a sterling zone, with the sterling penny functioning as a coin worth 3*d*., 4*d*., or 5*d*. in continental currencies. By 1180 great quantities of silver were flowing into England, thanks to rising European supply from newly discovered mines in Germany and Italy. In consequence mint production rose. Indeed in 1180, sensing the prospect of making greater profits, Henry II replaced the old system of licensed moneyers with one based on salaried officials at mints and exchanges in London and Canterbury. He had already ended the old system of frequent recoinages, and after this they became increasingly rare.

Records of production at the London and Canterbury

mints survive from the 1220s onwards. Before then the number of coins struck and the volume of coinage in circulation can only be 'guesstimated' on the uncertain basis of the ever increasing number and type of coins found. Statistically minded numismatists estimate that from the mid eleventh to the mid twelfth century the currency remained at somewhere between 5 million and 12 million pennies, approximately £20,000 to £50,000. (Earlier phases of higher production in the 990s and in the aftermath of the Danish Conquest saw a significant proportion of the newly minted silver being taken to Scandinavia.) Despite the huge variation, such estimates are revealing. Even taking the penny's high value into account, the amount of coin in circulation was small. Some scholars have estimated a currency in the region of only 3d. or 4d. per head. Even combining a high estimate of the currency with a low estimate of the population at the time of Domesday Book (1.5 million) produces a figure of no more than 8d. per head. By 1180 there was probably about £80,000 in circulation, but in view of the rising population perhaps no more per head.

After capturing Carlisle in 1136 David I became the first Scottish king to issue his own coin. For the next 200 years and more the Scottish currency shadowed the English one. Its silver penny was based on English standard weight and fineness; halfpennies and farthings were minted from 1279. By this time there was a Scottish currency in the order of £150,000, although finds suggest that a high proportion of the coin circulating in Scotland was English. Twelfth-century Irish kings minted a few silver coins, known as bracteates, at Ferns and Clonmacnoise, but it was only after the English invasion that the monetisation of Ireland took off. The new government began to mint coin principally, but not only, at

Dublin, including early issues of halfpennies and farthings. In 1204, as part of a deliberate policy of the anglicisation of Ireland, John ordered a recoinage to English standards of weight and fineness.

During this period coin could be, and clearly was, used to pay major outgoings such as taxes and rents, but was of no use in ordinary everyday transactions – for purchasing anything less than half a sheep. Most country people, smallholders and tenant farmers, must themselves have produced most of what they needed. Archaeological excavations have shown that many possessed some pots and pans; presumably these were acquired through barter or local credit, the equivalent of 'putting it on the slate'. These then were largely self-sufficient local economies in which payments were made in goods rather than cash, though it is likely that the practice of exchange involved the use of money as a standard of value. As lord of Ireland, King John issued halfpennies and farthings there, but otherwise kings and their advisers preferred to let consumers create their own small change by cutting coins in half or quarter – a procedure facilitated by the cross shown on one side of coins after 1180. There would have been no need to strike even smaller coins; a reduction in silver content would have done the trick. But not until November 1279 did the English government finally address the matter; over the next two years the Tower mint at London issued 72 million pennies, 20 million halfpennies and 13 million farthings. Thus day rates for men labouring on Edward I's castle-building in Wales were set at 1¼d. or 1½d. The fact that for so long there had been no real attempt to provide small change reveals that not even in England had there been a money economy.

By 1320 it had become one. Records of mint output reveal

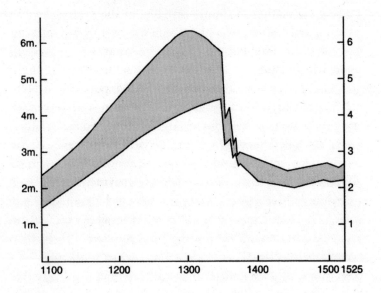

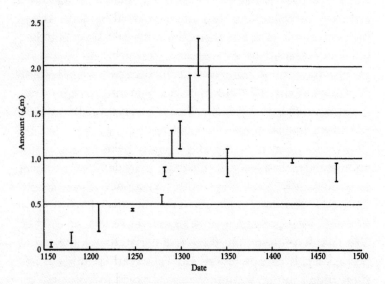

3: Long-term population trends, 1086–1525. 4: Estimates of the English currency, 1250–1450 (silver and, from 1351, gold).

a rising circulating medium: £450,000 in the mid thirteenth century, £1.1 million by 1300, £2 million by 1320. Population was rising too, but at nowhere near the same rate. Depending upon which estimates of population size are adopted there was 50–75*d*. per head in 1300, and 80–120*d*. per head in 1320, conceivably forty times as much per head as in 1086. Moreover the production of halfpennies and farthings made it much easier to spend money. Labour services were replaced by money payments. Coins had become the normal medium of exchange, increasingly used by villeins in payment of the dues such as heriot (death duty) and merchet which they owed their lords. The more important coin became as a medium of exchange the more useful it was to have coins of different denominations. In 1257 Henry III experimented with a 20*d*. coin. It was of pure gold and twice as heavy as a penny, but it failed when the sudden release of large quantities on to the London market led to the price of gold dipping below the coin's face value. In any case striking gold in imitation of the Florentines was a vanity project for which there was as yet no economic need. To some extent this was true also of Edward I's decision in 1279 to issue a higher-value silver coin; the groat, worth 4*d*. This was twice the daily wage of a skilled workman, and minting soon ceased.

Over the century wages had been held down by the presence of a plentiful labour supply provided by a growing population. Inevitably the increase in money supply led to monetary inflation. Livestock and grain prices trebled – but over so long a period this was an annual rise so small as to give contemporaries the impression that they were living through a period of stability. Only in the early years of John's reign and in the 1270s were people alarmed by rising prices, which in both cases they blamed on the practice of coin clipping. These anxieties were effectively allayed by recoinages in 1205 and 1279. The late thirteenth-century sense of stability and prosperity lasted until the heavy taxation of the years from 1294.

Foreign trade

As early as 1130 Henry of Huntingdon drew attention to Britain's export of raw materials and foodstuffs. German silver, he wrote, 'is brought down the Rhine in exchange for great quantities of fish and meat, of costly wool and milk, as well as of cattle without number'.[36] In all likelihood wool was already Britain's chief export. Although this is only demonstrable from the time that national customs statistics survive, i.e. from 1275 for England and Ireland, and from 1327 for Scotland, the favourable balance of trade noted by Henry was almost certainly based on growing demand for wool from the expanding Flemish cloth industry. For bulk goods such as wool, counted in sacks, each weighing 364 lb, or wine, stored in tuns each containing 252 gallons, water transport was much more efficient than land, especially over longer distances. It cost as much to move a tun of wine fifty miles overland as to bring it from Bordeaux to Southampton. From the twelfth century onwards a newly developed type of ship further increased the economic advantages of sea transport. The round-bellied cog could carry larger cargoes, and at a much lower cost per ton than earlier ships. Its deeper draft required deep-water harbours. Hence many of the new towns (see p. 32) were new ports equipped with quays and cranes and sited at river mouths or on coasts.

Seaborne trade led to a growing number of connections in all directions, including north and west to Iceland and

Greenland, but the most important trade routes led to the
richer and economically more sophisticated regions to the
south, above all to northern France, the Low Countries and
the Rhineland, but increasingly also to Spain and the
Mediterranean. In the 1160s a Jewish traveller, Benjamin of
Tudela, noted the presence of English merchants at Alexandria.
By the later twelfth century there was an English business
community in Genoa. From Spain and the Mediterranean
came silk, sugar, rice, almonds and oriental spices such as
cumin, cinnamon, cloves, ginger, nutmeg and saffron, in the
first instance for the royal court. A series of 'southern' queens
– Eleanor of Aquitaine, Isabella of Angoulême, Eleanor of
Provence, Eleanor of Castile – brought courtiers into closer
contact with southern tastes and spicier food that possessed
the prestige attached to Arabic science and Byzantine culture.

> Gold from Arabia, from Sabaea spice
> And incense; from the Scythians arms of steel
> Well-tempered; oil from the rich groves of palm
> That spring from the fat lands of Babylon;
> Fine gems from Nile, from China crimson silks;
> French wines; and sable, vair and miniver
> From the far lands where Russ and Norseman dwell.

With these verses FitzStephen proudly listed some of the
luxury goods that could be bought in the London of the
1170s.[37]

A duty on goods entering and leaving the country was
imposed by Richard I; the earliest records to survive in any
quantity relate to trade going through the ports of the south
and east coasts in 1203–4. Although the figures probably
underestimate London's share of the trade (17 per cent, not

that much more than Boston's 16 per cent and Southampton's 14 per cent), they do reveal the continuing importance of east-coast ports. Between them Boston, King's Lynn, Lincoln, Hull, York and Newcastle produced 54 per cent of the total recorded customs revenue. New centres of international trade had sprung up, sometimes in unexpected places. For three or four weeks every year after Easter the little country town of St Ives in Cambridgeshire, for instance, was transformed into a major commercial emporium. Wooden stalls were set up; the front rooms of town houses were rented out as shops; cart parks were full to overflowing. This was the 'great fair' of St Ives. People came here not only from all over eastern England, but also from overseas, from Flanders, Brabant and France. Most English towns enjoyed the right to hold an annual fair, but most served a local or regional market and lasted for only two or three days. The 'great fairs' which developed in the later twelfth century at Boston, Winchester, King's Lynn and Stamford as well as at St Ives, lasted for several weeks. They were open for business to all comers, free from the restrictions of trade which towns normally imposed in order to protect their own merchants and shopkeepers. This made them very attractive to foreigners of all sorts, Londoners and buyers for big aristocratic households, as well as merchants from overseas: Spain, Gascony, Toulouse, Normandy, Norway, Germany and the Low Countries, especially Flanders.

At the same time the six fairs of Champagne functioned as the key points of exchange between north-western Europe and Italy, linking north and south into a single European trading zone. Late in the thirteenth century the economic integration of Europe was taken a stage further when Italian merchant ships sailed from their home ports to Southampton and London via the Straits of Gibraltar, and returned with cargoes of English wool. All this ensured a volume and regularity of business sufficient to generate the changes in business techniques, credit and banking which have been dubbed the thirteenth-century commercial revolution. By 1300 Londoners were using negotiable credit instruments and bills of exchange. Contacts with the Continent, including the Mediterranean region, were now on a scale not seen since the days when Britain had been a province of the Roman Empire. In economic terms Britain and Ireland were fully integrated into a new Europe.

Inevitably these developments did not suit everyone. English winegrowers could not compete with the better-quality wines brought in by the wine fleets from La Rochelle and Bordeaux. In three months in 1303 no less than 271 wine shipments left Bordeaux, some containing over 200 tons. Towns celebrated for cloth-making in the twelfth and early thirteenth centuries such as Stamford and Lincoln suffered partly as a result of imports from Flanders and Italy. The superiority of Italian banks and credit systems gave firms such as the Ricciardi of Lucca access to funds that allowed them to buy up wool clips years ahead. By lending to the Crown they gained royal patronage and protection; in 1275 Edward I appointed the Ricciardi as collectors of customs on wool, woolfells and hides, in Ireland as well as England. By the later thirteenth century even Flemish businessmen were being elbowed out of England's international commerce by Italians, though they retained their leading position in Scotland's, as reflected by the presence of a Scottish business community at Bruges in the 1290s. Significant though economic growth in Britain had been, the economies of Flanders and northern Italy had developed faster. By 1300 England and Ireland were provinces that produced raw materials for an Italian commercial empire. Native businessmen had a smaller share of the trade of Britain and Ireland than for many centuries. The Business Charter (*Carta mercatoria*) issued by Edward I in 1303 laid down that in disputes between native and foreign businessmen, half the jury was to be composed of the foreigner's nation, '*de sa langue*'. The total volume of trade was now so much greater that arguably both groups gained. Certainly both gained from the developing network of courts, including 'piepowder' courts for foreign merchants, that helped to settle commercial disputes, register debts and pursue debtors.

In the countryside, 1086–1315

In Britain and Ireland as a whole the proportion of people living in towns was higher in 1300 than in 1066, yet it has been estimated that even in England at least 80 per cent still lived in the countryside. The most obvious way to feed the growing population was to bring more land into use. The introduction of rabbits and rabbit warrens into twelfth-century England (and then into Ireland) meant that an entirely new way of exploiting infertile land such as the Breckland (Norfolk) and Dartmoor was found. In most of Britain and Ireland there was room for expansion; in the Highlands of Scotland 'medieval warm period' weather allowed arable to be pushed higher than today. But varying soil quality meant there was always a limit to the physical expansion of cultivation. In some parts of England this point may already have been reached by 1086, but elsewhere large areas of forest, fen, marsh and upland were cleared, drained and farmed. One consequence was that numbers of wild pigs and wolves dwindled and by 1300 they had been hunted to extinction in England and Wales (though they survived for much longer in Ireland and Scotland). As a result of this, observed Sir John Fortescue in the fifteenth century, sheep did not have to be guarded at night as they lay in their folds fertilising the soil. The gradual reduction of woodland made it less easy to provide pigs with autumn foraging for acorns and beech mast, so the practice of keeping pigs in sties became more common. Some parts of England became virtually treeless, and what remained had to be managed by coppicing, which, carefully done, ensured a regular supply of wood of different thicknesses. As timber for building became more expensive, it made sense to turn to brick-making, visible in eastern England from the late thirteenth century on. Similarly the increasing cost of firewood meant that the economics of coal mining became increasingly attractive; by 1300 Newcastle was supplying coal to east-coast towns, above all London, and to the Continent.

Some of the new land was potentially good soil, as in the rich silt belt around the Wash. But there continued to be more grassland than arable. More ploughing required more draught animals so a great deal of reclamation was for pasture rather than tillage. By building dykes and diverting river courses, the monks of Glastonbury reclaimed thousands of acres in the Somerset Levels, creating high-quality meadow, growing the hay vital for horses and cattle. From the south of England to the Cheviot Hills in southern Scotland sheep farming became an increasingly big business. The survival of their records makes this particularly clear in the case of the great ecclesiastical estates. In 1322 Canterbury Cathedral Priory had a flock of 13,700 sheep; Melrose Abbey had 12,000. Because sheep dung is more efficacious as a fertiliser than that of other animals, as a form of livestock husbandry sheep farming made good sense at a time of growing population and increasing demand for grain. Customs revenue records (which survive from 1279–80 on) indicate annual English wool exports reaching the equivalent of 12 million fleeces by 1304–5. 'The wool of England', asserted a petition sent to Edward I in the name of the community of the realm, 'is worth half the value of all the land.'[38] The earliest Scottish records (for 1327–33) point to the export of 1.5 million fleeces and 35,000 hides per annum. These export totals show that more wool must have come from the thousands of small flocks kept by tenant farmers than from the large flocks of the great landlords, though in many cases the latter acted as the middlemen between farmers and the international market. The equivalent Irish records (which do not distinguish fleeces and hides) point to a late thirteenth-century export peak of 1 million fleeces or 400,000–450,000 hides.

In continuation of trends already visible long before 1066 a midland zone of nucleated settlements (villages rather than hamlets or scattered farmsteads) extended into northern England and southern Scotland. After the Norman Conquest many planned villages were laid out with linear house-plots along street-frontages. In the village, farming could be a more communal enterprise. By co-operating with his near neighbours, the ordinary farmer who owned two oxen could take advantage of the most up-to-date farm machinery, the heavy plough. Drawn by eight oxen yoked in pairs, heavy ploughs were much harder to turn than the old-fashioned scratch plough, so it made sense for the land they worked to be divided into long strips. Each householder held many strips scattered throughout the two (or three) large fields attached to each village. By this method good and bad soil was shared out fairly, and all lived more or less equidistant from their work. English emigration took this pattern of settlement and open-field farming into south-eastern Ireland after 1170.

One consequence of the proliferation of markets and the increasing volume of coin in circulation was that on many manors lords chose to take rents in money rather than as before in produce or in labour services. This trend can be traced in southern Scotland by the 1140s, and in thirteenth-century Wales and Ireland. Those who owed money rents were, by and large, free to raise the cash by whatever means they chose. Hence they enjoyed more freedom than those tenants who had to work on their lord's demesne (home farm). In eastern England where landlords had early given up labour services and regulation of the tenantry, the result had been both partible inheritance and an active land market. Free tenants were better placed to take advantage of market forces – but were also more vulnerable to them. Up to a point servile tenancies were protected by manorial custom; hence by 1300 free tenants were more likely than serfs to hold five acres or less of land. Smallholders with families could not have survived unless they supplemented their income by part-time employment as craftsmen producing goods for sale or as labourers on neighbouring farms. But rising population meant a greater pool of labour and low wages. The real wage rates of English farmworkers, which can be calculated from the early thirteenth century onwards, were at their lowest in the decades either side of 1300. (See graph on p. 60.)[39]

Rising population also meant, of course, a rising demand for basic foodstuffs, above all cereals. It has been estimated that c.1300 no less than 80 per cent of an English farmworker's intake of calories came from grain, in bread, ale and the thick soup known as pottage (to which peas and beans might be added).[40] It is quite likely that his diet was rather more varied than record-based calculation suggests. Garden produce such as leeks, onions and garlic was grown in quantities too small to be worth the cost of taxing, and so escaped notice. Similarly, for all that the Anglo-Saxon Chronicler was incensed by the intrusiveness of the Domesday survey – not an ox, or a cow or a pig left out – it did not occur to him that chickens, ducks and geese might have been counted. Even the poorest cottager should have had the benefit of poultry meat and eggs.

None the less, it is clear that growing crops for the market became an increasingly profitable activity, especially in the more urbanised south and east of England. Hitherto most of the manors belonging to the greatest lords had in fact been leased by tenants, either in return for knight service or for a money rent. From the lord's point of view this had the benefit of producing a predictable income at minimal administrative cost. But it also meant that it was the tenants, especially those who enjoyed long leases, sometimes for the term of a life or several lives, who made the profits to be derived from agriculture. Beginning in the late twelfth century, therefore, lords began to take their manors back into their own hands, appointing bailiffs and reeves as managers. Jocelin of Brakelond's life of the businesslike Samson, Abbot of Bury St Edmunds (1182–1211), contains a vivid account of the process which, not surprisingly, provoked fierce resistance from many tenants.[41]

Under the new regime expenses and profits were bound to vary from year to year, making it easy for the manorial managers, unless carefully checked, to cheat their lords. So, on each manor, detailed records were kept and then checked by auditors who represented the central administration of a great estate. The auditors had a policymaking as well as a fraud-detecting role, fixing targets and taking investment decisions. A new literature emerged, treatises on agriculture and estate management, such as that in which Walter of Henley, with an accountant's eye allowing for what he referred to as 'the malice of ploughmen', compared the costs and benefits of horses and oxen as plough animals. The author of *The Husbandry* recommended employing a woman to look after livestock kept in the yard – pigs, chickens, geese – 'at much less cost than a man'.[42] All these changes presuppose a society capable of producing numerate and literate men in numbers, and must be associated with an expansion in the number of schools (see p. 268–9).

The survival of thousands of manorial account rolls, especially from southern and midland England for the period *c.*1270 to *c.*1380, all using the same measures (four pecks = one bushel, eight bushels = one quarter), has enabled historians to study the English manorial economy in great detail. On the demesnes of many great estates one half or one third of the arable was allowed to lie fallow each year and seed was sown at the rate of only two to four bushels an acre; farm managers achieved returns of no more than three- or fourfold. Combining this evidence with Domesday Book, recent scholars have estimated that by 1300 there was twice as much land under the plough than in 1086 – up from 6 million acres to over 12 million. Given the probability that over the same period the population doubled, it is not surprising that historians generally painted a gloomy picture of a countryside choked with people, a land threatened by soil exhaustion as each year ordinary farmers were forced to plough an increasingly high proportion of their fields. In thirteenth-century England there were protests when wealthy landlords enclosed common pasture. In Scotland an assize required lords to live off rents as lords should, 'not as husbandmen or shepherds, despoiling their lordships and the country with a huge numbers of sheep and beasts, bringing poverty and destruction upon God's people'. If the wealthiest employed the most advanced agricultural techniques, and yet yields remained stubbornly low, this seemed to imply that by 1300 England was on the brink of a Malthusian catastrophe.

But more recent research has shown that in the most densely populated regions such as parts of Norfolk, Kent and Sussex, it proved possible to achieve much higher yields. In part this was done by growing legumes such as peas and beans. Whereas human and animal dung recycled nitrogen, legumes added new nitrogen by converting atmospheric nitrogen to soil nitrogen which could then be taken up by subsequent cereal crops. The science of this would not be understood until the late nineteenth century, but experienced farmers were well aware of the importance of legumes in keeping the land 'in good heart'. Moreover legumes were used as fodder for animals kept in stalls, whose manure was collected and then spread on the soil at the optimum moment – just before ploughing, far more efficient than relying on the droppings of grazing animals, much of which would be washed away by rain. Human excrement (known as nightsoil because collected at night) was similarly recycled. By ploughing more often, and by speeding up the ploughing – using horses instead of oxen – and by more frequent weeding, better results could be obtained. Yields of over twenty bushels an acre could be achieved, standing comparison with yields obtained by Norfolk farmers in the eighteenth century.

The key was evidently the intensive use of labour; many hands behind the plough, weeding, spreading manure. For most wealthy landlords, however, as their auditors would have told them, there was no point in achieving such high yields if it meant higher labour costs. The low yields on their estates made good financial sense. But ordinary tenant farmers were their own labour force, and could count on the additional labour of their wives and children. They may well have been prepared to put in the time and effort involved in cultivating their own fields as intensively as possible. Similarly their farm animals may have been better fed, and hence more productive. Since approximately three quarters of the land of England was occupied by farmers of this kind, over much of the country productivity per acre was probably a good deal higher than it was on the well-recorded great estates. But productivity per capita was another thing altogether. For all their hard work the standard of living of the poor fell during the later thirteenth century. For smallholders and low wage-earners *c*.1300 it was a struggle just to stay alive. Bad harvests such as those of 1294 and 1295 meant that those with smallholdings suffered very badly, while those with larger farms made bigger profits than in years of good harvest. When bad harvests were relatively frequent, rich farmers got richer and poor ones poorer. For many English farmers and their families, emigration into Wales, Scotland and, after 1170, into Ireland, had long offered a way out, though a risky one. But at the end of the thirteenth century political changes turned both Ireland and Scotland into war zones into which it became even more dangerous for English people to venture. The frontiers were being shut down.

The great European famine

In the winter of 1309–10 the Thames froze over. The bonfires on the ice may be an early signal that after several warm centuries Europe's climate was entering a colder phase. But it is hard to detect any consequential changes in vegetation or farming practices in Britain and Ireland. In contrast bad weather had an immediate impact. A poor harvest in 1314 meant that rather less grain could be put aside for seed than usual. Then in spring 1315 torrential rain and floods affected all regions of Europe north of the Alps until the summer of 1316. Two successive years of harvest failure meant record prices for foodstuffs, not just cereals but also meat and all animal products, because wet weather and hay shortage combined to spread disease among cattle and sheep. Attempts to fix prices, such as the London magistrates' order that a gallon of the best ale should cost no more than 1½d., proved useless. Once again, those who possessed acreages so great that even in these years they had grain surpluses to sell made yet bigger profits, as did also, for example, London's corn-dealers. But for the labouring poor, those reliant on daily wages, 1316 was the worst year on record, creating the worst subsistence crisis of the period during which as many as half a million people may have died in England.

From many parts of Europe, including Britain and Ireland, came reports of starving people eating grass, cats, dogs and dung, digging up dead bodies or turning to murder and cannibalism, in some cases feeding upon their own children. Many such reports may be exaggerated or false, but record evidence where it survives – principally from England and Flanders – demonstrates significant increases in the rates of both mortality and accusations of theft, including thefts of as little as a pennyworth of bread. In Maidstone jail alone no less than seventy-one prisoners, most of them awaiting trial, died in 1317. These are indices of desperation and catastrophe. A good harvest in that year helped to turn things round, but not until 1318 did prices drop back to normal levels. Even then another round of livestock diseases in 1319–21 added to the miseries of the years after 1315. Those who grew enough grain to be able to take some to market even in years of poor harvest made a huge profit. Such men were able to buy more land from those so desperate that they were ready to sell their few acres in order to survive for another year. In the north of England and in Ireland the great famine coincided with the devastation caused by the war with the Bruces (see p. 120, 135–6). In Ireland, this combination meant that the English colony went on the retreat. Here pollen analysis shows the decline in cereal and rise in grass that signals a shift from arable farming towards pastoralism from the early fourteenth century onwards.

Not surprisingly, there are indications of a widespread sense of crisis. From England in this period there exists a new literary genre, the song of social protest; if such were composed and written down in earlier times they do not survive. Even if not written by the poor themselves – though some may have been – they reflect a recognition that the lot of the poor was worsening as a consequence of a crisis in the manorial economy, with bad weather and heavy royal taxation piling on the last straws. In the 'Song of the Husbandman', composed c.1340, the husbandman laments that after being 'picked full clean' by manorial officials, 'I sold my seed to seek silver for the king, wherefore my land lies fallow and learns to sleep.' To him there seemed no point in struggling on any longer in 'a world full of consternation and woe'. In another song written at about the same time, the 'Song against the King's Taxes', such were the ills of the time that 'common folk must sell their cows, their utensils and even their clothes'.[43] At least they did not sell their children into slavery as they had in the famines of the eleventh century and earlier. What they did instead was put increasing numbers of them into service with better-off farmers.

Black Death

The pestilence, christened the Black Death in the nineteenth century, was a form of plague (bubonic, pneumonic or septicaemic) which in the fourteenth century affected virtually the whole of the known world. It spread death at a speed and on a scale that has not remotely been paralleled since. It arrived in south-west England in June 1348; a few weeks later it reached Ireland. In 1349 the mortality attained staggering proportions. William Dene of Rochester wrote that 'men and women carried the bodies of their children to church and threw them into mass graves, from which there came such a stink that it was barely possible to walk by a churchyard'.[44] On the manor of Cuxham every one of the twelve tenant farmers died in 1349, and so did four of the eight cottagers. According to Henry Knighton of Leicester, 'sheep and cattle wandered through the fields and among the crops. There was no one to round them up, and for want of a keeper they perished in out of the way places amongst the furrows and under hedges in numbers beyond reckoning, for there was such a shortage of hands and servants that no one knew what to do.' The Scots, wrote Knighton, mockingly called it 'the foul death of England . . . God's judgement on the English' and were preparing an army of invasion when they too were struck down in their thousands by the 'monstrous death'. In Ireland Friar John Clyn of Kilkenny wrote that 'more people in the world have died in this short time than has been heard of since the beginning of time'. In March 1349 he described himself:

> waiting among the dead for the coming of death. I have committed to writing those things that I have truly heard and seen, and lest the work of recording perish

together with the writer, I leave parchment just in case any human survivor should remain who might wish to continue the work that I have begun.

He died soon afterwards, as did millions of others. Modern scholars, basing their estimates on many local studies, are now inclined to revise the traditional estimate of mortality throughout Britain and Ireland upwards from about one third to nearer a half of the population.

Yet society did not collapse in the face of this barely imaginable catastrophe. Excavation of a clearly identified plague cemetery, at East Smithfield, has shown that graves were laid out in an orderly fashion. Parliament was postponed but at Westminster, Exchequer, Chancery and the law courts continued to operate. Although it would be some years before the King of England felt able to go to war again, taxes continued to be collected. In 1349 more than any other year the two certainties were death and taxes.

After the Black Death

Labour shortage after 1348 led to the rich and powerful fearing conspiracies of the many against the few. In London servants were accused of banding together and refusing to work until their wages were doubled. In response the English government issued the Ordinance of Labourers (1349), aimed at keeping wages down to pre-1348 levels. The able-bodied were to work not beg. Offenders were to be imprisoned; hence a proliferation of stocks at village level. When Parliament finally reconvened in 1351, the Statute of Labourers reiterated the provisions of the ordinance in language that reflected the feelings of men alarmed by the prospect of a world turned suddenly upside

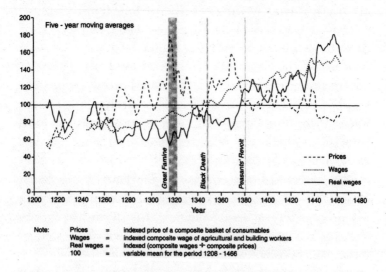

Note:

Prices	=	indexed price of a composite basket of consumables
Wages	=	indexed composite wage of agricultural and building workers
Real wages	=	indexed (composite wages ÷ composite prices)
100	=	variable mean for the period 1208 - 1466

5. Prices, wages and real wages in England, 1208–1446 (five-year moving average).

down by 'the malice of servants' who 'for the sake of their own comfort and greed completely disregard the said Ordinance' and demand 'outrageous wages'.[45] Justices were appointed to enforce the statute in Wales and Ireland as well as in England. The apparent lack of equivalent action in Scotland is probably to be explained by the fact that the king was a prisoner in England (see p. 120).

Despite their fears, wealthy landowners did quite well in the 1350s. A reservoir among the poor and younger sons meant that there was no difficulty in finding tenants to replace those who died. Heriots (death duties) and entry fines boosted landlords' incomes, enabling them to pay higher wages (economic reality proving stronger than the endeavours of Justices of Labourers). The combination of post-pestilence dislocation and poor harvests kept grain prices relatively high.

But developments in the 1360s and 1370s – first the second epidemic, the so-called Grey Plague, in 1361–2, then a series of good harvests in the later 1370s – ensured that the generation born around the time of the Black Death lived through one of the greatest reversals in British economic history.

Grain prices came tumbling down, and stayed low. Labour was in such short supply that even the most powerful lords faced stiff competition from other employers; hence they had to pay high wages and look after their workers better than before. Harvest workers received allowances of twice as much ale per day as before the plague, and of bread made of wheat instead of barley. The poet William Langland looked askance at the pretentions and ambitions of even the landless, those who had, as he put it, 'no land to live on but their shovels', yet who could be imagined as parroting the French of the upper classes.

Draught-ale was not good enough for them any more, nor bacon, but they must have fresh meat or fish, fried or baked and chaud or plus chaud at that, lest they catch a chill on their stomachs. So it is nowadays. The labourer is angry unless he gets high wages.[46]

The economic power of lords and employers had been decisively weakened. A craftsman's real wages were now at least three times as high as c.1300. Some workers had paid holidays, and more people than ever before could afford to travel or go on pilgrimage. The labour shortage created more opportunities for paid employment for both women and the young, and although both groups continued to be paid lower wages than grown men, it may be that these opportunities allowed some women to become more independent. Whether the numbers who gained from this were large enough to justify labelling the period 1350–1450 'a golden age for women' remains controversial.

The long-term removal of population pressure dramatically changed the appearance of the countryside. Settlements contracted and gradually over the century and a half after the Black Death many, such as those high on the Lammermuir Hills, came to be abandoned altogether. In England perhaps as many as 3,000 former settlements became 'ghost villages', the traces of which still show up clearly in aerial photographs. In many places land reverted to its former uncultivated state. Drainage systems and dykes were neglected; reclaimed marshland, in Sussex for example, was abandoned. Dendrochronological studies demonstrate a post-1350 regeneration of woodland. When heavy clay land was returned to pasture, the evidence of former generations of ploughing could – and can – be seen in ridge and furrow undulations in the grass. Since demand for meat, leather and wool was much more elastic than demand for grain (except, of course, grain used for brewing), it made sense for landowners to switch from arable to grazing sheep and cattle. The increasing use of horses as plough animals (visible from the thirteenth century) allowed a greater focus on cattle as providers of meat and milk. Rising demand for fresh and tender meat (including veal) meant that farmers slaughtered their livestock at a younger age, chickens and 'green geese' too. In some regions, such as the English Midlands, the shift from arable to livestock husbandry may have been on a scale sufficient to curtail female employment. The relaxation of pressure on land allowed animals to be better fed, and in consequence – as zooarchaeological evidence suggests – to increase in size. As settlements contracted so too did the need to maintain common rights over pasture, making it easier for some farmers to create private enclosures so that animals could be grazed without supervision from a herdsman. Another alternative to growing grain was to try a niche product such as saffron, prized both as a spice and dyestuff. The people living in and around one Essex market town specialised in this so much that it was soon to become Saffron Walden.

Compared with other estate owners, those manorial lords who had resisted the temptation to turn the labour services of their villeins into money rents were now in a relatively strong position – so long as they could keep their serfs on their manors. Consequently many lords made leaving as difficult as possible. On the other hand the fierce competition for labour at key times during the agricultural year led to other employers welcoming runaway serfs and treating them as freemen. Now that the terms of the free market in labour were on the side of the employee, serfdom – the condition in which hundreds of thousands of people still lived – became an explosive issue. In purely economic terms labour shortage might have led to the reintroduction of forced labour, but after two centuries without slavery, its reimposition was evidently inconceivable. Indeed the abolition of serfdom became one of the central demands of rebels in 1381 (see p. 165). It was in the most prosperous south-east where opportunities and hence frustrations were at their greatest that men rebelled. According to one account, the rebellion in Kent was triggered by the high-profile recapture of an escaped serf. In the event serfdom was never formally abolished, but the fundamentals of the economic situation both before and for long after 1381 meant that it slowly withered away. After 1381 few attempts were made to enforce the labour laws.

Many lords decided to move out of the direct management of their estates. They returned to the practice of leasing out their manors, even though land plenty meant that they were in no position to make harsh terms. One consequence was that masses of manorial records were no longer needed. Hence estate administration throughout Britain and Ireland in the century after c.1380 is much less well documented than in the previous hundred years. This only means it becomes less visible to the historian, not that it became less sophisticated. The leaseholders who took over the manors (together with their home farms) had a stronger personal incentive to keep a close eye on the market and make decisions accordingly than had the bailiffs and auditors who managed them in the previous era. The emergence of a new word, 'yeoman', reflected the rise of a class of substantial tenant farmers, many of them able to take on extra acres, particularly if they switched to the less labour-intensive pastoral farming. Sir John Fortescue, writing in the mid fifteenth century, liked to imagine an England in which 'there is no hamlet, however small, in which not only a rich knight, esquire or franklin could be found, but also many other free tenants and yeomen'.[47] On many manors servile tenure was replaced by copyhold; the tenant was given a copy of the entry in the manor court roll that recorded his title and terms of tenure. From the fifteenth century the Court of Chancery protected the copyholder's tenure making his position more secure than before. In some parts of England copyhold (which survived until 1926) became the most common form of landholding.

Crop yields per seed sown declined especially in East Anglia and the south-east. This was partly as a consequence of the colder and wetter weather characteristic of much of the fifteenth century and partly also because less effort was put into the selection of better seed stocks as well as into back-breaking tasks such as weeding. On the other hand more animal husbandry meant more manure and it is clear that productivity per capita improved. The poor no longer died of starvation. Wet weather in successive years in 1437 and 1438 caused the worst harvests of the century. Yet there is no evidence of greater mortality and the fact that chroniclers report that people in southern England were reduced to the extremity of eating barley, peas and beans instead of wheat, demonstrates just how much had changed since the Great Famine of the early fourteenth century.

If people no longer depended quite so much on a diet of vegetables and fruit, but ate less healthily – more roast meat and fried fresh fish (rather than dried or salted) – at least this gave them the satisfaction of imitating aristocratic manners, as also in drinking ale rather than cider, indeed developing a taste for stronger ale. Increasing demand for 'high class' birds led to the creation of swanneries and even, though more rarely, heronries. Chaucer's monk loved 'a fat swan best and roasted whole'.[48] The growing consumption of a wider range of wildfowl is both reflected and caricatured in the provision for one famous feast, the enthronement of the Archbishop of York in 1465, which in addition to thousands of domesticated fowls, included more than 1,000 quails, 500 partridges, 400 woodcocks, 400 herons, 400 plovers, 200 cranes (which hunting was making an endangered species in England), 200 bitterns, and a hundred each of curlews and egrets. In the fifteenth century beer made with hops was increasingly offered for sale in eastern England. Beer could be stored for longer than ale and distributed over longer distances; this encouraged brewing and buying in larger quantities. The rise of breweries brewing a thousand gallons of beer at a time helped to preserve the venerable English tradition for boozing. But ale remained the dominant drink. It was in this period that the ale house – as well as the stocks – was added to the amenities of the typical English village.

More people were able to afford to be fashionable. Instead of wearing loose woollen tunics, men began to wear stockings (hose) and a close-fitting tunic, often lined and therefore using double the amount of cloth; 'doublet and hose' became the standard male costume. In 1363 Parliament passed laws against people dressing 'above their station' – inevitably to no effect. Greater per capita wealth encouraged the London haberdashers to take their wide range of inexpensive consumer goods to fairs around the country. Long before the Black Death the whole population of England had become accustomed to going to markets and fairs and using money, and they did not lose the habit.

Shortage of evidence means that compared with England little is known about the economic impact of the Black Death in Ireland and in the rest of Britain. Presumably everywhere declining population gave the survivors opportunities to accumulate more land, as is implied by rental evidence for some Douglas estates in 1376–7. Aeneas Sylvius Piccolomini (see p. 17) was struck by just how much meat and fish was consumed by 'the poor, rough common people' of Scotland.[49] But even if in the north and west demographic contraction was on an English scale, this would not have had so dramatic an economic impact on regions which previously had suffered less from land hunger. In Scotland monetary inflation caused by the government's policy of debasing the coinage from 1367 onward may have meant that demands for higher wages seemed less 'outrageous' than in England. In 1426 James I instructed the aldermen and council of each burgh to vet prices and set wages, but overall the matter seems to have been much less contentious in Scotland. There was no equivalent of the 1381 rebellion.

In Wales too families were keen to leave bond land in the search for greater freedom and/or better soil. Since here all the owners of great estates were English, there was an ethnic edge to the tensions between landlords, tenants and labourers. Owain Glyndwr's revolt (1400–c.1410) precipitated a collapse of landlord control and the end of serfdom, allowing tenants to obtain more favourable terms. In Ireland the reversion to pastoral farming was hastened by the Gaelic recovery (see p. 136–7). Many English returned to the greater security of England, reversing the earlier direction of migration. The abandonment of many English settlements under the twin pressures of war and disease may have contributed to the belief of Richard FitzRalph, Archbishop of Armagh, that plague destroyed two thirds of the English nation in Ireland.

Towns and markets 2: after the Black Death

Many village markets disappeared, but the network of towns remained and the infrastructure of roads, bridges and waterways was maintained. Even so there is no doubt that almost everywhere towns were declining in size, including towns as important as York, Bristol, Lynn, Boston, Coventry, Winchester and Lincoln. Some overambitious urban foundations reverted to the status of villages. It is not surprising that the overriding impression given by town records – which survive from these centuries in much greater number and variety than from earlier – is one of gloom. But the number of town inhabitants is one thing, their per capita income quite another. Indeed it may be that population loss acted as a stimulus to the manufacturing sector of the urban economy, since high wages and increased spending power, by women as well as men, boosted the demand for all manner of goods, cloth, pots and pans, and furniture with which to fill better houses (see p. 47). The increasing number of household utensils, kitchen ware and personal items such as finger-rings, found in the excavation of late medieval sites suggests more widespread spending. All of this created employment for carpenters, butchers, fishmongers, tanners, shoemakers and workers in the woollen textile industry. 'Fifteenth-century towns, even when they had shrunk in population, were likely to be pleasanter places to live in than their thirteenth-century predecessors, with less unemployment, less destitution and less squalor.'[50] More space inside town walls meant more room for gardens.

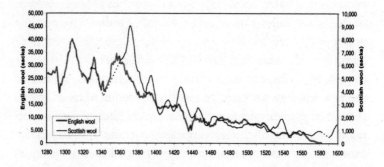

6. English and Scottish wool exports 1280–1600.
Scottish wool exports stayed at around one fifth of English throughout this period, and both, except briefly in the 1370s, 1420s and 1530s, followed a very similar and declining course, to the long-term detriment of customs revenues in both kingdoms. A similar graph for woollen cloth would show rising English exports, presumably to the overall benefit of the English economy – there being considerable added value in turning wool into cloth – but Scottish cloth exports showing little or no buoyancy.

There was certainly a massive revival of the English cloth industry after its earlier difficulties in the face of foreign competition (see p. 47). Customs records make it possible to measure cloth exports from 1347 onwards. From a total of just over 4,400 cloths (a cloth was twenty-four yards long, and 1.5–2 yards wide) in 1347–8, exports of woollen cloth reached 10,000 by 1360, 40,000 by the 1390s and 60,000 by the 1440s. The effects of the mid-fifteenth-century bullion famine on international trade meant that cloth exports dipped between 1450 and 1470, but they then resumed the upward rise, which in contrast to the decline in exports of raw wool (see p. 203) took them to almost 80,000 by the end of the century. The burgeoning cloth export trade created employment for a wide range of skills, some of them traditionally women's work such as carding and spinning – for which the spinning wheel increasingly replaced the distaff or spindle. Much of the dyeing, weaving, fulling and finishing of cloth was done in newly prospering rural areas such as Stroudwater in Gloucestershire or the Stour Valley on the Essex–Suffolk border, where water power was used to drive fulling mills. Here places such as Lavenham and Hadleigh grew in size and specialism sufficient to rank as towns – though without borough status. Moreover the new fashions for close-fitting clothes required much more cutting and sewing from an increasing number of tailors – in many towns one of the most numerous crafts. In London the most common occupation of those who had their wills registered between 1374 and 1488 was that of tailor, and the next brewer. Even in towns which got smaller such as York and Coventry the cloth-making industry expanded. London too was smaller than before 1348 but a visiting Venetian was impressed by its wealth c.1500. He counted fifty-two goldsmiths' shops in Cheapside 'so full of silver vessels, great and small, that in all the shops in Milan, Rome, Venice and Florence put together, I do not think there would be so many of the magnificence to be seen in London'.[51] In his view English pewter dishes were hardly inferior to silver in quality. Pewter goods, using the tin of Devon and Cornwall, were – after cloth – England's second most valuable manufactured export. London metalworkers supplied the finest memorial brasses and church bells all over England; many survive to this day, including no less than seven bells made in the Aldgate foundry (which in the early fifteenth century had a workforce of eighteen) while it was being run by Johanna Hill (d.1441). London was unquestionably the driving force in the English economy. Assessed at five times as much as its nearest rival in 1334 (Bristol), by the time of the next reassessment, in 1520, it was rated at eleven times as much as Norwich, then its nearest rival.

A new feature of urban life was the appearance of large inns in towns on major roads, especially those leading to and from London. Since the richer lords had reverted to leasing their manors in return for a money rent, they no longer had the option of consuming on the spot the produce of the manors while keeping an eye on local managers. Hence they travelled around their estates a great deal less than before. Instead, like more recent landed aristocrats, they divided their time between a London house and just two or three country houses, letting their other manor houses fall into decay. With fewer homes to call their own, when they and their households needed somewhere to stay the night, they called in at the inns. One of the scenes in a phrase book written in 1396 for people wishing to learn French envisaged a man arriving at an inn and being offered a choice between 'two beautiful girls as usual'.[52] That this was more than just an attempt to spice up a rather arid manual is suggested by the fact that the Habsburg envoy,

Nicolas Poppelau, reported receiving similar offers when staying at English inns in 1484.

Population 2: fourteenth and fifteenth centuries

After the 'great European famine' of 1315 and 1316 population levels seem to have recovered fairly quickly, but there was no such recovery from the Black Death and its aftershocks (including further visitations in 1361–2, 1375, 1390 and then a dozen local outbreaks during the course of the fifteenth century). Most estimates of the late fifteenth-century population of England put it at not much over 2 million, perhaps no bigger than it had been in 1086. Not until the sixteenth century did population levels rise again. Calculations of the life expectancy of Essex farmers at the age of twelve indicate that it was falling from forty-two in the late fourteenth century to thirty-six in the later fifteenth. A study of male replacement rates of the English aristocracy suggests that they averaged only 0.75 in the period 1350–1450. Why population levels remained low for so long after 1348 is a puzzle.

Economic circumstances (land plenty, high wages, low food prices and rents) appear to be ideal conditions for early marriage and a rising birth rate. Was it simply a consequence of disease and higher mortality rates, perhaps as a result of higher vulnerability to influenza and other diseases (tuberculosis, dysentery) to which people were more susceptible in a damper and colder climate? One historian speculated that this period represented a 'golden age of bacteria'.[53] Although it does seem that the earliest cases of venereal syphilis in Britain date from this period, what study has so far been made of human skeletal remains gives little support to this hypothesis.[54]

One possible explanation for low birth rates might link it with the established convention that led to children, usually in their early teens, leaving their parents' home in order to enter service with other families until they were in their twenties while their parents in turn took other children, both male and female, into their home. To a Venetian visitor to England the presence of so many 'life-cycle servants' seemed puzzlingly strange and cruel.

> When I asked the reason for this severity, they answered that they did it in order that their children might learn better manners. But I, for my part, believe that they do it because they like their comforts and they are better served by strangers than they would be by their own children. Anyway it saves them money because they do not have to feed them so well.

Severe or not, such customs may have had the effect of delaying marriage. Apprentices in late medieval England were typically bound to their masters for seven years, and during that time they could not marry. The Venetian imagined that at least they had prospects, writing that the master's widow 'usually bestows herself in marriage upon the apprentice living in the house who was not displeasing to her while her husband was still alive'.[55] In a contract drawn up in 1371 between a master bowyer of York and an apprentice, the master promised to teach the apprentice everything he knew about the craft, provide board, lodging, clothes and shoes; in return the apprentice promised to be obedient and not to play at dice, or go to gambling houses, inns or brothels. In the event of sex with his master's wife or daughter, the period during which he was bound was doubled from seven years to fourteen.

More common than apprentices were young servants taken on at hiring fairs and employed on contracts renewable after each year or half-year. This adolescent mobility may well have led them to hope they might better themselves. Evidence of the hopes of 'life-cycle servants' is naturally hard to come by. One thirteenth-century preacher described a servant girl walking to market with milk and poultry to sell, and daydreaming about advancing first to dealing in pigs and sheep and then in oxen, until she was rich enough to ride on horseback and marry a nobleman.[56] In such cases they might defer marriage until they felt they had reached the point beyond which they were unlikely to climb.

If in England a late medieval pattern of later marriage marks a shift from an earlier pattern of earlier marriage, it is not easy to explain so fundamental a change in people's expectations except – perhaps – as a response to a perceived crisis. Was one of the consequences of 'the world of consternation and woe' (see p. 57) that significant numbers of young men and women chose to postpone marriage? And in the world of opportunity that opened up for those who survived the Black Death did delayed marriage remain an attractive option? Such questions are probably unanswerable. Whatever the causes it looks as though more couples had no children and in consequence provision for old age began to shift from family to charity, whether private charity, as in the foundation of almshouses, or communal, as in the parish 'common box'.

Age of gold

In the fourteenth century the currency of Britain was transformed. A rapid growth in the supply of gold (from newly discovered mines in Hungary, combined with continuing supplies of gold from the Sudan) permitted Edward III to emulate his rival, Philip VI of France, in striking gold coin. This he ordered in 1343, and at better than 99 per cent gold, a level of purity maintained until 1526. Such were the complications of managing a bimetallic currency, however, that it was not until 1351 that a workable gold:silver ratio was achieved. In addition to the noble valued at half a mark (6s. 8d.), half and quarter nobles were also issued. In 1357 the Scots followed suit. Gold, increasingly crucial in international transactions, both commercial and political (such as the subsidies paid to allies in the Hundred Years War), was obviously not for everyday use. In 1351 the English government successfully increased the flexibility of silver by issuing groats (for the first time since 1281) and half-groats (2d.) – useful in the light of the wage rises following the Black Death (see p. 61).

But over the next hundred years European stocks of silver gradually ran out. In Edward I's recoinage of 1279 about 100 tonnes of silver had been reminted; when Henry IV carried out the same exercise in 1411–14 only 2 tonnes were. Because Henry had gold equivalent to 70 tonnes of silver reminted, the total volume of currency remained at about £1 million, where it had been since 1351, but by 1411 there was probably no more than £200,000 worth of silver coin in the kingdom. By 1422 the stock of silver per head had fallen to at most two shillings, four or five times less than it had been in 1320. In response to the rising price of silver on the international market, the penny was reduced in weight on three occasions between 1344 and 1351, again in 1412 when its weight was fixed at 0.97 grams, and then again in 1464, when it was reduced to 0.78 grams. Stray finds of coins on excavated village sites indicate that accidental coin losses, after reaching a high point between 1279 and 1351, fell back to twelfth and early thirteenth-century levels, with cut half and quarter pennies once again making an appearance. The dearth of small change was keenly felt. In 1379 the king was advised to strike more halfpennies and farthings, but the Europe-wide silver shortage made it impractical. Commons petitions in 1380, 1394 and 1445 complained that the shortage of halfpennies and farthings not only made it hard for the poor to buy things but also inhibited the charity of the better off.

Not surprisingly European governments analysed the difficulties which their subjects faced in monetary terms – the 'scarcity of bullion' – and devised policies intended to keep bullion within the country. In 1429 the Bullion Ordinance required payment in gold or silver and in full for all English wool bought at the Staple at Calais (see p. 205). This angered the Duke of Burgundy, contributing to his switch of sides in the Hundred Years War in the 1430s (see p. 111). But a favour-able balance of trade enabled the English Crown to avoid the instability and inflationary effect of debasement far more successfully than all other contemporary governments. When the supply of gold also dwindled in the 1440s, the mint at the Tower of London was at times the only mint in north-western Europe that managed to stay open. Throughout the long period of silver shortage the English Crown, unlike govern-ments elsewhere, never minted 'black money', a billon or copper coinage. Yet what can be interpreted as government success – the maintenance of a relatively high silver standard – had its downside in the shortage of small change, though to some extent lead-alloy tokens and local credit may have plugged the gap. Archaeological evidence (see p. 68) suggests that people somehow found ways of spending. At the level of 'big business', new credit arrangements were offered by the several Italian banks, the Alberti, Bardi and Medici for example, with branches in London. Ledgers recording transactions made by the London branch of Borromei and Company (a Milanese bank) in the 1430s show that about 180 merchants were using its facilities to write and accept bills of exchange and to settle debts by book transfers without any coin changing hands. Whether this created paper money on a scale sufficient to offset the mid-fifteenth-century shortage of bullion remains, in the absence of other similar evidence, a moot point.

The Scottish government took a different course. In 1367, wishing to attract more silver into the country to pay David II's ransom, it ended its centuries-old policy of shadowing England's currency and began a policy of debasement that over the next century whittled away at the Scottish penny until by 1470 it was mostly copper (3.5 grains of silver) and worth only one third of an English penny. (Debasement encouraged merchants to take coin to mints because at face value they received more money back than they brought in.) In Ireland in the 1460s mints under the authority of the Dublin government (Dublin, Waterford and Drogheda) began to strike not only pennies, halfpence and farthings at three quarters of the weight of English counterparts, but even half-farthings in copper. Beyond the Pale (the four counties of Dublin, Meath, Louth and Kildare), Gaelic imitations, known as 'O'Reilly's money', were minted.

The mid-fifteenth-century 'bullion famine' was not alleviated until new silver-bearing ores were discovered in the Tyrol and Saxony in the 1460s and improved pumps allowed old mines to be reopened, once again bringing the English currency up to about £1 million by the end of the century. In 1465 three new gold coins were minted: the rose noble (or noble ryal) worth ten shillings, plus halves and quarters worth

5s. and 2s. 6d. By 1485 there was a coinage of ten denominations (five of them gold, five silver) between a farthing and ten shillings, a very far cry from the one-coin economy that had existed until 1279.

Houses and homes

Houses represent one of the best indicators of the gradual development of material culture over these centuries – even though the kinds of houses in which the overwhelming majority of the populations lived can be traced only archaeologically. The only pre-1066 buildings of which remains still survive today above ground are a few churches. Despite the increasing wealth of the elites in the tenth and eleventh centuries, nothing of the houses they built for themselves survives above ground, except in timberless places such as the Orkneys and Shetland. Everywhere else the residences of the powerful consisted of an enclosure containing a number of timber buildings, principally a hall, chambers for the lord and his family, accommodation for visitors and senior servants, a kitchen, a brewhouse, workshops, stables and at least one privy, generally all of them single-storey buildings, visible today only as excavated post-holes, since they were constructed using earth-fast timbers which rotted away. The Old English word for 'to build' is (ge-)timbran.

The Norman conquerors of England, unlike their Danish predecessors, celebrated their triumph in stone. 'Let us picture in our mind's eye the wooden thatched houses that made up most human habitations . . . In colour and texture, with their timber and reeds, their turves and moss, they would have looked like something growing out of the natural environment, not a sharp artificial contrast to it . . . In such a world large-scale stone constructions stood out. They meant power.'[57] England *c*.1100 has been described as 'a vast building site'.[58] Buildings such as the Conqueror's Colchester Castle and White Tower of London, William II's Westminster Hall, and monumental churches such as St Albans, Winchester, Durham, Ely and York were the largest of their kind to be erected in northern Europe since the fall of Rome. Stone brought huge advantages. Fireplaces and chimneys could safely be set in the thickness of stone walls, so that it was no longer necessary to rely for warmth upon open fires or braziers in the centre of the floor space, with a louvre in the roof to draw out some of the smoke. Thick walls could hold lead pipes for running water from a well or from a cistern on the roof; they could also house corridors and private rooms, above all privies. Except in the borderlands with Wales and Scotland, the 'castles' built in England were 'power houses' in which comfort and fashionable display counted for more than defence. Financial records, surviving from the twelfth century on, show just how much more expensive it was to build in stone instead of timber. A timber hall, chamber block, kitchen and gatehouse all within a sixteen-foot-high palisade at Kinver in Staffordshire cost Richard I £24 18*s*. 9*d*. By contrast Henry II's great stone tower at Newcastle upon Tyne cost £912.

Unsurprisingly the kings of England set the fashion. Henry II built a wine cellar at Clarendon; an audit of King John's wines in 1201 revealed that he had 180,000 gallons (700 tuns) of wine in stock. By 1300 Edward I and his wife had separate bathrooms at Westminster; by the fifteenth century the provision of bathrooms at Caister Castle indicates they were widely fashionable among the aristocracy. Naturally everyone, including kings, great lords and country gentry, continued to build in timber, often using timber from their own estate, but increasingly on stone foundations. By the thirteenth century, what had once been separate buildings were being brought together to make a single whole, the standard 'English medieval house' with hall, chambers and service rooms (buttery and pantry) all under one roof, though owing to the risk of fire kitchens remained detached for longer. The increasing use of glass allowed rooms to be better lit; window seats set into walls enabled people to enjoy it, and gave them a better view of the gardens, fishponds, orchards and parks in which they took so much pleasure.

A few twelfth-century town houses still survive, in Lincoln and Waterford for example. Two storeys high and built in stone, such houses seemed to contemporaries to be urban palaces. By 1300 London's houses, counting stone cellars three or four storeys high, timber-built, roof-tiled, towered over the one- or two-storey houses typical of English market towns. In towns the poor lived in rented accommodation. Lady Row in Goodramgate in York is a surviving range of two-storeyed jettied houses with just one room on each floor, ten feet by fifteen, built in 1316. Those who crowded into them, with little or no space for cooking, must sometimes have relied on fast-food shops for hot meals (see p. 36). Thanks to the gradual adoption of improved methods of construction – setting timber houses on low stone walls or on pad stones – a few small village houses still stand that were erected in late thirteenth-century southern England. Elsewhere building materials and techniques were not such as would either leave much archaeological record or survive for centuries above ground – even if Gerald de Barri's description of Welsh houses in the 1190s as 'wattled huts, sturdy enough to last a year or two' may be unduly condescending.[59] Not until the later Middle Ages can stone houses, often in the form of 'tower houses', be found in both town and country in Ireland, Scotland and Wales. In Ireland the earliest were built in English areas, but by the fifteenth century the form had been adopted by the most powerful Irish. Bunratty, for example, was by then the principal residence of O'Briens. None the less, visitors to Ireland and to the north and west of Britain in this period remained struck by seeing what seemed to them primitive houses made of wattle and clay with turf roofs and oxhide doors. The greater settlement mobility that went with a more pastoral economy meant that in these regions relatively little was invested in house building.

In England, however, the redistribution of wealth that followed the Black Death meant that many thousand substantial houses were erected in both town and country in the century after 1375. With slate or tile roofs, stone hearths and chimneys, they were built to a standard that has allowed several thousand to stand to the present day, mostly in the south-east of England – perhaps over 2,000 in Kent alone. The insertion of a second storey, with a number of smaller rooms taking up the space once occupied by a 'public' hall, implies the continuing development of ideas of private domestic space. Inside the homes of even the less well off, people increasingly replaced their wooden tableware with ceramic or metal cups, jugs, pots and plates. Not that wood was being abandoned. Better-designed tools such as the frame saw and breast auger both saved on construction costs and improved the standard of workmanship. More houses were built by professional carpenters and furnished with finely joined stools, tables, chairs and cupboards.

Technology

The names of the inventors of these better tools are not known, just as all those significantly responsible for medieval technological advances, with the single exception of Johannes Gutenberg of Mainz, either remain anonymous or, like Roger Bacon, owe this claim to fame to later legend. In the absence of heroic figures, it has often seemed as though technology was at a virtual standstill throughout the eleventh to the fifteenth centuries. And so it was, of course, compared with the rapidly increasing speed of technological advance to which we have become accustomed. But compared with the 600 years that went before, these were centuries which witnessed accelerating change. Indeed the three inventions credited by Francis Bacon and Karl Marx with changing the world – printing, gunpowder and the compass – all came into Europe in this period. So did others which we take for granted: spectacles and the mechanical clock, for instance. Some advances were essentially the recovery of Roman techniques which had lapsed during the 'darker ages', but others were clearly innovative, as in the invention of mills designed to harness the renewable energy of the wind and apply it to the most basic need, the grinding of corn, work which had previously depended upon the power of women (often slave women), animals (as in horse-mills) and water.

Domesday Book records over 6,000 mills in England, and since the earliest explicit references to windmills date from the late twelfth century, it seems that they were all watermills. Water power had been exploited in Britain and Ireland for many centuries, using either the relatively low-cost horizontal wheel or the more complex vertical wheel with gearing. Windmills represented the adaptation of this gearing system to an entirely

7. A fourteenth century drawing of a postmill with stepladder leading up to the door. The long tall-pole was used to turn the sails into the wind.

new power source. The earliest known windmills are found either side of the North Sea and English Channel, suggesting that they were first developed in this part of the world, where mouths were plentiful and strongly flowing rivers comparatively few and far between. Known as postmills because they were balanced on a massive and firmly anchored upright post, the whole wooden superstructure could be turned so that its sails stayed facing the wind. So revolutionary a design attracted ambitious investors, and not all their mills turned a profit. But by *c.*1300 a significant design improvement meant that only the mill's cap needed to be turned, allowing the main structure to be built of masonry and made much taller (hence its name: tower mill), with longer and more efficient sails. The construction of windmills may have helped to reduce the pressure to build mills to the detriment of river transport, but water power continued to be used, of course, and was put to an expanding variety of uses: to drive hammers in the process of fulling cloth in the twelfth century, for example, and to power bellows in the iron and tin industries from the thirteenth century.

Transport was another sphere which saw advances, most importantly at sea. The earliest known description of a compass was composed by the English scholar, Alexander Nequam, in the 1180s. He said that sailors used it when cloud cover meant that they could see neither sun nor stars. In the eleventh century, boats and ships in the waters around Britain and Ireland were clinker-built, open-decked and single-masted, steered by side rudders and propelled by oars and a square sail. In the twelfth century the advent of the bulk-carrying cog, with its deep hull, high freeboard and sternpost rudder, meant a big increase in the volume of seaborne trade in northern waters (see p. 44–5). Taken south the cog was converted to the Mediterranean tradition of skeleton-building, and brought back north in the shape of the great Genoese ships the English called carracks. Henry V's response to their employment by the French in the war at sea was to order the construction of equally large warships, including the 1,000-ton *Jesus* and the 1,400-ton *Grace Dieu,* a three-master bigger than any English man-of-war built in the next 300 years. By the mid fifteenth century, after a few decades of rapid development in ship building facilitated by the spread of water-powered sawmills, ships could be three-masters, multi-decked and fully rigged; set with square sails on fore and main masts, and a lateen mizzen, this rigging permitted not only small caravels but even the largest three-masters to handle much better than their predecessors.

Innovation in the field of land transport was less dramatic.

In the Roman world horses had rarely been used for pulling anything heavier than a light chariot, but during the twelfth and thirteenth centuries, thanks to improvements in harness and vehicle design, they were increasingly used for ploughing and for pulling loaded carts. Horse-drawn ploughs and carts could go at least half as fast again as those pulled by oxen, and although horses could not cope with such heavy loads as oxen, their speed offered greater flexibility of use. To help speed up road traffic hundreds of new bridges were built and old ones widened. From the twelfth century onwards the most important bridges were built of stone, some of them by the employment of techniques, such as great arches, better known in other architectural spheres.

Most visible today is in the recovery of the engineering capacity to erect stone buildings of a size to match those of fourth-century Rome, hence the term 'Romanesque' for the ecclesiastical architecture of the Norman period. In this period (1066–1154) no less than nine churches were built which can be compared in size with Constantine's St Peter's in Rome: Winchester, St Augustine's and Christ Church at Canterbury, St Albans, York, Ely, Norwich, Bury St Edmunds and Durham. The Norman kings erected at London, Colchester and Norwich palatial great towers unlike anything that survives from Anglo-Saxon England, as well as halls of a type familiar from pre-Conquest days but now on a truly imperial scale, as at Westminster. This is the only period of English history in which its principal buildings outstripped in size, quality and number the equivalent buildings elsewhere in Europe – a phenomenon made possible by the Conquest and its concentration of great wealth in a few hands.

Two twelfth-century innovations, rib vault and flying buttress, opened the way for an entirely new architectural style. Rib vaults allowed roofs wide enough to span choirs and naves to be built of stone instead of wood, thus reducing the risk of fire. Flying buttresses supported upper walls thin enough to permit large windows and additional storeys. These innovations (first seen at Durham), when used in combination with the pointed arch, enabled master masons to build walls which appeared to be sheets of coloured glass, creating soaring inner spaces filled with light. The new style, now usually known as Gothic, and first seen in mid-twelfth-century France, was widely taken up, both to build new cathedrals such as Salisbury, Dublin and Glasgow, and to update old ones. The patrons' striving for dominating height led to remarkable feats of engineering as when spires reached up to 400 feet (as still standing at Salisbury) and over 500 feet at Lincoln and London.

Turning from worship to war, so great was the impression which the hundreds of castles built in Norman England made on the landscape and on the mind of the Anglo-Norman chronicler Orderic Vitalis, that he believed that if the English had had castles then the Conquest would not have happened. Welsh princes began to build castles in stone in the 1170s, as (probably, given the absence of written sources) did Scottish kings. In technological terms the main threat to stone fortifications came from Roman-style artillery; that was considerably increased by the introduction of the counterweight trebuchet c.1200. Gunpowder was brought to Europe soon afterwards, though it was originally employed more as a grenade than as a firearm. At the siege of Stirling in 1304 Edward I employed a dozen trebuchets capable of hurling stones weighing a hundred kilos or more, but also used them to throw clay pots packed with gunpowder. Firearms proper were introduced in the fourteenth century, initially as light anti-personnel weapons, and used as such in naval as well as land warfare. By the

1370s gun-founders, working in iron or bronze, had discovered ways of making much bigger guns capable of delivering massive horizontal blows very different from the high trajectory of previous siege artillery. In 1405 just one shot from one of Henry IV's cannons was enough to make Berwick surrender. Except along the south coast the threat of war was never pressing enough to push town authorities into transforming their defences by pulling down their now vulnerable stone walls and replacing them with bastions, essentially wide earthwork gun platforms, as was happening throughout the Continent. But siege guns now made it rather harder for the magnate in his castle to dominate the surrounding countryside in times of crisis. Kings such as James II of Scotland and Edward IV of England took care to build up considerable artillery trains.

Much less persuasive as an example of advance in the technology of war is the largely mythical tale of the longbow. For many centuries there had been bows as long as those used at Agincourt or found in the wreck of the *Mary Rose*. From *c*.1300 English warbows may have been marginally more powerful than before, but essentially it was not so much a new type of bow as the effective use of massed ranks of strenuously trained archers which helped bring about those victories in battle against the French which remain famous in English eyes. A stronger case for developmental change in the technology of war can be made for the crossbow, seemingly first brought to Britain at Hastings in 1066.

The revolutionary method of reproducing script by means of movable type came to Britain in 1476 when Caxton set up his printing press at Westminster, having learned the technique in Cologne and published the first printed books in English the previous year at Bruges. No matter how small early printed editions may have been, perhaps averaging only 200 copies, this represents an astonishing advance in information technology when compared with the productivity of a scribe.

Material conclusions

During these centuries Britain and Ireland in some ways had changed little. The overwhelming bulk of the population still lived and worked on small farms, kept animals and grew crops, including vegetables and fruit, but especially the grain used for making their daily bread and ale; people still took their bread to communal bakehouses to be baked. To observers from grain-growing countries it always seemed that pastoralists enjoyed an easy life. Although the climate may have entered a colder phase in the fourteenth century, it is hard to demonstrate consequential changes in farming practices. The family and the household always remained the basic unit of economic as well as of social life. Such industry as there was took place at home, whether indoors, in the yard, or on the street outside the shop. Everywhere inheritance customs favoured sons over daughters. For most children their home was also their school, and from the age of seven or eight they were expected to help their parents in the unremitting round of gender-divided work described in a fifteenth-century song with the title (given to it in the nineteenth century) 'Ballad of the Tyrannical Husband'. A ploughman, returning home after a day's work, suggests to his wife that his dinner is not yet ready because she has been gossiping to the neighbours; her furious answer is a very long list of the tasks that keep her busy night and day.[60]

But in some almost as fundamental ways Britain and Ireland had been transformed. In the eleventh century slavery was still an important source of labour. By the end of the period slavery no longer existed, and nor did its lesser cousin, serfdom. Men and women, especially women, the chief victims of the slave trade, were significantly freer than they had ever been before. None of this was the result of a more enlightened attitude on the part of the governing classes. It was the outcome of changing economic conditions, accelerated in England and Wales by the preparedness of people to rebel, in England in 1381, and in Wales after 1400.

By the end of the period writing was being used a great deal more, and a great deal more of it survives. Because this allows historians to write histories full of new kinds of detail, they always run the risk of giving the impression that new things were happening, when sometimes the only new thing was that they were recorded in forms that have survived. But it is also true that some changes created a greater need for written records. By the end of the period more than 600 new towns had been founded, and thousands of new markets had appeared. There was not only per capita more money in circulation, both in coin and in credit, than at the start of this period, but the widening range of denominations (from ten shillings down to farthings) in combination with inflation meant that coins were very much more useful than they had been when only pennies were minted. Although looking back from the twenty-first century it may seem to us that Britain and Ireland remained overwhelmingly rural economies, this is not how it seemed to those who participated in the process of urbanisation and commercialisation. The operation of the market meant that it was no longer so easy to rely on memory. Documents were needed if frequent short-term changes in prices were to be accurately registered.

In terms of loss of human life the Black Death of 1348–9 was catastrophic, the greatest disaster to strike the people of

Europe in recorded history. But although that great mortality undoubtedly resulted in some setbacks to the economies of Britain and Ireland, the institutional, technological and cultural infrastructure built up in the previous centuries did not wither, as such things had after the withdrawal of the Roman government from Britain. The innovations of the pre Black Death centuries survived, to the benefit of surviving generations. It is important not to exaggerate the extent of rural prosperity. Although the real wages of agricultural workers remained high throughout the fifteenth century, the intermittent demand for their labour meant that, when compared with workers in recent centuries, wages comprised a relatively small part of their annual earnings. Even so, in England GDP per head is thought to have been some 50 per cent higher in 1470 than in 1300. People everywhere lived in better houses and more of them could read.

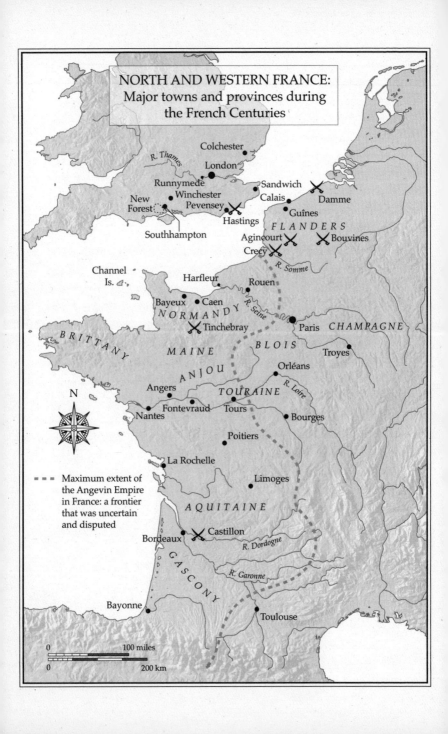

NORTH AND WESTERN FRANCE: Major towns and provinces during the French Centuries

Colchester

R. Thames

London

Runnymede

Sandwich

New Forest

Winchester

Calais

Damme

Pevensey

Guînes

Hastings

FLANDERS

Southampton

Agincourt

Bouvines

Crecy

Channel Is.

R. Somme

Harfleur

Rouen

Bayeux

Caen

R. Seine

NORMANDY

Paris

CHAMPAGNE

Tinchebray

BRITTANY

MAINE

BLOIS

Troyes

ANJOU

Orléans

TOURAINE

R. Loire

Angers

Fontevraud

Tours

Bourges

Nantes

Poitiers

La Rochelle

Limoges

N

AQUITAINE

- - - Maximum extent of the Angevin Empire in France: a frontier that was uncertain and disputed

Bordeaux

Castillon

R. Dordogne

GASCONY

R. Garonne

Bayonne

Toulouse

| 0 | | 100 miles |
| 0 | | 200 km |

Part II:
Political Contours

By 1066 the present-day configuration of Britain and Ireland was in many important respects already visible. We still think of the island of Britain as being divided into England, Scotland and Wales, with England as the richest and most powerful of the three. We think of Ireland as being, for the most part, a culturally distinct and politically separate island – as the whole of it certainly was in 1066. None the less, by 1485 the political map had been completely reconfigured. In 1066 there were dozens of kings. By 1485 there were only two left, the King of England and the King of Scotland.

According to Henry of Huntingdon, writing c.1130, 'Britain, the noblest of islands, is now called England.'[1] No doubt this would have irritated many of the other people of Britain, especially the Scots and Welsh, but it reflected the fact the island contained one political unit that was much larger than all the others, the kingdom of England. Although in the north, the Tees rather than the Tweed marked the limit of the King of England's power, in the west the kingdom's borders were already very similar to those of modern England. To the north and west stretched an arc containing a fluctuating number of smaller kingships, at times as many as ten, expanding and contracting as the ambitions and military fortunes of individual kings waxed and waned. By far the most important of these was Alba, the Gaelic kingship of the Scots. In the tenth and eleventh centuries belligerent kings of Scots such as Malcolm III (1058–93), driving outwards from their core territory in the rich farmlands of Fife, succeeded in imposing their rule over the Cumbrians of Strathclyde and the English of Lothian south of the Firth of Forth and, more uncertainly, over the men of Moray to the north – the Annals of Ulster mention an apparently independent King of Moray as late as 1130. In the south-west of modern Scotland, Galloway certainly still remained independent. In the north, Caithness was ruled by the earls of Orkney and they, like the kings of Man and the Isles in the west, owed allegiance – in so far as they owed it to anyone – to the King of Norway. In 1066 indeed a king of Norway, Harald Hardrada, claimed England too, though after the Battle of Stamford Bridge he had to be content with the traditional six feet of English ground.

In eleventh-century Wales there could be as many as five kingships at any one time: Gwynedd, Powys, Deheubarth, Morgannwg and Gwent. Some of these kings were ready to acknowledge the supremacy of the kings of England, but native poetry and tradition reminded them of the days when Britain had, for the most part, been ruled by Britons whose descendants the Welsh were – indeed they still called themselves Britons. 'Welsh' was what the Saxons called them, a word they used for people who were either foreigners or slaves. The Britons looked forward to driving the Saxons into the sea. In the mid eleventh century a king came to power in north Wales who looked as though he might fulfil these hopes. By conquering other Welsh kings, Gruffudd ap Llywelyn managed to dominate the whole of Wales by 1055. In the words of a Welsh chronicler, 'he hounded the pagans [i.e. Scandinavians] and the Saxons in many battles, he prevailed against them and ravaged them'.[2] But in 1063 he was defeated by Harold Godwinson, the greatest of the English earls (and soon to be king). This led to Gruffudd being killed by his own men, and his head sent as a trophy to the English court. The unity which he had imposed on Wales did not survive his death. Once again Wales became a land of rival kings, united by culture, language and law, but not by politics. Most of them owed tribute to the King of England.

Ireland, situated on the western edge of the known world, had been largely left to its own devices. Like Wales, it too was united by culture, language and law, but politically was even more fragmented. The learned thought of it as divided into two halves, northern and southern, into five provinces – Leinster, Munster, Ulster, Connacht and Meath – and into more than a hundred peoples (*tuatha*), each one ruled over by a chief (*toisech*) or by a king (*rí*), more commonly, to judge by the language of contemporary Irish annals, the latter. A mini-kingdom with a radius of ten miles was by no means impossibly small. Each *rí túaithe* owed tribute, gifts and military service to more powerful neighbouring kings. They in turn owed allegiance to kings who were, or claimed to be, supreme in one of the provinces. It was anything but a stable hierarchy. Scores of kings competed to be the strongest in a province, or even to be the greatest in all Ireland, sometimes known as *rí Erenn*, King of Ireland, or as 'high-king'. Ireland, even more than Wales, remained in a state of constant flux. Although dominant kings interfered in the internal struggles in other provinces and sometimes appropriated land, they did not eliminate other kingdoms, at least not the greater ones, in the way that had happened in Anglo-Saxon England. In this kaleidoscopic world of ferocious competition there was no way in which a father could ensure a son's succession to the position he had had to fight for himself. As in Wales, there was no established rule of hereditary succession. When a powerful king died the war game began again at the beginning – a struggle for kingship within the family while other more established kings in other kingdoms took full advantage.

A major theme of the next 500 years of political history is the English attempt to rule the rest. The kings of England, although they had no legitimate claim to rule the other kingdoms of Britain and Ireland, invaded Ireland, conquered Wales and took over the Isle of Man. English settlers colonised parts of both Wales and Ireland, especially the lowland and more fertile parts. When King Edward I (1272–1307) launched an invasion of Scotland, a contemporary English chronicler, Peter Langtoft, believed that he was witnessing the triumphant recreation of King Arthur's legendary empire under the English Crown:

> Now are all the islanders joined together
> And Albany [Scotland] reunited to the regalities
> Of which King Edward is proclaimed lord.
> Cornwall and Wales are in his power
> And Ireland the Great is at his will.
> There is neither king nor prince of all the countries
> Except King Edward who has joined them.
> Arthur never held the lands so fully.[3]

In Wales the English succeeded in overcoming resistance and rebellion, but in Ireland a Gaelic resurgence turned the tide.

Scottish patriotic resistance in the Wars of Scottish Independence (1296–1328) was sufficient to keep the King of England out, especially as with the Hundred Years War he grew increasingly interested in the crown of France. In any case by 1300 the kingdom of the Scots was too big to swallow easily. A series of aggressive campaigns by English-speaking kings of the Scots had extended the boundaries of their kingdom northwards and westwards into areas that had a strong Gaelic culture of their own, so that the realm comprised the whole of what we think of Scotland, including the far north and the Western Isles – a process that was to be completed when they acquired Orkney and Shetland in 1472. Inevitably this was not tension-free expansion. When John Fordun drew his unflattering portrait of Highlanders (see p. 17), he described them as 'consistently hostile towards people of English speech even when they are people of their own nation'. Yet for all the hostility he assumed that there was by then one nation and one kingdom, for he continued: 'Yet they are loyal to king and kingdom, and if well governed are ready to obey the law.'[4]

Norman Conquest

As this outline indicates, during these five centuries the flow of political power had generally been from south-east to north and west. The single most violent and abrupt moment in this flow was brought about by the north-westward course of the fleet of William Duke of Normandy during the night of 27–8 September 1066 as it sailed from Saint-Valery at the mouth of the Somme to Pevensey in Sussex on the south coast of

England. Two weeks later on 14 October on a ridge a few miles north of Hastings, William won a close-run, but by the end of the day, decisive battle against King Harold of England. William's troops included men equipped with the most up-to-date military technology in the form of crossbows. Henry of Huntingdon was the earliest historian to give a technological explanation for the Norman victory. In his view, it was because they enjoyed a clear superiority in archery.[5] Since missile weapons were the most effective means of disrupting infantry drawn up in defensive formation, as Harold's were on the ridge at Battle, Henry's was a plausible analysis. The Battle of Hastings was decisive because not only was Harold killed, but so too were his brothers and many of the English nobility. The 'great battle' as it was soon to be known was a mass slaughter that shocked contemporaries on the Continent where in warfare between fellow Christians people had become accustomed to a more chivalrous pattern of conduct, one in which the wealthy and well born were not killed but captured and held to ransom (see p. 286).[6]

William marched on London, exploiting to the hilt the lack of leadership which the calculated brutality of his generalship had created. The only potential English candidate for the throne, Edward the Confessor's grandson, Edgar the Ætheling, passed over in January when Harold seized his opportunity, was still an untried adolescent in his early teens. William forced London's surrender and had himself crowned king in Westminster Abbey on Christmas Day 1066. In January 1067 he returned in triumph to Normandy. The Conqueror's panegyrist, William of Poitiers, emphasised the vast quantities of gold and silver he distributed with a liberality that no emperor could match. He brought with him many of the leading Englishmen as hostages, paraded so that the Normans and visiting French nobles could satisfy their curiosity about 'the long-haired sons of the north . . . as beautiful as girls'.

> How gloriously he returned! . . . Though it was winter the sun seemed to shine with the clear brightness of summer. When he entered Rouen, all the citizens turned to welcome him so that you would have thought the whole city was cheering as Rome had done when it applauded Pompey . . . As they looked at the clothes of the king and his courtiers, woven and encrusted with gold, they considered whatever they had seen before to be of little worth.[7]

The Anglo-Saxon Chronicler (D) saw things differently.

> Before Archbishop Aldred would place the crown on his head, he promised that he would rule all this people as well as the best of kings before him, if they would be loyal to him. All the same he laid taxes on the people very severely, and then went in spring overseas to Normandy . . . and Bishop Odo [of Bayeux, William's half-brother] and Earl William [FitzOsbern] stayed behind and built castles far and wide throughout this country, and distressed the wretched people.[8]

According to William of Poitiers, Odo and Earl William 'paid the greatest respect to justice', but it had been one of the most hazardous military operations of the century, and in order to persuade so many, Normans and others, to risk life and limb, William had promised that if he succeeded in making himself, as he claimed was his right, King of England, he would reward those who shared the gamble with the lands

of the followers of 'the usurper' Harold.[9] Keeping that
necessary promise meant confiscating estates on a grand
scale, leading to massive resentment, and risings in every year
from 1067 to 1070.

Inevitably William had the greatest trouble in controlling
England north of the Humber, almost another country cut off
from the south by the Humberhead marshes and the Pennines,
and wide open to armed intervention from both Danes and
Scots. When Cnut's nephew, King Swein of Denmark, sent a
war fleet to assist Northumbrian rebels in 1069, William's
brutally effective response was the 'Harrying of the North',
the systematic destruction of an entire society and its stock of
food and seed; massacre by sword and famine. Reports of
cannibalism reached the ears of Marianus Scottus, a renowned
Irish scholar then living in Mainz. The Danes threatened to
come again in 1085 but, as it happened they did not – a non-
event which marked the end of the 'Viking period' of English
history. The Scots posed a far more permanent threat. The survivors of the English royal dynasty, led by Edgar the Ætheling,
fled to the Scottish court in 1068. Malcolm III married Edgar's
sister Margaret, and as late as the thirteenth century there
would still be English voices who claimed that the descendants
of their sons were the rightful kings of England.

For several years the Normans had to live like an army of
occupation, building castles in an effort to control the towns
and main roads while the countryside belonged to the
resistance. Memories of the struggle survived in the tales told
about Hereward the Wake, one of this guerrilla movement's
last leaders. Apparently nothing, wrote William of Poitiers,
could 'make the English prefer peace and quiet to turbulence
and insurrection'.[10] But the rebellions were poorly
co-ordinated and suppressed, each rebellion triggering a new

wave of confiscation. In the end the War of English Independence was lost, the English political nation destroyed. By 1086, as Domesday Book makes plain, the Norman Conquest had resulted in the old English landowning class suffering the virtually total dispossession of its property or status, or both, an event unparalleled in European history. By 1100 not a single bishopric or major abbey was ruled by an Englishman. From the point of view of the old English elite in town and country, 1066 and its aftermath was the greatest crisis – so far – in the entire course of English history. The destruction of the old English aristocracy and its replacement by a francophone elite meant that, in Henry of Huntingdon's interpretation, 'God had chosen the Normans to destroy the English people.'[11] They were not in fact wiped out, but had very good cause to feel that they were rapidly sidelined politically and overwhelmed culturally. So thoroughly did the bishops and abbots of the new regime demolish the old cathedrals and monastic churches that only at Sherborne does a major church still contain any pre-1066 stone standing above ground. Their new churches were built in a new style, influenced by models from France and the Rhineland. The new castles were characterised by distinctively French design features such as great towers and mottes. But what was most striking was sheer size (see p. 84). William I's Colchester Castle, Bishop Walkelin's Winchester Cathedral and William II's Westminster Hall were the largest buildings of their kind to be erected north of the Alps since the fall of the Roman Empire. The Conqueror's Tower of London carried a message that was repeated in town after town. The new regime imposed itself on a gargantuan scale; its mark on the English landscape can still be seen today.

The French centuries

It is the French connection that, at the level of the political classes, lends a kind of unity to this period of English history. One French dynasty after another came to power in England: the dukes of Normandy in 1066, the house of Blois in 1135, the house of Anjou in 1154. This accentuated the southern character of English kingship. William of Malmesbury writing in the 1120s observed that 'while the king is in our parts he is content with a retinue of household knights, but he does not visit northern parts without strong military reinforcement'.[12] In 1216 the French royal dynasty, the Capetians, came within an ace of becoming kings of England too. The two royal families had been closely related since 1140 when King Stephen arranged the marriage of his son and heir Eustace to Constance, sister of Louis VII. After 1154 Henry II ruled a territory four times the size of that ruled by the King of France. For virtually the whole period from 1066 to 1453 the kings of England also held substantial territories in France. In consequence most of them spent some time in France, and some of them spent most of the time in France. From 1340 onwards the King of England claimed to be King of France. For 500 years from 1066 most of the kings of England had French wives. The politics of England became and remained inextricably entangled with French politics. This would be much to the dismay of many historians in more recent centuries who assumed that the destiny of the English was to rule the 'British Isles', and who believed in consequence that kings of England who spent time in France were at best wasting their time, and at worst hindering the fulfilment of England's historic task.

The Anglo-Norman realm 1066–1154

William made no conscious attempt to integrate England and Normandy into a single kingdom. When he died in 1087 he divided his two lands between his two older sons, Normandy for Robert Curthose, and England for William, known as Rufus. Inevitably as the firstborn Robert was not happy to see his younger brother get the richer part, but if both had been married and had sons of their own, the union of England and Normandy might have proved short-lived. On the other hand it might not. Driven by reasons of short-term military and political expediency, William I had in effect created an entirely new class, a cross-Channel aristocracy holding lands in both England and France (not just in Normandy since quite a few were Bretons, Flemings and Poitevins). This new class, ecclesiastical lords as well as secular barons, constituted a powerful interest group favouring Anglo-Norman political unity. In consequence William II, as the younger brother, for several years enjoyed only a precarious hold on England. Then his problems were resolved in a totally unforeseeable way. In 1095 Pope Urban II came to France to urge Christians to join an armed expedition intended to recapture Jerusalem from the Muslims (who had held it for over 400 years). Thousands were inspired by his preaching of what turned out to be the First Crusade, among them Robert Curthose. In order to equip himself and his retinue for the long march, in 1096 Robert pawned Normandy to William for 10,000 marks.

But when Rufus was struck down by an arrow while hunting in the New Forest (on 2 August 1100), it was the youngest of the three brothers, Henry, who was on hand to grab the English throne. As it happened, Robert was now on his way back from crusade, celebrated as one of those who, against overwhelming odds, had marched all the way to Jerusalem and then taken the Holy City by storm. He resumed control of Normandy. Inevitably the old tensions re-emerged and this time, after a few years of covert or open war, Henry was able to take advantage of the greater wealth of England to outbid and outmanoeuvre his brother. At the Battle of Tinchebrai (1106) Henry defeated and captured Robert, keeping him in prison until he died. In 1135 when Henry himself died without a surviving legitimate son, the Normans who chose his nephew, Theobald Count of Blois and Chartres, as their duke, changed their minds and decided to support Theobald's younger brother Stephen as soon as they heard that the latter had already been crowned and anointed king in England. By this date, the most powerful Normans, holding lands on both sides of the Channel, regarded the maintenance of the union as an overwhelming priority.

In the event Stephen's right was challenged by Henry I's daughter Matilda and her handsome husband (he was known as 'le Bel'), Count Geoffrey Plantagenet of Anjou. The capture of Stephen at the Battle of Lincoln (1141) allowed Geoffrey to make substantial gains in Normandy, and although the subsequent capture of Earl Robert of Gloucester (the chief champion of Matilda's cause in England) led to Stephen's unexpected release, in exchange for Robert, the king was unable to recover the ground lost in Normandy. The war continued in England with both sides claiming to be the legitimate ruler of both kingdom and duchy. In this sense the idea of a single Anglo-Norman realm continued to exist even during those years (1145–54) when de facto it did not. In August 1153 Stephen's eldest son Eustace died suddenly. This blow so discouraged Stephen that he agreed to make peace and adopt Henry, elder son of Matilda and Geoffrey (who had died in 1151), as his heir in return for his own possession of the throne of England for life and a guarantee that his second son, William, would be allowed to keep all the family lands in England and France. When Stephen died in October 1154, Henry was in France, and in no great hurry to return to England. Not until 19 December was he crowned and anointed at Westminster. If earlier claimants to the throne had been as slow as this, they would have been beaten to it, but Henry's position was secure. His succession represented the restoration of peace after a long and damaging civil war; no one was going to challenge it.

The Angevin Empire

Henry II was, as contemporaries commented, in extent of his dominions greater than any previous King of England. What made Henry greater was the extent of his dominions in France. In 1152 he had married the richest heiress of the day, Eleanor of Aquitaine, the divorced wife of the Capetian King of France, Louis VII. His charters and his seal list his titles: King of England, Duke of the Normans and Aquitanians, Count of the Angevins. All the major ports and cities of western and northern France were his: Bayonne, Bordeaux, La Rochelle, Poitiers, Angers, Nantes, Caen and Rouen. As King of England he held Bristol, Southampton, London, Boston and York. All this placed enormous resources at his disposal. According to an anecdote told by one of Henry's courtiers, Walter Map:

On one occasion when I was in Paris and chatting with the king [Louis VII], he compared the wealth of various kings: the Emperor of Constantinople and the King of

Sicily, he said, glory in their gold and silk, but their men can do nothing but talk for in matters of war they are useless; the Roman emperor, whom we call the emperor of the Germans has fine soldiers and war-horses, but no gold or silk or other opulence. But your lord the King of England lacks nothing, he has men, horses, gold, silk, jewels, fruits, wild-game and everything else. We in [Capetian] France have nothing but bread and wine and gaiety. This saying I made a note of, for it was merrily said – and truly.[13]

The marriages of Henry's three daughters – Joan to William, King of Sicily, Eleanor to Alfonso, King of Castile and Matilda to Henry the Lion, Duke of Saxony and Bavaria – demonstrate just how unprecedentedly Europe-wide was the network of connections. Although Henry never envisaged passing on the whole of his empire to a single heir, he certainly assumed that a cross-Channel realm would survive his death. In 1169 he announced that his own inheritance, Anjou, Normandy and England, should go to his and Eleanor's oldest surviving son, Henry, leaving Aquitaine for their second son, Richard. He had already provided for the third son, Geoffrey, by bullying the Bretons into accepting him as their duke in 1166. Ireland was intended to ensure that the fourth son, John, did not long remain 'Lackland'. In 1170 Henry tried to secure the future by having his oldest son crowned king, the only time in English history that a son has been crowned while his father was still alive. In the event the young King Henry died before his father, and on Henry II's death in 1189 Richard became both the King of England and ruler of the whole of the family estate on the Continent.

When Richard I died in 1199 with no children apart from

an illegitimate son, his younger brother John took over the whole. John's political ineptitude, however, culminating in the fact that he was unable to quash rumours that he had murdered his rival, Arthur, son of Geoffrey of Brittany, meant that when King Philip II of France (Louis VII's son by his third wife) invaded Normandy and Anjou, there was almost no one who had the heart to fight for him (1202–04). In Poitou people were still loyal to Eleanor but when she died in March 1204 there was a rush of the barons, prelates and towns to do homage to the King of France. In Gascony, the commercial ties, above all the wine trade, of towns such as Bordeaux and Bayonne with England were so central to their interests that they remained loyal to John, as did the great wine-exporting port of La Rochelle and the Channel Islands. But the loss of inland Poitou, Anjou and Normandy was one of the most comprehensive defeats ever suffered by a King of England. It also meant that from now on almost every King of England was to spend far more time in England than in any other part of his dominions. From 1106 until 1204, except for one period of ten years (1145–54), England and Normandy had shared the same ruler, but Philip's conquest of Normandy established a new fact of European political geography, and one that turned out to be near permanent. From now on, apart from a few years under Henry V and his son, there were two rival nation states separated by the Channel, France the larger and richer of the two.

Not that John admitted defeat. He drove up royal revenues in England to unprecedented levels (see pp. 198–9), and by 1212 was ready to return to France in force. Philip forestalled him, announcing an invasion of England in April 1213, only to see his invasion fleet destroyed and plundered as it lay at anchor at Damme. 'Not since the days of King Arthur has so much booty been seen in England,' wrote one author.[14] In February 1214 John disembarked an army at La Rochelle while his expensively bought German and Flemish allies kept Philip busy in the north-east. But he retreated when Philip's son Louis threatened to attack. Disaster followed soon after when his allies paid the price for their own overconfidence and were overwhelmed by Philip's army at the Battle of Bouvines on 27 July 1214. Not only did this battle put an end to John's dreams of recovering his lost dominions in France, it also cleared the way for those who were angered by his exploitative government of England. In the words of J. C. Holt, 'The road from Bouvines to Runnymede was short, direct and unavoidable.'[15]

John's refusal to keep the promises made at Runnymede (Magna Carta, 15 June 1215) forced his enemies to see that he could not be constrained by a written constitution. It is a measure of how desperate and determined they were that they offered the throne to Philip's son and heir, Prince Louis of France. Louis landed at Sandwich in May 1216 and, with the Scots and Welsh as his allies, was soon in control of most of eastern England, including London. John's death on 19 October 1216 from dysentery – brought on, it was alleged, by gluttony 'for he could never fill his belly full enough to satisfy him' – came in time to save his dynasty.[16] John's supporters crowned the king's oldest son as Henry III at Gloucester on 28 October. He was only nine years old, too young to share the slightest responsibility for his father's misrule. Prevailing sentiment disliked depriving a child of his inheritance, and now that his father was dead there was no need to press on with so unpleasant a scheme. In any case the boy was English, and people were beginning to grumble about the French troops. According to one author, the French in London had done nothing except drink all the wine in the city and then complain about the ale.[17] Support for Louis rapidly ebbed away. In September 1217 he conceded defeat and returned to France. Had John lived longer he might have managed to lose his whole kingdom to Louis, in which case when Louis inherited the French throne an Anglo-French dual monarchy would have been created.

Soon after he succeeded his father, Louis VIII (1224–8) invaded Poitou. With the English government's attention held by events in England, Louis's invasion turned into a triumphal procession, climaxing on 3 August 1224 with the surrender of La Rochelle. Once again, as in 1204, Bayonne and Bordeaux held out. In 1225 Henry III's younger brother, Richard of Cornwall, was given the title Count of Poitou and sent to Bordeaux with £35,000, the proceeds of a generous grant of taxation in return for a promise of good government in the form of a reissue of Magna Carta. With the situation in Gascony stabilised, Henry III continued to hope to recover other ancestral dominions in France. He made perfunctory efforts to do so in 1230 and 1242, but the huge territorial gains made by Philip II and Louis VIII had transformed the French monarchy. The resources of wealth and of character at Henry's disposal were simply no match for the new King of France, Louis IX [St Louis]. In 1258 the reforming English barons (see p. 159) allowed Henry to go to France to sort out a French connection which was becoming irrelevant to the increasingly insular English political elite. In the Treaty of Paris of 1259 Henry formally gave up his claims to Normandy, Anjou and Poitou; in return Louis IX recognised Henry as duke of a truncated Aquitaine (Gascony). Given Henry's problems and the vulnerability of Gascony to sudden attack, the terms were notably generous – as many of Louis's advisers pointed out. But the wives of the two kings were sisters, Eleanor and Margaret of Provence, and in the interests of family they wanted peace. In 1254 Henry had formally granted Gascony and the Channel Islands to his eldest son Edward stipulating that they were never to be separated from the Crown of England. In the event although the English Crown was unable to retain Gascony for as long as the Channel Islands, it would none the less be another 200 years before it lost control of the duchy of Aquitaine.

The ties between England and Gascony became ever closer as wine exports from Bordeaux in exchange for English cloth and grain was stepped up to take over what had previously been La Rochelle's share of the market. Yet Aquitaine always remained a part of France, and disappointed litigants within the duchy were inclined to appeal to the French king's *parlement* in Paris. King Edward I (1272–1307) devoted more time and money to Gascony than any other English monarch. He stayed there in 1272–4, on his way back from crusade, and again in 1286–9. So cordial were the family ties between the two royal courts that Edward was deeply shocked in 1294 when Philip IV 'the Fair' (1285–1314) exploited routine disputes over the hearing of appeals to proclaim the forfeiture of the duchy and invade. Philip made life even harder by making the treaty with the Scots which traditionally marks the beginning of the Auld Alliance. To raise the huge sums of money needed to fight wars on several fronts Edward I consulted Parliament more frequently than ever before. Defending Gascony during the crisis of 1294–1303 had a significant impact on the structure of English politics, amounting to the creation of a state financed by parliamentary taxation (see p. 200–2).

Kings of France and the Hundred Years War

The French kings continued to make life awkward for the next two dukes of Aquitaine, Edward II (1307–27) and Edward III (1327–77). French forces invaded Gascony in 1324 and again in 1337, on the latter occasion in part because the first Valois King of France, Philip VI, wanted to help the Scots in their resistance to Edward III's aggression. This provoked Edward into taking the bull by the horns. In the absence of a direct male heir in the Capetian line, he formally assumed the title 'King of France' in 1340, justified on the grounds that his mother Isabella was Philip IV's daughter. Although France was richer and larger than England, neither Philip VI nor John II was able to match Edward politically and militarily. At times he was prepared to consider renouncing the royal title, but only in return for acceptance that he held the duchy in full sovereignty, free of homage to the French king. The capture of Calais, and victories in battle, especially at Crecy in 1346 won by Edward himself, and Poitiers in 1356 won by his eldest son, Edward – later known as the Black Prince – enabled him to negotiate the Treaty of Brétigny (ratified in October 1360). This gave him Calais, Guînes and Poitou as well as the promise of a 3 million écu ransom for John II (captured at Poitiers). In 1362 the Black Prince was given the title 'Prince of Aquitaine'. But his regime there took too little account of regional custom and the taxes he imposed in order to finance campaigns in Spain provided some of the more independent lords with the opportunity to challenge English sovereignty by appealing to the King of France. The astute Charles V renewed the war in 1369. Edward III, now fifty-five years old, left the war in his

oldest son's hands, but illness undermined the latter's effective-
ness as a commander. The Black Prince died in 1376, a year
before his father, and in 1377 the throne was inherited by the
ten-year-old Richard II (1377–99). In consequence the French
generally held the upper hand throughout the 1370s and 1380s.
In 1396 Richard made a twenty-eight-year truce with France.

But the catastrophic situation of the French court under a
king, Charles VI, who suffered from periodic fits of madness
– including the belief that he was made of glass and might be
shattered by the slightest touch – led to civil war in France.
Both main factions, Armagnac and Burgundian, turned for
help to the England of Henry IV (1399–1413). In 1411 an
English expedition crossed the Channel. Henry V (1413–22)
pursued this interventionist policy with greater determination
and ruthlessness. After the – from the English point of view –
fortunate outcome of the gamble of the Agincourt campaign
(1415), he set about methodically conquering Normandy
(1417–20). The assassination of the Duke of Burgundy in 1419
exacerbated the French civil war, allowing Henry to negotiate
the Treaty of Troyes (May 1420) with Charles VI. By this
Charles disinherited his son, the dauphin, and made Henry, his
future son-in-law, his heir. Henry married Catherine of Valois
in June and next day marched off to continue the war against
the dauphin. In December 1420 he entered Paris in triumph,
but died of dysentery in 1422 a few months before his father-
in-law. When Charles VI died in October 1422, both the
dauphin and the nine-month-old Henry VI (1422–61, 1470–1)
were proclaimed King of France by their supporters.

Many historians have judged that Henry V had led England
into conquests which, in the longer term, would have proved
impossible to maintain. Contemporaries, however, had few
doubts. Indeed the English, led by Henry V's brother, John,

Duke of Bedford, added Anjou and Maine to the area under their control. Not until 1429 did the pendulum swing back, and then it was in large part due to the inspiration given the French by the meteoric career of the most extraordinary war leader in the history of Europe, Joan of Arc. After Henry VI was declared of age in 1437, he never visited his kingdom of France. Piously inert, he watched from afar as all his continental dominions except Calais were taken from him. In 1450 French armies swept the English out of Normandy. With the fall of Bordeaux in June 1451 Gascony too was lost, after 300 years in the possession of the English Crown. At last Henry VI's government made a real effort. In October 1452 an expeditionary force led by the experienced John Talbot, Earl of Shrewsbury, recaptured Bordeaux. But in July 1453 the English were overwhelmed in the Battle of Castillon and Talbot himself was killed by a ball fired from one of the French guns.

This is conventionally taken to be the end of the Hundred Years War (a term invented in the nineteenth century), but it was not quite the end of the French connection. Calais remained, together with castles such as Guînes, Rysbank and Hammes in the March of Calais; these permanent garrisons represented the Crown's only standing army. Time and again this strongpoint and these troops played a key role in the wars which broke out when the rapid collapse of their empire in France shocked all Englishmen and precipitated the violent quarrels between the houses of Lancaster and York known as the Wars of the Roses. These civil wars became deeply enmeshed in the wider network of European politics, in particular the long-standing tension between the dukes of Burgundy and kings of France. After Henry VI had been pushed off the throne by the Yorkist Edward IV (1461–70, 1471–83), Louis XI of France's intervention allowed him to recover it in 1470. Edward fled to Duke Charles of Burgundy, and with his help turned the tables once again.

For as long as kings of England claimed to be kings of France – as they did until 1801 – there was always the possibility that, given the kind of opportunity presented to Henry V, they might reactivate the claim. Indeed Edward IV did so in 1475, but confronted near Agincourt by Louis XI, he allowed himself to be bought off by the promise of a pension worth £10,000 a year – to the fury, it was believed at the French court, of his brother, Richard of Gloucester. When Richard himself took the throne in 1483 (see p. 161), the French court, alarmed by his ruthless belligerence, gave a warm welcome to an exile hitherto languishing in obscurity: Henry Tudor. Now the French king provided him with not only financial and naval backing, but also troops. There is a case, Alexander Grant has argued, for seeing the Battle of Bosworth not just as the decisive battle of the Wars of the Roses, but also as the last battle of the Hundred Years War, and this one fought, as none of the earlier ones had been, on English soil.[18]

Scotland: the English connection

Malcolm III (1058–93) was undoubtedly one of the most successful of all Scottish kings, but we know nothing about his reign except what can be gleaned from archaeological and place-name evidence (i.e. precious little) and what is reported in sources composed either very much later or outside Scotland. This indeed is a feature of all Scottish history before the twelfth century. The earliest surviving chronicle that was composed in Scotland was begun by the English monks of Melrose Abbey in the 1170s. (The Latin word 'Scotia' at this date still referred just to the territory north of the Firth of

Forth, hence Melrose's near neighbour, Dryburgh, was described as being in the land of the English as well as in the kingdom of the Scots.) If any documents were issued in Malcolm III's name they do not survive. We would know virtually nothing about his reign were it not for the fact that in 1068 Edgar the Ætheling fled to Scotland, taking his sister Margaret with him. By marrying Margaret, Malcolm became the protector of the old English royal family, and hence of interest to the English compilers of the Anglo-Saxon Chronicle and to Symeon, a French monk at Durham. So we know about both Malcolm's invasions of northern England and William I's counter-invasion in 1072. But to attempt the conquest of north Britain was out of the question for a ruler whose priorities lay in France. All William could do was force Malcolm to give him hostages, including his oldest son Duncan, and withdraw. This did not prevent Malcolm from raiding Northumbria again in 1079 – provoking the Norman counter-raid in 1080 at the end of which Robert Curthose built a new castle on the Tyne – and then twice more after William I's death in 1087.

According to Symeon, under Margaret's influence, Malcolm laid aside his barbarous ways and became more civilised. In the life of Margaret composed by Turgot, Prior of Durham, she is depicted at councils of Scottish clergy, urging them to modernise their ways, speaking in English and getting Malcolm, who had learned English in exile, to translate her words into Scottish (i.e. Gaelic).[19] The names given to her children are revealing: Edward, Edgar, Edmund, Æthelred, Alexander, David, Edith and Mary – five of them names used by the English royal house, and none of them names of her husband's ancestors. When Malcolm and their eldest son were both killed while raiding England in 1093, a violent succession dispute broke out, during which Duncan II, who returned to Scotland with William II's blessing, had to promise that 'he would never bring Englishmen or Frenchmen into the country'.[20] Despite giving this promise Duncan was killed and replaced by his uncle Donald Ban in 1094, only for Donald himself to be either killed or mutilated and imprisoned in 1097 when Edgar the Ætheling was given command of an army that put his nephew Edgar on the Scottish throne as William II's client. A generation of peace on the Anglo-Scottish border then followed as a result of Henry I's marriage to King Edgar's sister Edith, renamed Matilda/Maud, and the succession of two more of her brothers to the Scottish throne, Alexander I (1107–24), and David I (1124–53).

David promoted the foundation of towns (burghs in Scotland) such as Edinburgh, Dunfermline, Perth, Stirling, Inverness and Aberdeen, and the development of others such as Berwick (Scotland's most important port) and Roxburgh. Burghal laws were based on the legal customs of Newcastle upon Tyne. By ordering the payment of a *teind* (tithe) from all living in the area served by a local church, he in effect founded the Scottish parish system. His foundation of abbeys at Kelso, Holyrood and Melrose not only brought in English and continental monastic fashions, they also – like his burghal foundations – involved the drawing up of the earliest extant and undoubtedly genuine charters of a Scottish king, and hence the employment of writing in the administration. This may mean that some of the innovations attributed to him had been anticipated by his predecessors, but not recorded in writing. He was certainly, however, the first Scottish king to issue his own coin, modelled on Henry I's, and overall there can be little doubt that his reign left a permanent mark on Scottish society, the 'Davidian revolution'. Since David had been a familiar figure at the English court since 1093, and Earl of Huntingdon since his marriage in 1113 to Maud, widow of the former earl, it is not surprising that the English historian William of Malmesbury should claim that 'the rust of his native barbarism had been polished away by his upbringing amongst us'.[21] He welcomed to his court French-speaking nobles of French descent – the Bruces, Stewarts, Morvilles, Montgomerys and Lindsays – and endowed them generously in Lothian. The opposition he faced from Alexander I's illegitimate son Malcolm mac Heth in 1124 and from Malcolm again and from King Oengus of Moray in 1130 may reflect the hostility of traditionalists to so many newfangled and foreign ways. But they were defeated, Oengus killed and Malcolm imprisoned.

9. Dunfermline Abbey nave. The abbey was founded by David I on the site of his mother's Benedictine priory. According to Scottish tradition, after Margaret and her sons had been buried there, Dunfermline replaced Iona as the principal mausoleum of the Scottish royal family. Its first abbot came from Canterbury; the nave piers reflect Durham influence.

The accession of Stephen to the English throne in 1135 instead of the empress Matilda (David's niece) meant that the King of Scots found himself excluded from the English court. In consequence he pressed his wife's claim to Northumbria, and invaded in 1136, 1137 and 1138. Although David's army was defeated near Northallerton at the Battle of the Standard (1138), Matilda's arrival in England next year so tied Stephen's hands that he recognised David's son, Henry (a French name), as Earl of Northumbria. Since David also acquired Cumbria, this meant that for once in British history, a Scottish king, in possession of Newcastle and Carlisle, was almost as rich as his southern neighbour. Henry died in 1152, however, and David's decision to designate his eleven-year-old grandson, Malcolm, as his heir, inevitably put this achievement at risk. In 1157, indeed, Malcolm IV agreed to return Cumbria and Northumbria to Henry II of England, perhaps the better to face a rival king to the west, Somerled, the Gaelic–Norse King of Argyll and the Western Isles.

In the event Malcolm, a victim of Paget's disease, died unmarried and childless, and was succeeded by his younger brother William, whom David had proclaimed Earl of Northumbria in 1152. Naturally William I (1165–1214), later known as 'the Lion', took advantage of rebellion against Henry II to invade and reclaim his earldom in 1173–4. But he was taken by surprise at Alnwick and captured. To obtain his release he was forced to do homage to Henry II for Scotland, and see English garrisons in the castles of Edinburgh, Berwick and Roxburgh. When Henry II arranged William's marriage to a cousin, Ermengarde of Beaumont, in 1185, he gave him back Edinburgh as a wedding present, but it was not until the accession of Richard I in 1189 that Scottish independence was fully restored, by the Quitclaim of Canterbury, in return for a payment of 10,000 marks. It was during what the Melrose chronicler called Scotland's 'servitude' that the throne-right of Margaret's line was challenged by another dynasty, the mac Williams, descendants of Duncan II. William never let kings of England forget his claim to Northumbria, but he had much more success in overcoming the macWilliam challenge – both Donald macWilliam and his son Guthred lost their lives – and in extending royal authority northwards across the Moray Firth.

His son Alexander II (1214–1249) was initially drawn into supporting the Magna Carta rebellion by the promise of the northern counties, but he withdrew once Henry III's hold on the throne appeared to be secure. This ushered in an eighty-year period of peace between the two countries, formalised by Alexander's marriage to Henry's sister Joan in 1221, and then by the Treaty of York (1237) in which he renounced his claim to Northumbria, finally establishing the Tweed–Solway line as the border between Scotland and England. He put an end to Galloway's status as a kingdom in 1234, and was on his way west to annex the Western Isles when he died in Oban Bay. Peace with England permitted his son, Alexander III (1249–86), to continue the policy of westward expansion, which then provoked a vigorous reaction from King Haakon of Norway. But after Haakon's death, King Magnus in the Treaty of Perth (1266) sold off all Norwegian rights over Man and the Western Isles. Apart from the Orkneys and Shetland, which remained Norwegian, the political geography of modern Scotland was now in place.

Yet within a generation the accidents of life and death threatened to bring the kingdom down. The early deaths of all his children led to Alexander III recognising his granddaughter Margaret, 'the Maid of Norway', as heir presumptive to the

Scottish throne. When he was killed in a horse-riding accident, she was accepted as Queen of Scotland and betrothed to Edward, Edward I's eldest son. But she died in 1290 on her way to Scotland, at Kirkwall on Orkney at the age of seven. Since there was now no one with an evident right to the throne, her death precipitated the great crisis in Anglo-Scottish relations. Edward I's seizure of the Isle of Man was a portent of what was to follow. In 1291 he declared that if the Scots wanted to oppose his lordship over their country they would have to do so by force of arms. No less than thirteen 'competitors' claimed the throne, recognised Edward I's overlordship and agreed to accept his verdict. In 1292 he awarded the throne to John Balliol, who probably had the best claim, but then treated him not as the king of another country but as though he were an English baron, driving him into opposition which Edward chose to interpret as rebellion.

The Scots turned for help to Philip IV of France (the Auld Alliance). Edward invaded, captured Berwick (Scotland's largest burgh) in 1296, took Balliol prisoner and carried off the Stone of Scone on which Scottish kings had been enthroned. The Scottish aristocracy recognised defeat, but two esquires, Andrew Moray and William Wallace, did not. They inflicted a humiliating defeat upon the overconfident English at Stirling Bridge on 11 September 1297, though Moray was mortally wounded in the battle. For the next ten months Wallace was the unrivalled leader of the Scots until in July 1298 he unwisely engaged Edward himself in battle at Falkirk, where the Scottish spearmen were overwhelmed by the massive English superiority in archers and cavalry. Wallace returned to relative obscurity, but fought on until betrayed and executed in 1305.

Although poor in material resources, the Highlands were far too extensive to be ringed round with castles like North

Wales, and here was a safe refuge for patriots inspired by Moray's and Wallace's heroic resistance. The War of Scottish Independence went on far longer than Edward had imagined possible. Even so, by the autumn of 1306 it seemed that Edward I, the 'Hammer of the Scots' (the words inscribed centuries later on his tomb in Westminster Abbey), had won, and was well on the way to reorganising Scotland under English administration as he had Wales and Ireland. The enthronement of Robert Bruce, grandson of one of the 'competitors' of 1292, on 25 March 1306 had led nowhere. On 10 February 1306 he had committed murder and sacrilege, killing John Comyn of Badenoch in the Greyfriars' church in Dumfries. For the last few years before then he had been on the English side, even employed as Sheriff of Lanark and Ayr. So tarnished a figure was easily disposed of, hounded by the English and the Comyns until he disappeared beyond the horizon of historians into a legendary world of caves and spiders.

The story of Bruce's re-emergence early in 1307, of how he overcame each setback and won the initiative until at last, at Bannockburn in 1314, he felt able to confront head-on an English army led by the King of England in person, is one of the great more or less true romances of history, and told as true romance in the earliest known life of Robert, John Barbour's epic poem from the 1370s, *The Bruce*. A letter drafted in Bruce's Chancery, known as the Declaration of Arbroath (1320), summed up the cause: 'we fight not for glory, nor for riches, nor honours, but for freedom alone, which no good man gives up except for his life'.[22]

Initially the fightback was made possible by Edward I's counterproductive policy of treating Robert's friends and kinsmen not as honourable enemies but as rebels whom he put to death as traitors (see p. 163–4). The political disarray in

England during Edward II's reign then gave Bruce the breathing space that allowed him to overcome his Scottish enemies, partisans of Comyn and Balliol, giving their estates to his own followers, before launching the series of raids into northern England that turned the fight for survival into a profitable enterprise. After Bannockburn he was able to open up another front, sending his brother Edward Bruce with an army to Ireland (1315–18), appealing to pan-Gaelic patriotism. In 1318 he recaptured Berwick. Ten years later in the Treaty of Northampton an enfeebled English government recognised Robert's kingship and the existence of an independent Scotland.

Once again the priority given to the claims of family put the kingdom at risk. In 1326 at the Parliament of Cambuskenneth, Robert I had arranged for the succession to be settled on his only legitimate son David, born in 1324. The accession of a child king, David II (1329–71), presented Edward III, a warrior king determined to avenge recent humiliations, with a golden opportunity. In return for the promise of much of southern Scotland, including Berwick, he encouraged Edward Balliol to claim the Scottish throne. From 1332 to 1338 a triple alliance of Balliol, the 'Disinherited' – those whose lands had been confiscated by Robert Bruce – and the King of England campaigned in Scotland, but met fierce resistance from those, notably the Douglas family, who had acquired what the 'Disinherited' had lost. When Edward III's ambitions turned south, David II, as a good ally of France, invaded England and was captured in the Battle of Neville's Cross near Durham in 1346. He remained a prisoner for eleven years while Robert 'the Steward', son of Robert Bruce's daughter Marjory, governed as Lieutenant of Scotland.

For a while Edward, having pensioned Balliol off, planned

his own inauguration as King of the Scots, but in 1357 he and David finally agreed terms; the latter was released in return for a ransom of 100,000 marks, to be paid in instalments. When David fell behind with the payments, fresh negotiations ensued, involving reductions in the ransom in return for the childless Scottish king recognising either Edward or one of Edward's sons as his heir. But what had been acceptable in 1290, was so no longer. The Scottish Parliament would have none of it. In consequence after David's death in 1371, Robert the Steward came to the throne, fifty-three years after he had been declared heir presumptive following Edward Bruce's death in 1318. Since he had five legitimate sons there was little danger of the Stewart dynasty dying out in the male line. Providing them with earldoms did, however, add to the amount of power that was in the hands of regional magnates rather than the Crown. As Robert II (1371–90) he made little effort to enforce law and order; indeed during the last six years of his reign he handed over responsibility for this to his sons. Then the renewal of the Anglo-Scottish war in 1384 led to the Scottish victory at Otterburn in 1388 and the recovery of territory. By the end of his reign only Roxburgh, Jedburgh and Berwick still remained in English hands.

By common consent Robert III (1390–1406) was a feeble king, unable to control feuding within the Scottish nobility or to take advantage of the years of political confusion in England after 1399. Scottish political life from 1388 to 1420 was dominated by his brother the Duke of Albany (also called Robert), who acted in turn as lieutenant for his father, brother and then for his nephew, James I (1406–37). In 1406 Robert III decided to send his son James to France for safekeeping but the twelve-year-old was captured by the English. The news may have pleased the Albany Stewarts, but was said to have hastened the king's death. According to Walter Bower's *Scotichronicon*, Robert III asked to be buried in a midden as 'the worst of kings and the most wretched of men'.[23] Although James I was at once recognised as king by Parliament (the Three Estates), he was kept in England until 1424, able to do little but write a poem, 'The Kingis Quair', about his experience of captivity, including falling in love with Joan Beaufort. To obtain his release he had to agree to meet the expenses of his imprisonment, assessed at 60,000 marks, less 10,000 marks as Joan's dowry. He returned to Scotland convinced that Robert of Albany and, after 1420, Robert's son Duke Murdoch, had done nothing to secure his release. He flung himself into furious activity, arresting, for breaches of the peace, and executing those he held responsible for his eighteen years in prison. By confiscating their estates he reclaimed control of the crown's material resources. He used Parliament to intro-duce a flood of statutes, including such famously paternalist ones as ordering the destruction of rooks' nests and prohibiting football. Not surprisingly, so interventionist a king made many enemies. In 1437 he was assassinated at Perth, leaving a six-year-old boy as his heir.

Revulsion at his father's murder helped to secure James II's own safety as various factions, mostly made up of families that had been prominent in James I's household, including the Douglases, struggled for possession and control of the boy king during the twelve years of his minority. His marriage (to Marie de Gueldres, a niece of Duke Philip of Burgundy) in 1449 marked his coming of age and resumption of his father's policy of attacking some of the most powerful families. Between 1452 and 1455, using a combination of murder and gunpowder artillery, he brought down the Black Douglases, adding their estates to the Crown lands. In compliant parliaments he proclaimed his concern for law and order, economic stability and royal authority. Although no King of England had invaded Scotland since Henry IV did in 1400, both the Percy-Douglas feud and the fact that the English still held Roxburgh and Berwick, meant that war with England was always on the cards. The Wars of the Roses gave James II the opportunity to array his guns before Roxburgh Castle. He was killed on 3 August 1460 when one of them exploded. None the less by 8 August Roxburgh had been battered into submission, and on 10 August the ten-year-old James III was crowned and anointed at Kelso Abbey. Next year Margaret of Anjou, desperate for help against the Yorkists, restored Berwick.

Like his father, James III both married and began to rule in person in the same year, 1469. His marriage to Margaret of Denmark led to the acquisition of Orkney and Shetland in 1472. In the same decade substantial inroads were made into the power of the last of the great regional magnates, the Macdonald Lords of the Isles, who had been semi-independent rulers of the Hebrides ever since they had ousted their rivals by backing the winning side in the civil wars of Robert Bruce's reign. The growing authority of the Crown meant not only that its reach extended further out into Gaelic and Scandinavian regions, but also that at the centre Edinburgh began to function as a capital city. Yet the social and cultural contrast between, roughly Highland and Lowland, west/northern and east/southern, Gaelic-speaking and English-speaking Scotland still remained strong. And so did a potent Anglophobia, the legacy of the previous 170 years. Even if few Scots used words as bloodthirsty as those in Blind Harry's *The Wallace*, composed in the 1470s, it struck the visiting Italian Aeneas Sylvius that there was nothing they liked hearing more than abuse of the English.

Wales: the English conquest

Norman invasions of Wales followed hard on the heels of the Norman conquest of England. At this stage of Welsh economic development a conquest in the manner of the conquest of England was ruled out by the logistical problems involved in maintaining armies for long periods in thinly populated regions. Even so the concentration of so much English wealth into so few hands allowed the new Norman king and his followers to drive further west than any previous ruler. By the 1090s the Welsh scholar Rhigyfarch ap Sulien lamented:

> The people and the priest are despised
> By the word, heart and deeds of the Frenchmen.
> They burden us with tribute and consume our
>   possessions.
> One of them, however lowly, shakes a hundred natives
> With his command, and terrifies them with his look.[24]

With the Frenchmen came a multitude of English settlers to populate newly founded towns such as Cardiff, Abergavenny and Brecon, building a new society on the model of the one they left behind. In the view of the author of the *Gesta Stephani*, Wales was being turned into a 'second England'. It amounted, according to the Welsh Chronicle of the Princes (*Brut Y Twysogion*), to the imposition of 'French tyranny'.[25] This initial stage of colonisation was largely limited to the south coast, lowland Gwent, Glamorgan, Gower and Pembroke. Civil war in England during Stephen's reign and what Sir John Lloyd called a National Revival in Wales threw the process into reverse. Welsh kings regained territory they had lost to the invaders and even played an important part in defeating

Stephen in the Battle of Lincoln. In the words of a contemporary poem in Anglo-Norman French:

> Well have the Welsh revenged themselves
> Many of our French they have slain,
> Some of our castles they have taken
> Fiercely they threaten us,
> Openly they go about saying,
> That in the end they will have all,
> By means of Arthur they will have it back . . .
> They will call it Britain again.[26]

The conquest of Wales was to be a slow and piecemeal process, undertaken on the initiative of individual baronial families (marcher lords) such as the Braoses, Clares and Mortimers, with only occasional intervention by kings of England far more concerned with events in the much richer land of France. Even when Henry II invaded Wales in the 1150s and 1160s, he made little headway, indeed at times a combination of Welsh rain and resilience compelled him to negotiate. Such successes against the odds won great reputations for Owain ap Gruffudd of Gwynedd and Rhys ap Gruffudd (known as the Lord Rhys) of Deheubarth. But they had to recognise English overlordship to the extent of no longer calling themselves kings. Moreover the fragmentation of their principalities after their deaths (Owain in 1170; Rhys in 1197) revealed how difficult it was, in the face of traditional succession customs, to consolidate a Welsh principality for more than a single generation.

If anyone achieved this feat, it was Llywelyn ap Iorwerth (who came to be known as Llywelyn the Great), ruler of Gwynedd, not the richest, but thanks to its mountains and tidal estuaries, the most defensible of the ancient Welsh kingdoms. As was customary in Welsh politics, his first enemies were his own kindred (rivals for power in Gwynedd). Against them he was, wrote one of his court poets, 'the swirl of a great windstorm in a surly February'.[27] His next enemies were neighbouring Welsh princes, in particular the rulers of Powys. Llywelyn was careful to recognise English overlordship, and in 1205 he married King John's illegitimate daughter Joan. But John turned against him, invading Gwynedd in 1211 and again, with overwhelming force, in 1212, forcing Llywelyn to capitulate and surrender Perfeddwlad (the Four Cantrefs or land divisions east of Conwy). Fortunately for Llywelyn, John's high-handed exploitation of this triumph united the Welsh people against him, and catapulted the Lord of Gwynedd into leadership of a national revolt.

The setbacks John suffered in France and England in 1214–16 gave Llywelyn a free hand which he used so effectively that he never lost his position as protector and overlord of the other Welsh rulers. From now on they were merely lords and only the ruler of Gwynedd was prince. He adopted a prudent policy of accommodation and alliance with the earls of Chester and other English marcher lords – though he made an exception when he hanged William de Braose for an affair with his wife. As a modernising ruler he built stone castles, preferred to collect revenues in coin rather than in produce, and in administration increasingly used written documents authenticated by a seal proclaiming his titles: Prince of Aberffro (his principal seat on the fertile land of Anglesey) and Lord of Snowdon. Perhaps his main achievement was to get the Welsh lords to swear allegiance to his son Dafydd.

But after Llywelyn's death in 1230, Henry III's government, posing as the guardian of Welsh tradition, set out to undermine the embryonic principality. By supporting all

Dafydd's rivals, it forced him to accept humiliating terms in 1241. English arrogance again provoked a Welsh rebellion which Dafydd was leading when he died in 1246, enabling Henry III to impose the Treaty of Woodstock in April 1247, annexing Perfeddwlad and leaving Dafydd's two nephews Owain and Llywelyn ap Gruffudd with just the lands west of Conwy. According to Matthew Paris, 'Now Wales has been brought to nothing.'[28] The threat of further subdivisions of Gwynedd provoked Llywelyn to fight. In 1256 he recovered Perfeddwlad where the Welsh, in the words of the *Brut Y Tywysogion*, 'preferred to be killed fighting for their liberty rather than suffer themselves to be unjustly trampled over by foreigners'. He was joined by the Welsh rulers in Ceredigion, Powys and Deheubarth, in part thanks to his policy of restoring territories recovered from marcher lords to their former Welsh owners, 'keeping naught for himself save fame and honour' as the *Brut* proudly records.[29] Henry III's political difficulties from 1258 to 1265 played into Llywelyn's hands to such an extent that the English king felt obliged, even after his restoration to power, to accept in the Treaty of Montgomery of 1267 the reality of Llywelyn's conquests and his authority as Prince of Wales.

But since 'Welsh' Wales produced no salt and not enough wheat, iron or cloth, it was economically dependent upon England; the new principality would survive in the long run only if the King of England learned to accept it. For this reason in return for English recognition Llywelyn agreed to pay a huge price, £16,667 – in instalments since it was about four times his annual revenue. But after 1272 he miscalculated badly. He paid no more instalments and avoided doing homage to Edward I; in 1275 by arranging to marry Eleanor de Montfort, he reminded the king of his earlier alliance with Edward's arch enemy, Simon de Montfort (see p. 159–60). In 1276 Edward proclaimed Llywelyn a rebel. In autumn 1277 an English army landed on Anglesey, the 'bread basket' of Wales, and harvested the grain. Llywelyn surrendered and, though by the Treaty of Aberconwy he was allowed to keep the title of prince, he had to hand over the Four Cantrefs and accept that Welsh barons owed homage not to him but to the king. It was agreed that all disputes within Wales should be settled 'according to the laws and customs of those parts', but in practice it was Edward who picked the judges. This, together with the building of great castles at Flint, Rhuddlan, Aberystwyth and Builth, created once again in the Welsh the feeling that they were being bullied. A widespread revolt broke out in March 1282. Llywelyn claimed to have been kept in the dark but joined it openly in the summer. On 11 December 1282 the first and last native Prince of Wales (Llywelyn the Last) was killed near Builth by a soldier who had no idea who he was. Edward pressed on with his stated intention of putting an end to 'the malice of the Welsh'. In January 1283 in an unprecedented winter campaign his troops overran Snowdonia. Llywelyn's head was sent to London, to be jeered at by the crowd. The principality of Wales was annexed to the English Crown, and divided into shires on the English model. The Statute of Wales of 1284, while tolerating Welsh law in some spheres, introduced the forms and substance of English common law. 'Is it,' asked a Welsh poet of the time, 'the end of the world?'[30]

In spite of rebellions in 1287 and 1294–5 the Edwardian conquest proved final. Further castles at Harlech, Caernarfon, Conwy and Beaumaris ensured its permanence. In 1301 Edward of Caernarfon became the first heir to the English throne to bear the title Prince of Wales. But Wales remained a

10. The great castle at Caerphilly, nine miles north of Cardiff, begun in 1271 by Gilbert de Clare, Earl of Gloucester and Lord of Glamorgan, in response to the growing power of Llewellyn, Prince of Wales.

fragmented country. Outside the principality the numerous large lordships known collectively as the March of Wales continued to be held by English baronial families. In terms of administration and the law they were largely independent of each other and of the Crown. To this fragmentation was added the division between the native Welsh and the English settler population. This caused tension and resentment, focusing especially on the commercial privileges of the burgesses of the English towns in Wales (the Welsh were not allowed to live in them or trade outside them), and the glass ceiling which made it difficult for natives to obtain high office in secular and ecclesiastical administration. Many of them felt, as one contemporary put it, as 'aliens in the land of their birth'.[31] Since all the owners of great estates were English, there was inevitably an element of ethnic hostility to post-Black Death tensions between landlords, tenants and labourers.

In September 1400 Owain Glyndwr, a descendant of the princes of Powys and Deheubarth, took advantage of the turmoil in England caused by the dethronement of Richard II to have himself proclaimed Prince of Wales. His rising was rapidly put down, but when the English parliament of 1401 reacted to it by sharpening anti-Welsh legislation, the revolt flared up again and spread more widely. Henry IV faced too many threats to be able to give Wales a high priority; each Welsh success produced another panicky and draconian response. By 1403 any Welshman caught within Chester city walls after sunset was liable to the death penalty. In 1404 and 1405 Owain was able to hold Welsh parliaments at Machynlleth and Harlech. Moreover he found friends outside Wales. In 1403 and 1405 the French sent military aid. In 1405 the Percys, Edmund Mortimer and Owain drew up the Tripartite Indenture, agreeing to divide England and Wales between them, with Owain's share being an extended Wales. In 1406 the Avignon papacy (see p. 258) freed the Welsh church from its subordination to Canterbury. But once Henry IV had survived his early political and financial difficulties, the much greater English resources were bound to tell. The English *ancien régime* was reinstated. Owain himself never submitted. His capacity to inspire loyalty meant that he was still at large when he died, place and date unknown. In the words of a Welsh annalist: 'Very many say he died; the prophets insist he has not.'[32] But although poetry and prophecy continued to fuel Welsh resentment, there was no further revolt. And long before now they had moved from calling themselves Britons (Brytaniaid) to preferring another ancient term, Cymry – hence not the BNP but Plaid Cymru.

Ireland: the land of war

The growing prosperity of the Ostmen towns – Limerick, Cork, Waterford, Wexford and Dublin, all in southern Ireland – offered the prospect of greater wealth and power to those kings who could control one or more of them. As the most northerly, Dublin lay within range of warrior kings from all parts of Ireland, and its central position in the Irish Sea economy, with close links to the Isle of Man and the Isles, made it the most desirable of prizes. One after the other the dominant kings of the day fought or negotiated their way into Dublin: Diarmait mac Mail na mBo of Leinster in 1052, Turlough and Muirchertach O'Brien from Munster in 1072 and 1089, Turlough O'Connor from Connacht in 1118, Muirchertach Mac Loughlin from Ailech (Tyrone) in 1149 and 1154, and Rory O' Connor from Connacht again in 1166. Their control of Dublin, while it lasted, gave all of these kings a prima facie case to be regarded as *rí Erenn*, even if not all the other kings of Ireland accepted this – a state of affairs acknowledged by the phrase, almost a title, 'King of Ireland with opposition'. Diarmait mac Mail na mBo, Turlough and Muirchertach O'Brien and Turlough O'Connor all appointed sons of theirs as kings of Dublin, clearly in the hope that its resources would enable that son to build up a power base of his own so that in due course he could succeed to the supremacy the father had won. Only in the case of Muirchertach O'Brien, made King of Dublin in 1075, can this strategy be said to have worked, and even then after his father's death in 1086 it took Muirchertach three years of intense fighting within Munster, during which time he lost Dublin to Godred Crovan, King of Man and the Isles, before he reasserted that dominance. Even after that, his repeated invasions of the north failed to subdue Domnall MacLochlainn, his rival for the kingship of Ireland.

In other ways too economic development may have had consequences for politics. The annals give the impression that twelfth-century kings were richer than their predecessors, able to raise larger and better-equipped armies and fleets, and hence able to exercise more power than their equivalents in earlier times. But when they died, the ensuing succession struggles were fought with the traditional ferocity. In 1141, for example, Diarmait Mac Murchada killed or blinded seventeen members of the royal families of Leinster. From the moment that he inaugurated his reign with his first raid, no king's position was ever secure. Each and every supremacy – whether local, provincial or national – was under permanent threat both from kinsmen and from other dynasties and had to be constantly reasserted. To an English observer such as William of Newburgh, twelfth-century Ireland looked like the England of centuries before. When Muirchertach Mac Loughlin, in 1161 styled 'King of Ireland without opposition', was killed in battle in 1166, Diarmait Mac Murchada of Leinster, one of the kings who had acknowledged Muirchertach's overlordship and had been protected by him, found himself overwhelmed by enemies and forced to flee. Taking his wife and daughter with him he set sail for Bristol. The sequence of events that were to lead to the English invasion of Ireland had been set in motion.

Diarmait went to Henry II and received permission to recruit soldiers. A contemporary poem summarised his offer:

If anyone wishes to have land or money,
Horses, equipment or chargers,
Gold or silver, I will give him very generous payment.

> If anyone wants land or pasture,
> I will enfeoff him generously.[33]

In 1169, attracted by these propects, a small force of English and Anglo-Welsh adventurers sailed to Ireland. In 1170 others joined them, most prominently Richard de Clare, known as Strongbow, to whom Diarmait offered the hand of a daughter and, in breach of Irish custom, succession to Leinster. By September Dairmait and his son-in-law had captured Waterford and thrown the last 'high-king', Rory O'Connor of Connacht, out of Dublin. When Diarmait died in the spring of 1171, Strongbow was left as de facto King of Leinster. This so alarmed Henry II that later that year he took a massive English army across the Irish Sea. Most Irish kings decided to submit, allowing Henry to claim lordship over the island. Many of the 'modernisers' among the Irish churchmen welcomed Henry's presence as a means of pushing ahead with reform. Letters from them led Pope Alexander III to express his joy at the news that vice was waning now that 'a barbarous and uncivilised people has been made subject to the noble king of the English'.[34] Writing only twenty-five years later, William of Newburgh, in a chapter he entitled 'The Conquest of the Irish by the English', observed that 'a people who had been free since time immemorial, unconquered even by the Romans, a people for whom liberty seemed an inborn right, were now fallen into the power of the King of England'.[35]

Not all Irish kings submitted. Among those who did not was Rory O'Connor. One of Henry II's clerks, Roger of Howden, believed that the high-king too would have been defeated had Henry II not been called away in April 1172 by urgent business in Normandy. This established a new pattern. Until 1541 kings of England retained the title 'Lord of Ireland', but in their eyes other things would always matter more. Only two of them visited Ireland: John in 1210 and Richard II in 1395 and 1399. Henry kept Dublin, Wexford and Waterford to be administered by royal officials, but before he left he confirmed Strongbow in his possession of Leinster and granted Meath to Hugh de Lacy. In this way too subsequent kings followed Henry II's lead, granting other – as yet unconquered – Irish kingdoms to English lords to see what they could make of them. In 1226, for example, Connacht was granted to Richard de Burgh. In 1276 the Ui Briain kingdom of Thomond was granted to Thomas de Clare. Ireland became a land of opportunity for English lords who seized land from the Irish in order to found towns and build castles and churches; opportunity too for thousands of settlers, farmers, craftsmen, merchants, labourers and clerks, who came over from England and Wales. They settled in such numbers along the south and east coasts and the river valleys from Cork to Carrickfergus that these parts became an England overseas (see p. 34).

Anglicisation became official policy. In 1210 John ordered that English law and customs were to be observed throughout his lordship. A statement of English law was put into writing and a copy sent to Dublin. In 1216 a copy of Magna Carta was sent to Ireland, and from then on legislation made in England was routinely dispatched to Dublin. The apparatus of English government was transferred to Ireland: central courts (Exchequer and bench) presided over by the justiciar (in place of the absentee king), chancellor, counties (three by 1212, twelve by 1300), sheriffs, councils and parliaments, the system of taxation. Although some lords were granted 'liberties' – territories from which sheriffs were excluded – their seneschals still had to enforce the king's law and account at the Exchequer for the profits of the pleas of the Crown. The modern Irish legal system, pattern of local government and parliamentary tradition all derive from the innovations made in this period.

Not surprisingly the incomers were rarely welcome. Sometimes, according to Gerald de Barri's narrative of the invasion of Ireland – which he called 'the coming of the English (*adventus Anglorum*)' – they were 'cruelly put to death without any respect for sex or age'.[36] But attempts by the Irish to co-ordinate resistance, such as the 1258 alliance between Aedh O'Connor and Brian O'Neill, were crushed. O'Neill's head was sent to London, and the defeat lamented by his court poet:

> Unequal they engaged in battle
> The foreigners and the Gael of Tara
> Fine linen shirts on the race of Conn
> And foreigners in one mass of iron.[37]

The pace of migration into Ireland gradually slowed down. But Edward I, determined to make Ireland contribute to his conquest of Wales and invasion of Scotland, imposed heavy demands on both administrators and taxpayers. In some parts of the country English lords seized power, but could not introduce settlers in numbers sufficient to replace the native inhabitants, most of whom continued to live by their own laws and customs, and were regarded by the English as wild and uncivilised. Other parts, such as O'Donnell and O'Neill territories in the north, escaped the colonising process altogether. There were always internal military frontiers, war zones in which Irish and English fought not only against each other but also between themselves.

In 1315 the whole of the island became a land of war when Robert Bruce responded to the English invasion of Scotland by sending an army under the command of his brother and heir presumptive, Edward, into Ireland. The Bruce brothers consciously appealed to the Irish by emphasising the common ancestry of the two peoples, and many Irish recognised Edward as their king. Edward campaigned across Ireland for three and a half years but was unable to win over many of the Anglo-Irish or capture Dublin. His death in battle at Fochart in October 1318 brought an abrupt end to the Scottish challenge to English rule in Ireland. That challenge proved, none the less, to be a turning point. The turmoil of invasion, coinciding with the great famine (see p. 56–7), caused a marked contraction in the area controlled by the Dublin government. Another battle fought in 1318, at Dysart O'Dea, saw the death of Richard de Clare and the restoration of Ui Briain power in Thomond. After 1315, government revenue from Ireland, which had averaged over £6,000 a year during Edward I's reign, remained at about £2,000 a year for the rest of the fourteenth century. From now on Ireland cost the kings of England more than it brought in. Moreover labour shortage in England after 1348 reversed the flow of migration, to the dismay of Anglo-Irish lords and employers. There was, however, no effective means of implementing the legislation of 1410 and 1429 which tried to stop tenants, craftsmen and labourers moving to the relative peace of England.

Only during the interludes of peace in the Hundred Years War with France were the English prepared to divert substantial resources to Ireland. From 1361 to 1367 Edward III's son, Lionel of Clarence, governed Ireland as lieutenant (the title now replacing justiciar). He was funded from English resources to the tune of £43,000, but since there was no united organised Irish enemy for him to find, let alone defeat, his troops could make little military impact. Richard II took an even larger army to Ireland in 1394–5. He recognised, as he wrote to the council, that Irish rebels are rebels only because of wrongs done to them and lack of remedy, but neither on this occasion nor in 1399 was he able to stay there long enough to provide that remedy. The Dublin government was trapped in a downward spiral of diminishing authority and declining revenue.

Great Anglo-Irish lords such as the earls of Desmond and Ormond ruled their territories much as Gaelic lords did, as autonomous units which used summer cattle raids as one of the means by which they jockeyed for position within their regions. In the 'land of war', the lifestyles and fashions of the two peoples became hard to distinguish. Both Gaelic and Anglo-Irish lords built the stone tower houses which still characterise the Irish landscape. Those English who adopted 'degenerate' Irish customs in dress and hairstyle were condemned in the Dublin parliament of 1297 and again in the Statutes of Kilkenny (1366) which prohibited marriages and alliances between English and Irish. The Irish who submitted had to swear to learn English and wear English clothes. In the 1350s Richard FitzRalph, the English Archbishop of Armagh, felt obliged to remind his compatriots that killing an Irishman, though not a felony in law, was none the less a sin. Yet an Anglo-Irish magnate such as Gerald 'the Rhymer', 3rd Earl of Desmond (d.1398), chose to write Irish verse displaying his familiarity with Gaelic tales. A century later close ties to Gaelic society could make an office-holder vulnerable to accusations of treason; this led to the summary execution of the 7th Earl of Desmond in 1468.

Since the English government was unwilling to provide lieutenants with adequate salaries and resources, only men such as the earls with great estates in Ireland could afford to take the office, a circumstance which meant that Dublin became increasingly independent of the Crown, particularly so in the 1470s and 1480s under successive earls of Kildare. In the fifteenth century, receipts at the Irish Exchequer averaged only £1,000 a year. By the 1470s taxes could be collected only within Waterford, Wexford and the Pale. More exposed colonists had to pay 'black rent' to neighbouring Gaelic chiefs in order to buy temporary protection from their ravages. Yet the kings of England upheld their claim to be lords of Ireland, and this, together with the presence of Anglo-Irish chieftains beyond the Pale, meant that very few outsiders thought of the Gaelic chiefs as kings, whatever their own bards continued to call them.

Compared with England very few administrative documents of any kind survive from Gaelic Ireland. On the other hand, from a very early period vernacular annals survive in far greater numbers in Ireland than in England. Irish history as portrayed in the annals – a seemingly endless round of raids and battles – established a perception of Ireland in English historiography as being irredeemably violent and primitive.

Part III:
Political Structures

Kings

The expectations placed in kings were high and everywhere broadly similar: to keep the peace, ensure that justice was done and protect their people in times of war. 'Kings,' wrote Henry of Huntingdon, 'are like gods to their subjects, so great is the majesty of this earth's highest, that people never weary of looking at them, and those that live with them are looked upon as being above the rest of mankind. No wonder that crowds of women and children rush to gaze at them, so too do grown men and not only men of a frivolous type.'[1] In 1485 just as much as in 1066, it was taken for granted that kingdoms, like landed estates and businesses, were family firms. When quarrels broke out within these families, the result was often a political crisis that shook whole kingdoms. This was true of internal wars such as the 'anarchy' of King Stephen's reign in the twelfth century or the Wars of the Roses in the fifteenth. It was true also of seemingly external wars such as the Hundred Years War. When peace was made it took the form of a family arrangement, as when Stephen adopted Henry of

Anjou as his son in 1153, or when Henry Tudor married Elizabeth of York in 1486.

Then, as now, some expected their rulers to increase the prosperity of their subjects. This was Sir John Fortescue's view: 'it is the king's honour, and also his office to make his realm rich . . . God give him grace to augment his realm in riches, wealth and prosperity.'[2] It was not, however, a king's job to make himself rich. It was perfectly well known that a rich king was potentially a powerful king. The duty of those of his servants who had financial responsibilities was to make him rich. As Richard FitzNigel, Henry II's treasurer, writing in the 1170s, observed in the preface to his *Dialogue of the Exchequer*, 'the power of princes fluctuates according to the ebb and flow of their cash resources'. But he also said to Henry II, 'Your Majesty's glory lies not in hoarding treasure, but in spending it as it should be spent.'[3] And how should it be spent? That was a matter of opinion. Like all other rulers, kings were sustained politically, or brought down, by contemporary opinion. What was emphatically not wanted was a king whose heart, in the words of Thomas Hoccleve, 'lurketh in his coffers'.[4] Kings could be very rich, as records show Edward II to have been in 1326, and Richard II in 1399. It did neither of them any good. By contrast, as the reigns of Edward III and Henry IV demonstrate, kings with good political judgement could weather the most acute financial difficulties.

Throughout these centuries the single most important political factor was the personality of the head of the family, his capacity to get on well with those to whom he was closest. *His* capacity, not hers, because it was also taken for granted that the head of the family would be a man. Nowhere in Britain and Ireland did a woman come to the throne in this period. Two came close. Henry I of England, lacking a legitimate son, and one of the most terrifying of kings, could bully assemblies into swearing that his daughter, 'Empress' Matilda, would inherit his throne, but once he died in 1135, their oaths counted for little compared with their preference for a man, in this case Henry's nephew, Stephen. In 1286, when Alexander III of Scotland died, his granddaughter Margaret, 'Maid of Norway', in the absence of nearer male relatives, was recognised as Queen of Scots, but she died at Kirkwall on Orkney on her way to Scotland in 1290, aged only seven. Rulers were expected to be warriors, and the most successful kings were. Not even peace-loving kings such as Henry III and Henry VI of England were able to avoid wars. In the fifteenth century, just as before, it was assumed that competent adult rulers would accompany their armies and share the risks themselves when they sent their people to war – not stay behind their desks as rulers are expected to do today. Extraordinary circumstances led to a few women such as 'Empress' Matilda and Margaret of Anjou becoming in effect commanders-in-chief. Even fewer took part in battle. In 1136 Gwenllian, wife of Gruffudd ap Rhys, King of Deheubarth, rode at the head of her army 'like a second Queen of the Amazons', and was killed in battle against the Anglo-Norman invaders of Wales.[5] Leadership in war was for men.

Queens

Since kingdoms were family firms, kings' wives were hard to dispense with. Of the twenty-nine kings of England (not counting Edward V) and of Scotland who came to the throne after 1100, only Malcolm IV never married. Queens and their ladies were expected to add beauty, glamour and a frisson of sexual tension to the other excitements of life at their husband's court. As wives, queens were exceptionally well placed to give confidential advice; no doubt many did and many husbands such as Henry III were happy to follow it. Occasionally the sources represent queens as counsellors on public occasions and a few, such as Margaret of Scotland and Margaret of Anjou, were reputed to wield great influence. But it was always taken for granted that they should submit to their husband's authority. Eleanor of Aquitaine's involvement in rebellion against Henry II in 1173 came as a great shock, whereas contemporaries disapproved of, but were not surprised by, the rebellions of his sons.

Kings' wives enjoyed fewer opportunities to show their mettle than aristocratic wives. The latter were often entrusted with important managerial work, running the estates while their husbands were away, usually at court or with the king's army. But, by definition, adult kings could never be 'away' from the permanent centre of patronage and political power – except on those extraordinary occasions such as Stephen's captivity or Henry VI's mental breakdown, when their wives, Matilda of Boulogne and Margaret of Anjou, stepped into the breach, the former proving to be a very effective campaign manager, the latter a divisive one. Only William I, Henry I until 1118, and Henry II until 1173, i.e. those married kings of England who had large dominions in France, routinely asked their wives to act as their representatives on the other side of the Channel from the one they themselves were on. Kings of smaller kingdoms were never tempted to do this, and after 1173 kings of England almost never let their wives off the leash until Edward II allowed Isabella to go to France in 1325, with fatal consequences for her husband when she returned in 1326 together with a lover, Roger Mortimer, and an army. Not surprisingly it did not happen again.

A queen who was a first wife was expected to bear her husband's children; her sexuality was closely guarded. In England the violation of the queen was declared high treason in 1352. Queens were expected to oversee the education of their children, both daughters and, in the boys' early years, sons. The care that some queens took over their children's education may well have encouraged clerks to look to them for patronage, and see in them, as in aristocratic women more generally, suitable dedicatees of works of religious and secular literature, particularly works in the vernacular. It was as widowed mothers that a few queens came to possess significant political influence. Sometimes this was while their sons were underage, as in the case of the several minorities which dogged the history of fifteenth-century Scotland. In England, by contrast, neither John's nor the Black Prince's nor Henry V's widows counted for much during the minorities of their sons (Henry III, Richard II and Henry VI), yet other kings' mothers were thought to be influential advisers to their adult sons: 'Empress' Matilda to Henry II, Eleanor of Aquitaine to Richard I, Cecily Neville to Edward IV and Margaret Beaufort to Henry VII.

In the public mind the queen was often seen as an intercessor, much as the Virgin Mary was perceived. This was potentially very useful in allowing the king to appear gracious rather than weak when changing – or appearing to change – his mind, as in the famous case of Edward III pardoning the burghers of Calais. The fact that after 1100 nearly all queens of England and Scotland came from outside their husband's kingdom made it easier for their intercession in internal quarrels to be seen as non-partisan. In Scotland the only exception to this occurred in 1364 when David II married Margaret Logie; when she bore no children, he divorced her.

In England the Black Prince broke with more than 250 years of convention when he fell in love with and secretly married Joan of Kent in 1361 during the lifetime of her first husband, from whom she was divorced (possibly illegally). When Edward IV followed the Black Prince's example by marrying Elizabeth Woodville in 1464, he created a tense political situation that had not been seen since the reign of Edward the Confessor: a Queen of England with many English relatives looking to her for support and advancement. 'Now take heed,' wrote a contemporary Londoner, 'what love may do.'[6]

Choosing rulers

The extent to which kings succeeded or failed in living up to their responsibilities depended much more on themselves as individuals, on the quality of their personal rule, their ability to manage their own family, than on any machinery of government. This applied as much in the fifteenth-century kingdoms of England and Scotland, as the violent ends to the reigns of James I and James III, of Henry VI and Richard III, all testify, as it had done in the much less bureaucratic kingships of eleventh-century Britain and Ireland. In these circumstances choosing a king was a matter of the greatest importance. It was taken for granted that he would be a member of the reigning family. Kings who had sons almost always wanted one of them to succeed. But in Ireland and Wales the way to the throne remained open to any member of the dynasty who had followers and resources, the levers of power. Since candidates for kingship could come from fairly distant segments of the ruling dynasty, anthropologically minded historians have called the succession disputes that resulted 'segmentary strife'. A son who had been favoured by his father, perhaps chosen as 'tanist' (deputy), certainly possessed an advantage over his rivals, but what counted above all were the skills to win men to his side – political intelligence, military prowess, resourcefulness, if necessary ruthlessness. In Ireland and Wales there were no boy kings. In those regions where kingdoms were small and economic conditions combined with fierce com petition for resources to make cattle-raiding a sine qua non of kingship, it was crucial to have a king who could do this. In Ireland tradition required a king to inaugurate his reign with an armed raid, his *crech ríg*. The 'open' system of succession in Wales and Ireland created a more or less permanent stock of eligible kings and, not surprisingly, more bids for kingship. It resulted quite often in shared kingships and in partitions of kingdoms. Kingdoms fluctuated in size depending upon the outcome of each round of 'segmentary strife'. To English observers from the twelfth century onwards, politics in contemporary Wales and Ireland always seemed chronically unstable.

Father-to-son succession, by contrast, seems to have been accepted as the norm in England by 1100, and in Scotland fifty years later – though here the norm faced a number of challenges from the mac William dynasty, descendants of Duncan II. Boys less than ten years old came to the throne in England in 1216 (Henry III), 1377 (Richard II), 1422 (Henry VI), and 1483 (Edward V); in Scotland in 1249 (Alexander III), 1329 (David II), 1437 (James II) and 1460 (James III). In lands where kings did not have to go to war every year, then boy kings could be tolerated in the expectation that they would grow up to be warriors, though in the event Henry III, Richard II and Henry VI all proved to be extremely reluctant. Evidently by the thirteenth century there were systems of government in both England and Scotland capable of functioning for some years without the king himself having to play an active managerial role. Richard I's three-year absence on crusade and in German captivity suggests that England had reached that point earlier; the fact his father, Henry II, spent most of his reign out of England may have contributed here. The kingdom of England survived long minorities such as Henry III's and Henry VI's. Even more remarkably, the Scottish kingdom survived the interregna of 1290–2 and 1296–1306 as well as the series of minorities and absences (including absences in English captivity) that characterised the reigns of Alexander III, David II, James I, James II and James III. In crisis the Scots showed that they were loyal to more than a person. In 1296 when Edward I forced John Balliol to renounce the throne and royal regalia, leaving him only his bare surcoat, 'toom tabard', the Scots continued to resist English aggression. At the siege of Stirling in 1304 they proclaimed their allegiance not to a person but to the Lion of Scotland. None the less in this period none of the peoples of Britain and Ireland deliberately chose to do without a king.

If a king had more than one son, then the question arose: which son? Was it up to the ruler to decide which of his sons to promote? Or were there rules which circumscribed his choice? In 1066 England was conquered by William the Bastard. This contemporary name reveals one fact: many churchmen regarded him as illegitimate. The fact that he was Duke of Normandy reveals another: in eleventh-century Normandy the churchmen did not make the rules. But things were changing. Henry I's son, Robert of Gloucester, one of the most admired politicians and patrons of the age, would surely have become King of England when his father died in 1135, had it not been for the fact that the relationship between his parents was not recognised as conferring legitimacy upon him. The same may also have applied in Scotland in 1124 when Alexander I's illegitimate son Malcolm mac Heth was defeated by Alexander's brother, David. In Wales these new ideas of legitimacy came to count for something by the thirteenth century; in Ireland they still had not by the fifteenth. Where the sons of many different women could bid for the throne, then kingship was an office open, if not to all, then at least to many talents. By contrast the acceptance of the ecclesiastical theory of illegitimacy in England and Scotland added to the number of boy kings. In 1483 the theory suggested to Richard of Gloucester a way of getting rid of one of them, Edward V.

In eleventh- and twelfth-century England it was not a foregone conclusion that legitimate sons would succeed to the throne in order of seniority. There was no prescribed order of succession. In cases of dispute – and in these centuries most successions were disputed – the outcome was always decided by politics and war. In that sense the successful claimant was always the one chosen by the people. None the less it is clear that the wishes of the previous king, in particular his testamentary dispositions, were widely regarded as creating an acceptable title. In 1087 William I designated his younger son, William Rufus, as his heir in England. In the absence of legitimate sons, as in 1066, 1135 and 1199, the old king's right to designate a successor was all the more evident. In both 1066 and 1135 the rivals based their claims to the throne upon the assumption that the political nation would respect the previous king's wishes. According to a contemporary account, in 1199 Richard bequeathed the kingdom of England and all his other lands to his brother John. But ideas were changing. By the 1220s authors were interpreting 1199 in terms of an argument about order of succession. Who was the nearer heir: the younger brother (John) or the son (Arthur) of an older brother? In a more legalistic age people in England and Scotland were increasingly inclined to apply the laws governing descent of property even at the highly politicised level of a kingdom. In the 1280s Alexander III had tailzies (entails) drawn up combining the principle of primogeniture in the male line with female succession to the throne in the absence of male heirs. In 1290 Edward I followed suit in England. In 1292 he adjudicated the 'Great Cause' by awarding Scotland to John Balliol as the nearest heir. (Other claimants included descendants of five of William the Lion's illegitimate children.) In many ways the emergence of rules of succession eased the king's task of managing his own family. Henry II's relationships with his sons were always likely to have been more awkward than Edward III's. Although a tendency towards primogeniture has been discerned in Irish succession practice, to a contemporary writing c.1500 it seemed that 'he that hath the strongest army and hardest sword among them, hath best right and title'.[7]

The right of women to inherit or transmit title to thrones was never recognised in Welsh or Irish law; Strongbow's claim to inherit Leinster on the death of his father-in-law, King Dermot, used foreign law to justify foreign conquest. In England Henry II's accession in 1154 could be seen in retrospect to have strengthened the claim (his mother's) that had failed in 1135; at the time he succeeded only by exerting enough military pressure to force Stephen to adopt him. In Scotland the threat of a challenge to Alexander II via the female line of the mac Williams was sufficient to cause the murder of an infant child, her brains dashed out against the market cross at Forfar in 1235. Edward III's claim to France ran through the female line. Despite this in 1376 he entailed the throne of England in the male line. But, as the struggle between York and Lancaster reveals, this did not end the matter. Richard of York's claim, pressed in 1460, went through the female line. When Henry VI regained the throne in 1470, the entail in the male line was reasserted in Parliament. What one king did, a later king could undo. Richard of York's son, Edward IV, not only fought his way back to the throne in 1471, he also had the records of Henry VI's Parliament destroyed.

Royal households

Throughout these centuries and beyond, a ruler's political as well as social life was played out within the arena of his household. All lords had their households and above them all was the king's. Wherever a king went, his household went with him; part domestic, part administrative, part political, it was indispensable. Irish bardic poetry, Welsh legal texts, English and Scottish administrative documents all reflect this same basic reality. The most elaborate household ordinance of the entire period, Edward IV's *Black Book of the Household*, envisaged England as a hierarchy of households, at the head the king with a household of 500, then dukes with households of 240, earls 140, barons forty, knights sixteen, and esquires with ten. 'Duke' was a new title, created in the fourteenth century, but there was nothing new or particularly English about the substance. Between households in the various kingdoms the differences were above all ones of scale.

The nature of the surviving evidence means that we know little about early royal households except when they went to war. The increasingly elaborate records from late medieval households make their function as centres of conspicuous consumption more apparent. This creates the impression of a development from warband to court. While it is the case that after the 1340s the King of England's household played a smaller role in military organisation than previously, it is not the case that the earliest royal households were nothing but bands of warriors. Royal households had always included people who catered for entertainment (huntsmen, keepers of hounds, musicians, poets), religious (chaplains) and domestic needs (cooks, brewers, candle-makers and the like). The food, drink and entertainment which the household provided allowed the king to demonstrate his generosity and display his magnificence. Later English records make a formal distinction between the 'house of magnificence' and the 'house of supply' (*domus providencie*), in effect between 'upstairs' and 'downstairs'; in one form or other these two parts had always existed, and both were integral to the political process. 'Day by day, dining in his chamber, he sought to influence chosen guests. At the great feasts, dining in the hall, he aimed to impress the wider body politic.'[8] In their households kings held council with their most trusted advisers. Here they heard disputes between their subjects, in a court that in England became known as King's Bench.

The leading men of the royal household were not there full-time. They spent only a part of the year at court; the rest of the time they lived, like all other gentlemen, on their own estates. According to the *Black Book*, it made sense for the squires of the household, 'chosen by the advice of [the king's] council from men of possession, worship and wisdom' to come from different shires throughout the kingdom 'by whom the disposition of the countries [i.e. counties] may be known'. If there were forty squires, then twenty were to be at court, 'attending upon the king's person, in riding and going at all times and to help serve his table'. Afternoons and evenings, as of old, they were supposed to exercise their talents 'in talking

of chronicles of kings and other policies, or in piping or
harping, singing or other laudable acts, to help occupy the
court and entertain guests'.[9] Whether for them the reality of
their days at court was quite so entertaining may be doubted.
When at court they were deprived of most of their own
followings. Owners of huge estates and great mansions were
compelled to share bedchambers, even beds, when staying at
court. Stripped of the protective cocoon of their own
households, the most ambitious men in the kingdom faced
each other at close quarters in a highly competitive society.
Henry of Huntingdon, himself a court poet who fell out of
favour, recalled seeing Robert Bloet, Bishop of Lincoln and
once Henry I's chancellor, shedding tears:

> He felt such despair about the king's friendship that
> when he was told the king had spoken highly of him, he
> said 'the king only praises one of his men when he has
> decided to destroy him'.[10]

To call the court a form of hell was already a cliché by the
twelfth century, but at the gates of this hell there were always
thousands desperate to get in. For it was here in the court, the
political heart of the household, that 'the great engines of
power lay, stoked by bribery, flattery and constant agitation; at
their centre, like Dante's Lucifer pinioned at the very heart of
the Inferno, presided the one great figure of the king'.[11]

Common to royal households everywhere were three
senior officers: steward, chamberlain, and constable (or their
equivalents). The steward, normally a lord, was responsible
for overall management of the household, but often the
chamberlain, controlling access to the king's chambers, where
the king slept and where a store of money and treasure was

kept, would have been more influential. The responsibilities of the constable (*penteulu*, 'head of the retinue', in Welsh) were primarily military. Together with the marshal, who originally had been responsible for the king's horses, he had the job of mobilising the household knights and of ensuring that they were paid their annual fees and then wages reckoned according to the number of days they served. When a king went to war, the core of his army – and sometimes the whole of it – comprised an expanded household, drawing in not just the king's domestic household (*domus*), but also the wider household (*familia*), composed of men (the *familiares*) retained by the king to perform political and military services when called upon. When within his own kingdom, of course, it created a bad impression if the king kept an armed bodyguard about him, as though he were in enemy country. This political mistake was made by King John (from 1212) and by Richard II (after 1397).

Only in England was the use of the written word for government already so common by the eleventh century that the royal household included an official responsible for the seal and writing-office, a chancellor. Throughout Europe rulers made increasing use of the written word, the documents most likely to survive being charters recording grants of estates or privileges, copies of which were made and kept by the beneficiaries. Then rulers themselves began to archive their records. For historians of English government the year 1199, when the royal Chancery, as the secretariat was now being called, began to keep registers (in the form of rolls) of copies of outgoing letters, marks a major turning point. The first full year for which all three new types of Chancery roll survive is John's sixth (1204–05). They contain over 1,300 documents – more than ten times as many per year as survive from the 1190s. Kings of smaller kingdoms had less need for a secretariat, but in the twelfth century many of them, the Scottish king first, also came to employ clerks attached to their chapels to draw up written documents. When crisis struck the Scottish monarchy in 1289, nearly 800 rolls were sent to Edinburgh Castle for safekeeping. Although historians, English ones especially, have been impressed by the increasing use of documents, contemporaries were more impressed by those men close enough to the king to hear his orders out of his own mouth than by those who received his commands in writing. They were even more impressed when they themselves heard the king's words. Hence kings were constantly on the move, making their presence known and felt.

Kings and their households had always travelled in this way from one centre to another consuming the customary renders in cows, pigs, sheep, cheese, loaves of bread and vats of ale brought in by local agents. The term 'renders' covers both rent paid by those who lived on the king's estates, and tribute (*cain* in Scotland and Ireland) owed by the whole population of the district. The larger the royal household, the more likely it was that this system of consumption would get conspicuously out of hand. The arrival of hundreds of humans and horses (the equivalent of a small town) requiring food and drink in a region which lacked the infrastructure to accommodate a sudden surge in demand, inevitably caused disruption as well as business opportunities. According to the Anglo-Saxon Chronicle for 1104, 'wherever the king went, there were burnings and killings as his wretched people suffered from the ravages of his household'. As the use of money increased and markets proliferated, royal households were less constrained to visit the places of production. Richard FitzNigel said he knew people who had seen supplies brought to the court at fixed times, but that this practice had been discontinued as being convenient neither to the king nor to the farmers – as they had demonstrated by marching on the court brandishing their ploughshares.[12] It had been replaced by the payment of money rents. The cash was then used to buy goods on the market, either in towns or from merchants who came to court. According to Walter Map, a properly managed royal household followed a well-publicised itinerary and attracted so many traders from all over England and overseas that 'there was no market anywhere as busy as the market that travelled with the king'.[13] In England this process was largely complete by 1130. In Scotland it was still ongoing in the thirteenth century. In 1264, for example, the Sheriff of Forfar accounted for £485 in money plus thirty-seven cows, seventy-five pigs, 1,578 stones of cheese, 291 hens, 206 measures of oats, thirty-two of barley and ten of flour, and 800 eels. Political imperatives – and the pleasure of hunting – meant that even the kings of England continued to travel, in order to measure the political temperature in the regions, to see and be seen. Hence kings insisted on retaining 'purveyance', the right to commandeer provisions, notionally in return for fair payment. But it was a system wide open to abuse. For this reason when Edward I announced his intention of spending Easter at Nottingham, he reassured the townspeople by promising to leave as fast as he had come. But purveyance was still causing complaint in the seventeenth century.

Thanks to the survival of the Chancery rolls, the itineraries of the kings of England from 1199 onwards can be established with much greater precision than those of other rulers. John averaged no less than three moves a week, winter and summer, throughout his reign (1199–1216). Since he and his predecessors were as much French princes as kings of England, they spent a great deal of time in France, particularly in the fifty-year period between 1154 and 1203. After 1203 English royal itineraries were increasingly confined to England. Even after Edward III claimed the throne of France, the only King of England to spend much time in his other kingdom was Henry V. Moreover although from Henry II onwards they all claimed to be lords of Ireland, only Henry himself (in 1171–2), John in 1210, and Richard II in 1395 and 1399, ever went there. Wales too, even after 1300, they rarely visited except at the head of an army. By the fifteenth century English kings were significantly less mobile than John had been, averaging two moves a week in the summer, and tending to spend the winter months in and around London/Westminster. It seems likely that the rise of a money economy also enabled other rulers to travel less, though in the absence of records it is hard to be sure. In Gaelic Ireland, however, sixteenth-century chiefs continued to demand their 'coign and livery' (billeting rights and produce-rents), a traditional practice that to contemporary English observers now seemed wicked.

Peace and war

Whereas in Irish Ireland, and in some parts of Wales and Scotland, warfare was a way of life, England was an exceptionally peaceful country. The Wars of the Roses were far from being typical. Contrast the thirteen civil-war battles on English soil in the thirty-three years between 1455 and 1487 with just nine in the previous 350 years (two in Stephen's reign, one in Henry II's, three in Henry III's, one in Edward II's, one in Richard II's). Compared with their continental contemporaries, English townspeople spent little on town walls. English armies did their destructive work in other countries.

War at home was a remote eventuality. After the eleventh century, except in the occasional periods of crisis and on the borders with Wales (until *c*.1300) and Scotland, castles were built more for display and comfort than for defence. The evidence of the earliest extant household accounts and inventories shows that very few of the wealthy spent much on weapons and armour. Recent work by landscape historians and archaeologists has shown that away from the Scottish and Welsh marches, designed landscapes, ornamental fishponds and gardens, dovecotes, viewing pavilions, roof walks, a concern for comfort rather than defence, were all characteristic of medieval England – it is just that, above ground, they barely survive, and certainly make less impression than ruined walls which appear to speak of war.

Occasionally, however, there were crises severe enough for men to risk life and limb in taking up arms against their opponents, as there were indeed in the sixteenth and seventeenth centuries. In essence there were two different types of political upheaval: the one, a war of succession triggered by the death of the old king; the other a rebellion against the way the reigning king was exercising power. Between 1066 and Stephen's reign (1135–54), the crises were all of the first type, following hard upon the deaths of Edward the Confessor (1066), William I (1087), William II (1100) and Henry I (1135), although in this last case it took three years before the war between Stephen and Matilda spread from Normandy into England. The last time that the death of a king precipitated an armed struggle in England was 1135. The successions to both Stephen and Henry II were de facto settled before they died, and succession to Richard I in 1199 was disputed only in Anjou. In England the successions from 1154 on passed off peacefully, as indeed they did in Scotland. For as long as it seemed natural that a war of succession would routinely follow the death of the previous king, new reigns were not formally held to begin until the day of coronation or inauguration. But Edward I's reign began on the day of his father's funeral, and from Edward II onwards it was conventional to date a new king's reign from the day after his predecessor's death. In 1329 the Scots went one better, starting the new reign on the day the old king died.

From the 1173–4 rebellion against Henry II onwards, all political crises apart from two were caused by acute dissatisfaction with the performance of a king whose own accession to the throne had been undisputed. The first exception was the rebellion launched by John in 1193 when he heard that his elder brother Richard I was a prisoner in Germany; his bid for power flopped, however, since rather than help him almost all Richard's subjects preferred to pay a king's ransom. The second exception occurred in 1483 when Richard III seized the throne before Edward V could be crowned. In that sense Richard put the clock back several centuries. Henry Tudor's response led in 1485 to a King of England being killed in battle for the throne for the first time since 1066, and the accession of a king whose dynastic title was as weak as William I's had been.

Magna Carta and reform

In view of its impact upon English history and myth, the Magna Carta rebellion and subsequent civil war (1215–17) is a particularly significant case. By 1215 it was plain that John, though intelligent, was a poor war leader and an untrustworthy and oppressive ruler. By eliminating his nephew Arthur of Brittany, he had ensured that there was no alternative ruler in the family. His sons were too young to be plausible leaders of a rebellion, as Henry II's elder sons had been in 1173–4. In this situation the opposition barons took the revolutionary step of inventing a new kind of focus for revolt: a document, a charter of liberties which they forced John to grant 'to all the freemen of the realm and their heirs for ever' (see p. 4). Rather than risk being identified with a programme that suited only their own sectional interests, they drew up a long charter containing something for nearly everyone. Its sixty-three chapters were primarily a commentary on John's rule but included much that applied to English royal government in general, including some chapters that became and remain iconic statements of the rights of the subject. Chapter 39: 'No free man shall be taken or imprisoned or deprived or outlawed or exiled or in any way ruined except by the lawful judgement of his peers or by the law of the land.' Chapter 40: 'To no one will we sell, deny or delay right or justice.' Two chapters undermined the sovereignty of the Crown by making John's decisions subject to a review committee composed of his enemies. For this reason John sealed the charter at Runnymede on 15 June 1215 only in order to gain time to hire an army of foreign mercenaries and persuade the pope to declare the charter null and void, which he duly did. But few if any of John's opponents were moved by Innocent III's threat of excommunication.

Civil war broke out in September 1215. In desperation the rebels looked to Louis, heir to the throne of France, to provide an alternative king. In consequence when John died in October 1216, the war turned into a succession dispute between Louis and those who supported John's oldest son, Henry (see p. 106). A boy of nine proved a more acceptable ruler than John had been, particularly when his advisers cut the ground from under the feet of the opposition by issuing a modified Magna Carta. In 1217 Louis withdrew and Henry III's government reissued the charter again, with further modifications, including a supplementary charter dealing exclusively with forest law. It was in contrast with this shorter Forest Charter that the Big Charter (*magna carta*) acquired its familiar name. The reissues of 1216 and 1217, followed by a further reissue in 1225, ensured that Magna Carta, to all appearances a dead duck in the autumn of 1215, survived to become in effect a written constitution – the earliest in European history – limiting the powers, especially the money-raising powers, of thirteenth-century English government. In time it came to enjoy mythic status as the foundation stone of freedom.

Henry III proved to be a feeble king with an overambitious and expensive foreign policy. In 1258 he was forced, under threat of rebellion, to acquiesce in the Provisions of Oxford. These imposed on him a council of fifteen chosen by four electors, only two of whom were the king's men. This council was authorised to appoint the king's principal officials, chancellor, treasurer and justiciar, and was answerable to the barons in Parliament. Henry was in effect treated as if he were a child. As a constitutional experiment 1258 was even more radical than 1215. But once the unity of 1258 broke down, and this happened once Henry had been forced to renounce his unrealistic foreign policy, then only a few hardliners such as Simon de Montfort insisted on depriving the king of what he considered his right: to choose his own counsellors and servants. On this issue civil war broke out in 1264.

The Montfortian victory at Lewes led to the establishment, in the name of the captured king, of a conciliar government. Among its decrees was the order that Magna Carta should be proclaimed in the county courts twice every year so that in future no one could claim to be ignorant of it. But for all his efforts to shore it up (see p. 189), Earl Simon's political base was a narrow one. In 1265 he was defeated by Edward (later Edward I) at Evesham. The earl and thirty of his friends were killed in the battle. The mutilation of Simon's corpse symbolised the determination of the king's men to destroy root and branch the revolutionary experiment which had reduced the king to the position of being a figurehead, a constitutional monarch.

Shedding royal and noble blood

Although later attempts to limit royal authority, such as the Ordinances of 1311 and the scheme forced upon Henry IV in 1406, did not go as far as 1258, the events of Edward II's, Richard II's and Henry VI's reigns in England – as also of Robert II's and Robert III's in Scotland – all suggest that opposition magnates still preferred to think of institutional ways of limiting a king's freedom of action rather than of dethroning him. In the last resort, however, there was no way of preventing an adult king taking over the reins of government if he were free and wished to do so – as Richard II demonstrated in 1389 and Henry VI in the 1450s. That being so, men and women sometimes resorted to more extreme measures.

In 1326 when Queen Isabella and her lover, Roger Mortimer, had Edward II in their power they chose to depose him. The same fate was suffered by Richard II in 1399, by Henry VI twice (in 1461 and 1471) and by Edward V in 1484. All four kings were subsequently murdered. In contrast not one of the three kings or would-be kings of England who fell into the hands of their enemies during the twelfth and thirteenth centuries – Robert Curthose (captured in 1106), Stephen (captured 1141) and Henry III (captured 1264) – had been put to death. Nor indeed was Alexander III of Scotland, twice kidnapped in 1250s. By 1484, when all Europe took it for granted that Richard III had had Edward V killed, the chancellor of France publicly commented on the English habit of murdering their kings. In that he was blamed for the deaths of children, Richard was believed to have gone beyond what the political community found acceptable, and his reign was correspondingly brief (two years, two months and one day). Although Henry VII had an alabaster memorial made for Richard's grave in the Grey Friars church in Leicester, such was the lack of respect for him that by the early seventeenth century the site was, according to the antiquarian John Speed, 'overgrown with weeds and nettles'.[14] Then forgotten, not until 2013 was it rediscovered, and within it Richard's skeleton with scoliotic spine. By contrast, and despite their responsibility for the violent deaths of their predecessors, both Henry IV and Edward IV had been able to rule successfully. Their tombs, in Canterbury Cathedral and St George's Chapel, Windsor, remained carefully tended through subsequent centuries.

This acquiescence in political killings was one symptom of a change in English political values visible after 1300. Following the hanging of William de Alderie in 1095, not for well over 200 years did another English noble suffer the death penalty for rebellion. Despite the fact that taking up arms against the king was always regarded in law as treason, none of the nobles who risked this course of action in the twelfth and thirteenth centuries was executed for it. The worst treatment meted out publicly to high-status English rebels against the kings from Henry I to Edward I was exile and confiscation of property.[15] Indeed it may have been this that led Edward and his supporters to kill the leading Montfortians in battle at Evesham in 1265 rather than bring them to trial. Hence the shock when Edward II had his cousin Thomas of Lancaster beheaded and two dozen other rebels hanged after the Battle of Boroughbridge in 1322. In the words of a contemporary chronicler, Edward II 'brought all the chivalry of England unto death'.[16] The bloodbath of 1322 was followed by further high-profile executions in 1323, 1326 and 1330 as well as the murder of Edward II himself in 1327.

Nothing like this had been seen in England since the reign of King Cnut. The legality of the executions was questioned by contemporaries, on the grounds that the accused were not tried before their peers in Parliament and were not given a chance to defend themselves. They had instead been tried in courts and by procedures in which the newly emerging class of professional judges, men whose family origins were distinctly non-aristocratic, played an important role, as was happening in France at about the same time. It seems that such men were less inclined to respect the old conventions which had allowed men of rank to 'get away' with rebellion when less mercy was commonly shown to those of lower rank.

The killings of 1322–30 set precedents and marked a turning point. In the event, Edward III's gift for man-management meant that the rest of his reign passed off without such bloodshed, but the execution of leading opponents became a feature of the reigns of Richard II and of all the rulers of England for the next 300 years. First developed in 1424, Acts of attainder condemning people for treason by simply listing their names in Parliament, with no evidence produced, no witnesses examined, no defence possible, became standard instruments of vengeance in the struggle between York and Lancaster. The politics of medieval England has often been portrayed as 'medieval' in its brutality, a representation supported by a statistic showing that medieval dukes were more likely to meet a violent end than were dukes in later centuries. But this argument cannot be applied to the twelfth and thirteenth centuries since there were no dukes in England before 1337. Moreover it was not until Henry VIII's reign that a king began to execute women – and not only his wives – for impurely political reasons.

Even during the 'chivalrous' twelfth and thirteenth centuries, however, the English dealt with the Welsh and Irish with much less restraint than they showed in their internal quarrels, or in their wars against the French. The English perceived the Welsh and Irish as barbarians and believed that they understood only savage medicine. In part this was because the killing and mutilating of enemy leaders remained a characteristic feature of internal wars in Wales and Ireland throughout the twelfth century. Indeed although a trend towards mutilation rather than outright killing has been observed, Gaelic Irish politics stayed a bloody business throughout the medieval centuries. Between 1274 and 1315 nine kings of Connacht were killed either by their brothers or cousins. In Wales, by contrast, princely politics became noticeably less bloody after 1200, with Llywelyn ap Iorwerth (see p. 126) setting an example of a more merciful treatment of his rivals. By contrast, Edward I, the victor of Evesham, chose to hang, draw and quarter David of Wales in 1283, and other leaders of Welsh resistance in 1292 and 1295.

Bloodshed (for an example see p. 148) also characterised Scottish succession disputes in the twelfth and early thirteenth centuries, but because those put to death came from either Scandinavian or Gaelic (the mac William dynasty) Scotland, it can be said that the anglicising kings of David I's line were merely dealing with outsiders in the English manner. This did not prevent Edward I from having William Wallace executed in 1305 nor, more significantly, from reacting to the shock of Robert Bruce's sacrilegious murder of the Red Comyn in 1306, by unleashing a reign of terror in which six of Bruce's brothers and brothers-in-law, as well as Edward's own distant cousin John, Earl of Atholl, were put to death. John was the first earl executed by a King of England since the beheading of Earl Waltheof of Northumbria in 1076. The executions, many carried out in England, that resulted from Edward I's invasions of Wales and Scotland, may have contributed to the brutalising of English politics visible from Edward II's reign until the seventeenth century.

Political conflict in later medieval Scotland was in one respect more violent than in England. The fierce conduct of the Gaelic clansmen, 'wyld wykkyd Heland-men' as Andrew of Wyntoun called them, including such episodes as the burning down of Elgin Cathedral in 1390, frequently alarmed English-speaking Lowlanders (see p. 171).[17] On the other hand, apart from Robert Bruce's execution of three nobles for their part in a Comyn-linked conspiracy in 1320, the civil war between Bruce and Balliol, although it inflicted great damage on the Scottish countryside, largely because of the English intervention on the Balliol side, was fought without captured magnates being put to death (except by Edward III, in 1346). Despite occasional acts of violence – as when David II's mistress, Katherine Mortimer, was murdered in 1360, and the chief suspect, the Earl of Angus, died in prison – high politics in later medieval Scotland long remained less bloody than contemporary English politics. Only in the generation after 1425, when James I returned home after many years in England, were Scottish nobles executed or murdered similarly frequently. One consequence of the new ruthlessness was the murder of James himself in 1437.

Rebellions of the people

English rule in Scotland and Wales triggered popular risings in which leaders such as William Wallace (from 1297 until his capture in 1305) and Owain Glyndwr (from 1400 until 1408) acted as the champions of national resistance. One other, and very different, kind of popular rising occurred in England and nowhere else in Britain and Ireland. The rebellion of June 1381 was a revolt of the taxpayers of south-east England against a government whose policies were perceived as fundamentally unjust, favouring the employers at the expense of labouring men and at a time when, for once, the economic tide was in the latter's favour (see p. 61). Military setbacks in France in the 1370s added to the government's unpopularity and laid it open to charges of inefficiency and corruption. The last straw came with the imposition of a flat-rate poll-tax in 1380 and the stringent measures taken, particularly in the wealthiest counties of England, to enforce its collection in the early summer of 1381. Although commonly known as the Peasants' Revolt, townspeople and artisans were just as prominent when rebel armies from Essex and Kent marched on London, taking the government completely by surprise – hardly surprising since nothing like this had ever happened before.

The rebels took London (including the Tower), executed several government advisers and ministers including the treasurer and chancellor (who happened to be the Archbishop of Canterbury), and seemed to have the thirteen-year-old king, Richard II, at their mercy. But they did not hold him responsible for 'his' government's failings and many went home on 14 June when he agreed to their demand that serfdom should be abolished. Those who remained in the capital, many hoping for further reforms and still trusting the king, allowed themselves to be dispersed the next day when one of their leaders, Wat Tyler, was killed during a conference with the king's party at Smithfield. Richard then revoked his concessions and the remaining rebel leaders were rounded up and punished. Many, such as John Ball, preacher of fiery sermons reminding his audience of the theoretical egalitarianism of Christianity, were hanged. Risings elsewhere, notably in East Anglia, though provoked by local grievances, were inspired by the news of the march on London, and did not long survive its collapse.

The year 1381 signalled the violent entry into politics of a group that had hitherto been excluded. Although nothing quite like 1381 was ever to happen again, the fear that the poor would rise was a haunting one. Their more active participation in 'high' politics – whether in the form of lynching five nobles in 1400 and 1450, or in the considerable support attracted by a gentry-led rising such as Cade's revolt in 1450 – shows that the fear was not entirely groundless. It would be a long time before the English government would try to interfere so plainly with the laws of supply and demand, and even longer before one would try to introduce a poll-tax.

Land and Lordship

Throughout these centuries as earlier too the lordship of some people (nearly always men) over others was fundamental to social and political life throughout Britain and Ireland. All lords had followers, some of them living more or less permanently in their lords' households, others with lands of their own. In pre-Conquest England the commonest word for a lord's follower was *cniht*, from which the later 'knight' was derived. All men were expected to have lords. The 'lordless man' was a source of anxiety. Kings and princes were lords who depended for their own political and military success, and indeed survival, on the support of their leading tenants, i.e. people who held property, principally land, from them, and who looked to them in the hope of obtaining further advancement.

The number and wealth of such subjects, as well as the formal and informal terms of their tenancies, naturally varied considerably over time and space. As always, the surviving English evidence allows us to see developments there more clearly than elsewhere. Even in relatively well-documented England, however, the amount of evidence relating to property holders and their rights before 1066 is very small, and great uncertainties remain. It is clear at least that long before 1066 many of a lord's dependants had also been his tenants, paying rent in many forms, including an obligation to provide military service. On the other hand many landholders were entitled, in the words of a recurring phrase in Domesday Book, 'to go to any lord they chose with their land'. It was possible, in other words, to hold land, on a lease for example, from a landlord, but to acknowledge someone else as one's lord (in a sociopolitical sense). In such a case the key element in the relationship between lord and man was personal, not tenurial. Lords wanted retainers who could give them good service, which might not be the case with their tenants, and ambitious men sought out lords who could promote their interests, not necessarily their landlords. As David Carpenter has put it, 'no ambitious lord could afford to be stuck with a circle of dud tenants, just as no ambitious tenant could afford to be stuck with a dud lord'.[18] He was writing about English society in the later twelfth century, but the same would have applied before 1066. No doubt it was possible for a tenant to transfer his land to a new landlord – with the consent of the old one – but more commonly the

terms of his lease remained unaltered when he entered the
service of a new lord.

Whether or not all the landholders in England saw
themselves as tenants or subtenants of the king, it is clear that
before as well as after 1066 the king was the source of lawful
authority over all the land in his kingdom. The king alone
could 'book' land, i.e. issue a charter (*boc* in Old English)
exempting a particular estate from the customary rules which
applied to all other estates. Wealthy pre-Conquest men and
women who held some 'bookland' enjoyed the privilege of
being able to make written wills bequeathing it to whomever
they wished, irrespective of the usual inheritance customs.[19]
They were also freed from having to provide many of the dues
and obligations (such as escort, carrying and messenger
services) generally expected from those who held land on
lease. But they were still required to ensure that all military
service was properly performed, and if they failed in this, then
their bookland passed into the king's possession, while any
land they held from another lord reverted to that lord. Cnut's
law code (regarded then and in the twelfth century as the
authoritative written statement of pre-Conquest law) makes
this explicit. As Cnut's code shows, royal legislation set out or
altered the terms on which land was held: what was to happen,
for example, if a man died intestate, what the rights of widows
were, in what circumstances the death duty known as 'heriot'
should be remitted, and what were the appropriate levels of
heriots depending on the status of the deceased.[20] Even if, as is
sometimes claimed, there had been some land in pre-Conquest
England held from no one at all, it is clear that those who held
it were still subject to the king's authority, and might find their
land confiscated if they offended. After 1066 the privilege of
being able to bequeath bookland to heirs of one's choice was

no longer on offer. Those Frenchmen who received great estates from William I were in no position to bargain individually about the terms on which they benefitted from massive royal generosity. In consequence after the Conquest written bequests of land became increasingly rare.

The Conquest was an event unparalleled in European history; following it the King of England's position was uniquely strong. William I's creation of a new landed aristocracy led to an exceptional strengthening of royal power. The new French lords knew that they possessed great estates in England because they had been given them by the king, and not because they had inherited them from parents or grandparents. Equally the foreign followers of the new landowners owed their prosperity in England to their lords. For a while, moreover, 'multiple lordship', i.e. the situation in which a person held land from more than one lord, would have been uncommon. For a generation or two the glue binding tenants to lords was extraordinarily strong. In societies in which custom allowed landholders to give away or sell off parts of their land or gave them great flexibility in providing for their kin, especially younger children, estates tended to fragment – a process which made extracting rent or services more complicated. Consequently where lords were strong, the rate of fragmentation was relatively slow. Undivided succession to estates held from them suited lords, including the lord king, so it is not surprising that in post-Conquest England the right of one heir (usually the eldest legitimate son) to succeed to the whole estate (male primogeniture) became the rule. The individual estate, called a manor (itself a word coined soon after 1066), acquired a degree of permanency which pre-Conquest estates, the boundaries of which were in constant flux, lacked. From after 1066 it becomes possible to trace the 'descent of manors' through several centuries. None the less every succession both diminished the degree to which landholders felt they owed their position to the king, and simultaneously strengthened their sense that they owed it to inheritance from their ancestors. This was a process which no legal doctrine such as 'all land belongs to the king', even supposing that such an oddity had been formulated in the aftermath of 1066, could have staved off for long. In the absence of a legitimate son, equal division between daughters became the common-law rule. These 'English' inheritance customs were increasingly adopted in Scotland from the thirteenth century, in contrast to Celtic custom which still tended to give all sons a share, and exclude daughters.

Outside England the absence of relevant pre-twelfth-century evidence makes it very difficult indeed even to speculate about changes which may – or may not – have occurred within the structures of lordship. Although Lowland Scotland, for example, is commonly said to have been feudalised in the twelfth century as the result of an influx of English settlers of Norman descent, this is because it is from that time that the earliest royal charters survive (see p. 114). Whether the terms of land grants they record fitted easily into pre-existing structures or not, these charters do not say.

Patronage

In kingdoms with relatively stable borders such as England and Scotland, political stability always depended primarily upon the ruler's ability to manage the relationship of mutual interdependence between him and the noble lords who comprised his wealthiest tenants – nearly all of whom, of course, had tenants of their own. Even in societies, notably Ireland, where frontiers between kingdoms were chronically unstable, skilful leadership in war was not enough. Rulers everywhere were expected to be sources of patronage, to manage and distribute resources in ways that kept their most powerful subjects, usually including members of their own family, content and active on their behalf.

In England some of the greatest nobles were given the title 'earl', but they were allowed such limited comital authority that, apart from the earldom of Chester (which was taken over by the Crown in 1254), they never constituted the kind of regional power that, for example, some French counts and Scottish earls did. The fact that William I in effect created a new aristocracy, both lay and ecclesiastical, naturally reinforced royal power, notably the power of patronage. Norman and subsequent kings not only appointed bishops and important abbots, they also held on to a church's estates for as long as there was no bishop or abbot – and were, not surprisingly, accused of deliberately prolonging vacancies so as to increase their own revenues. They offered some prelates, often former royal chaplains, lucrative positions in government, and could just as easily take them away. In the case of the king's secular tenants (later called tenants-in-chief), adult heirs had to pay an inheritance tax known as a relief; if underage, they and their father's estates were taken into royal custody, allowing the king either to pocket the profits of the estate, or to grant the custody and, if he chose, the marriage of ward, to whomever he chose. Some people, it should be remarked, felt that the lord was a safer bet as guardian of an underage tenant than were kinsmen, on the grounds that all too many of them would have designs on the child's inheritance. High mortality meant that heirs were often either boys under age (usually set at fifteen) or females (daughters or nieces). Of the 189 baronial estates in existence in 1166, fifty-four had passed through the female line at least once since 1086. If there were no close heirs then, after provision had been made for the widow, whose own remarriage was also under royal control, the king could make a new grant of the estate. The chance survival of a document drawn up in 1185, entitled 'the ladies, boys and girls in the king's gift', listing the widows and wards in Henry II's custody, plus the information that allowed him to assess their market value, reveals that this was a carefully administered system. Taken together with the king's right to appoint men to offices of profit, both at the centre and in the localities, this degree of control over the inheritances and marriages of the richest people in England meant that he enjoyed immense powers of patronage. In the eyes of ambitious men wardships and marriages were desirable assets, well worth bidding for. Thirteenth-century evidence shows that by then, and perhaps earlier, the kings of Scots enjoyed similar rights, and used them for both financial profit and to advance the careers of trusted men.

Since in the nature of things there were never enough offices, estates, wards and widows to satisfy all aspirants, this only made the royal court an even livelier and more competitive place. This store of patronage could yield some tidy sums (see p. 196), but two things are clear. First, political considerations such as the king's need to reward good servants meant that it was not always the highest bidder who won the auction. Second, the system was more useful as an instrument of political control. Kings often made little or no effort to collect the sum offered and agreed. By 1130 Henry I, for example, had accepted offers to the value of nearly £26,000 but only about 14 per cent of that amount was actually paid into the treasury that year. Counting on this, the politically ambitious sometimes offered more than they could afford. In consequence many influential people were permanently in debt to the Crown. They had a powerful motive for serving faithfully, for otherwise the king might demand immediate payment, and then, if they could not pay, forfeiture of their lands. At a crucial moment the fate of William de Braose and his family alarmed many. One of King John's closest advisers, William had offered 5,000 marks for a great lordship in Ireland. For seven years he paid virtually nothing, but in 1208 he lost John's favour, was driven into exile and his family imprisoned, never seen again. The king's proclamation that all this was merely 'action for non-payment of debt in accordance with custom and the law of the Exchequer', was hardly calculated to reassure other debtors.[21]

The powers which the lord king had over his tenants undoubtedly gave him a very strong hand in his dealings with the nobility, but it was a hand which had to be played skilfully if he were not to alienate too many of those families on whose co-operation he ultimately depended. In the eleventh and twelfth centuries, for example, there was no firm rule about the level of relief; instead it was negotiated on a case by case basis. Here was fertile ground for friction, as is indicated both by the Coronation Charter promulgated by Henry I in 1100 and by the Great Charter extorted from King John in 1215. To a greater or lesser degree all twelfth- and thirteenth-century kings of England exploited the system, but none pressed it as hard as King John. Indeed it was very largely by overplaying this strong hand that he brought about his own downfall. In Magna Carta he was forced to make concessions on relief, wardship and marriage. The levels of reliefs were fixed at £100 for an earl's or a baron's estate, and £5 for a knight's.

The Crown's rights over wardship and marriage were much

less easy to circumscribe, indeed could still be exploited by the Tudors and Stuarts. A father's premature death could still deliver the wardship and marriage of his heir to the crown – in 1380, for example, this allowed John of Gaunt to buy the marriage of an heiress for his son Henry Bolingbroke (later Henry IV). Even so, the development of legal devices such as jointures and 'uses' by late medieval lawyers made a difference. The jointure meant a widow could keep more than the traditional common law dower (a third of the estate's value) under her control for her lifetime, including the period of an heir's minority. By the device of granting some of their estates to a group of trustees for specific purposes or uses, privileged landholders were once again, as before 1066, permitted to bequeath land by will. Moreover parents often arranged betrothals while their children were still young. In these ways late medieval English kings were weaker than their Norman and Angevin predecessors. On the other hand the fewer the structural causes of tension between Crown and nobility the easier the co-operation between them, to the advantage of both.

Feudalism

Given that a new monarchy, a new royal family, a new aristocracy, a new language and a new elite culture all came into England after 1066, it is not altogether surprising that the Conquest should be imagined to be the appropriate time for revolutionary change in other spheres too, such as the terms on which land was held. But to state that in England after 1066 lords had greater power over tenants than before, something which may, after all, have been a matter of degree, is very different from claiming, as some historians still do, that an entirely new 'feudal' principle of land tenure was introduced into England after 1066. For these historians the alleged absence in Anglo-Saxon England of either 'feudal incidents' (i.e. royal rights over wardship, marriage and relief) or 'feudal military service' (i.e. knight service), or indeed both, is critical. Elsewhere in Europe, it should be said, historians have preferred to deal with understandings of the word 'feudal' much broader than in insular British tradition. Indeed when the seventeenth-century antiquarian Henry Spelman invented the notion of an English 'feudal system', he also commented upon its insularity, observing that 'the Servitudes and Grievances of Feuds, viz. Wardship, Marriage, and such like, to this day were never known to other nations that are governed by the Feodal Law'.[22]

Beyond doubt Henry I's Coronation Charter promising to 'abolish all the evil customs by which the kingdom of England has been unjustly oppressed', demonstrates that the 'feudal incidents' had been important sources of tension between the lord king and his tenants (and probably also between lords and their tenants) during the reign of Rufus. Henry addressed these matters in chapters 2–4 of the charter. (In chapter 1 he had, as was proper, promised to set free the church of God.) In chapter 2 he promised that in future heirs would pay no more than a just and lawful relief; in chapter 3 that he would not deal with the marriages of women, in particular heiresses, in ways which brought profit to him but which they and their family resented. Widows too were not to be given in marriage without their consent, and if they had children, he promised that either they or their relatives were to have custody of the deceased's land and children. This last (chapter 4) would seem to abolish a royal right of wardship. But for how long had these issues been causes of friction?

In practice there were undoubtedly reliefs before 1066, even if they were called heriots (see p. 168). Although in theory heriot was paid by the person who was going to die – despite the practical risks entailed by payment in advance – while relief was paid after their death by their successor, in practice death must often have struck a property owner before a heriot was actually handed over, leaving the transaction to be either completed or made in its entirety by the heir. Not surprising, then, that the mid-twelfth-century compilation known as the Laws of William based its list of reliefs on the heriots in Cnut's code of law.

Given the impact of the Conquest on lord–tenant relations, few would question the proposition that pre-Conquest lords in general had less power over the marriages of women belonging to their tenants' families than did lords after 1066. Matters such as those highlighted in 1100 were almost certain to have been less prominent before 1066, but they had not been altogether absent. Cnut had laid down that 'neither a widow nor a maiden is ever to be forced to marry a man whom she dislikes', a provision which was presumably directed against people with power over women, a category which might include lords as well as family members. In 1100 Henry I promised to uphold the 'law of King Edward', just as Edward himself on coming to England in 1041 had promised to uphold the law of Cnut. It is true that there are no pre-1066 references to wardship, but it is hard to argue from this silence that wardship existed after 1066 but not before it, since there are no mentions of wardship between 1066 and 1100 either. In any case the earliest evidence to throw some light on how the system of 'feudal incidents' actually worked in practice, the Exchequer roll of 1130, shows that wardship was financially much less central to Henry I than marriage and relief, producing only about one fifth as much as marriage, and about a tenth as much as relief.

Other proponents of the 'feudal revolution' theory prefer to focus their attention, as J. H. Round did in 1895, on knight service. In doing so, and bearing in mind that knight service could involve either service in the field or as part of a castle garrison, they have helped to establish knights and castles as the iconic images of the 'feudal system' – whereas feudalism as understood on the Continent requires at least one more image, that of a downtrodden peasant. Round's remarkably narrowly focused argument was that the conqueror required each of his tenants-in-chief (a term first used in Henry II's reign) to provide a contingent of knights, his knight-service quota, and he insisted that this was based on an arbitrary deal between tenant and king, one which bore no relation whatever to a previous Anglo-Saxon rule by which every five hides of land had to provide one well-armed soldier. Historians have come to refer to a force summoned under the five-hide system as the 'select levy', and envisioned levies mustered shire by shire under the command of shire-reeves. Although in the last fifty years Round's theory has often been challenged, even today it still has its adherents.[23]

In part this is because while the terms of pre-1066 charters insisted that those who held bookland had to ensure that military obligations would be met, only one of the surviving charters explicitly states how much service was required, leaving open the possibility that this was generally not written down because there was some well-known rule of thumb by which the amount could be calculated – rather than, for example, leaving it unwritten so that it could be varied according to specific political and military circumstances. The growing volume of evidence surviving from the twelfth century shows that charters recording land grants in England and Scotland did occasionally spell out how many knights'

service tenants owed in return for their 'fees' – the usual term
for estates held in this way. But the earliest clear-cut evidence
for knight-service quotas in England comes no earlier than
1166, from an inquiry into knight service commissioned by
Henry II. The returns to this inquiry demonstrate that the
number of knights owed was not related to the number of
hides held, and in Round's view this disproved any continuity
between 1166 knight service and the Anglo-Saxon system. Not
surprisingly any interpretation which emphasised discontinuity
looked to the Conquest as the most likely moment for
something new. When Henry II invaded Ireland in the 1170s
he made grants in the style of a conqueror, giving Meath to
Hugh de Lacy for the service of fifty knights, and Leinster to
Strongbow for one hundred.

Undoubtedly Henry's Norman predecessors as kings of
England had been more involved in warfare than Edward the
Confessor, partly as a consequence of their intense engagement
in continental politics. It is, none the less, certain that Anglo-
Saxon magnates, both secular and ecclesiastical, had men of
knightly rank in their armed followings, and inconceivable
that these men would not have been required to contribute
when kings summoned their lords to war.[24] Are we to say that
the size of the contingent owed by an Anglo-Saxon lord could
always be calculated by dividing the number of hides he held
by five?[25] Given the perennial pressures of politics and
patronage the concept of a uniformly administered national
system seems implausibly neat – no matter how strong we
suppose Anglo-Saxon government to have been. Or might
additional arrangements have been made to ensure that when
it came to risking war that same lord would bring a well-armed
following commensurate with his rank and level of commitment to the king's cause? By the time we reach the much

better-documented reign of King John, it is plain that soldiers were called up under a combination of coexisting systems, and it would be odd if this had not been the case 200 years earlier. In practice too it is clear that knight's fees were commonly fragmented; many tenants owed the service of fractions of a knight. Clearly this obligation was really a financial one, a levy known as scutage (shield money) which could be demanded when a king when to war, and which was assessed at so much, for example £1, per knight's fee. Income from scutage could be used to help meet the cost of paid troops or of military households, the two core elements in armies throughout the period, both before and after 1066.

There can be no doubt that the majority of the 1166 quotas post-dated 1066. The great estates held by laymen before 1066 had been dismembered in the aftermath of the Conquest, and entirely new ones created. But one of the oddities of Round's theory of the knight-service quota itself being a post-Conquest innovation is the fact that the inquiry of 1166 shows that no abbey or bishopric founded after 1066 owed knight service, only those which had been founded before 1066. (In Normandy abbeys founded after Duke William came of age also did not owe knight service, only the older ones.) Clearly it is possible to interpret this as proof that William imposed an additional burden on the ancient churches of England in order to punish them for their support of Harold, while at the same time he allowed new foundations to benefit from the ideas of ecclesiastical liberty characteristic of eleventh-century Gregorian reform. But if this is what happened then it is extraordinary that neither Pope Gregory VII nor a single contemporary or near contemporary author from one of those ancient English churches complained about this punitive new burden. Voices lamenting the impact of the Conquest on them can indeed be heard from many of the ancient churches, from Durham, Evesham, York, Canterbury, Worcester, Bury St Edmunds and Wells, yet one imposition which none of them mentions is knight service. The earliest known complaint about knight service, from Ely, dates from the late 1160s, around the time of Henry II's inquiry. It was not until the thirteenth century that a chronicler, Roger of Wendover, explicitly stated that after the Conquest a new burden of military service was imposed on bishoprics and abbeys previously free from all secular service. The only reasonable explanation for the long silence on the subject by authors writing in the first fifty and more years after 1066 is that the ancient churches had already been familiar with knight-service quotas.

Government in England

The Norman Conquest, following upon conquests by West Saxon and Danish kings in the tenth and early eleventh centuries, meant that by the time of Domesday Book (1086) England was already a 'well-conquered, much-governed kingdom'.[26] Given that it lacked a bureaucracy, a standing army and a police force, a phrase such as 'much-governed' can seem odd. But if we compare it, not with the states of much later centuries, but with other eleventh-century European polities, then the force of the remark is clear. In England, centres of wealth and local power such as towns and castles were enclosed within a remarkably uniform network of shires and their sub-divisions, hundreds (first visible in England in the tenth century and not abolished until 1867) and vills which, with some exceptions such as the palatinates of Durham and Cheshire, covered the entire kingdom. Sheriffs (shire-reeves) and hundred reeves held meetings (the latter every three or four weeks), and together with village reeves they were responsible for policing their districts. In the light of the demonstrable capacity of the pre-1066 government to manage the currency and collect taxes, it seems reasonable to believe that the shire, the hundred and the vill also functioned reasonably well as a law-enforcement and peace-keeping system. Men who were in some sense agents of the national government were unusually thick upon the ground. They received no pay for the work they did. What they got was something better: prestige and local influence, commodities which, in turn, brought material rewards, often in the shape of gifts. Indeed, so profitable was the office of sheriff that men habitually bid for it.

Domesday Book reveals that the king and queen held land in all but five of the thirty-five English counties, and valued at 17 per cent of the value of everything recorded in Domesday Book. The fact that the three wealthiest secular lords, Odo, Earl of Kent (who was also Bishop of Bayeux in Normandy), Robert of Mortain and Roger of Montgomery, were all close relatives of King William reveals what a hold the new king and his family had on the realm. Royal landholding loomed large within England. By contrast the lands held by kings across the water, in France and Germany, were to be found only in restricted regions of their much wider kingdoms. More than other European polities, England was king-centred. In consequence royal power over many centuries created and preserved records in quantities hard, perhaps impossible, to parallel elsewhere. Not surprisingly by focusing on these records historians have reinforced the sense that royal power was what mattered, and made themselves vulnerable to the accusation that they have been 'the king's friends', unsympathetic to other foci of power.[27]

In some respects fifteenth-century England looked much

11. Whereas during Edward the Confessor's reign only the king is known to have possessed a seal, by 1300 even serfs were expected to have them. This is one half of a chirograph drawn up c.1225, recording an agreement between the Earl of Chester and about fifty of his tenants, smallholders of Freiston and Butterwick (Lincolnshire).

like eleventh-century England. The increasing use of writing in government meant more paid employment for increasing numbers of clerical staff, but the localities continued to be governed by unpaid part-timers, members of the local elite, the gentry. Even so there were some important differences. New tasks were being imposed on the old officials. For example, sheriffs were required to publish proclamations in cities, boroughs and market towns, and inform Chancery of the dates and places at which they had done so. During the thirteenth century new kinds of local officials had been set up to help the overworked sheriff: coroners, escheators and keepers of the peace. Keepers of the peace became JPs after 1361 when they were allowed to determine cases (see p. 192). The numbers of JPs tended to grow. In Wiltshire there were six in 1368, twelve in 1427 and seventeen by 1478. In addition special commissions were appointed ad hoc, to recruit soldiers for example. By 1400 there were as many as fifty individuals active in the government of a single large shire such as Norfolk. The institution of Parliament enabled some of them to participate more actively in national politics. If eleventh-century England was much governed, by the fifteenth century it was even more so. The increasing elaboration of local government meant a growing number of links between centre and localities, which in turn involved a more bureaucratic central government.

Capital cities

The trend towards bureaucratic government led to the emergence of capitals – central places for much routine government business, no matter where the king was – first in England, then in English Ireland and finally in Scotland. In

England this process began before 1066. At the old West Saxon centre of Winchester the kings already possessed a permanently staffed royal treasury, a depository for fiscal records such as Domesday Book as well as for silver. When Matilda entered Winchester Castle in overconfident mood in 1141 she found there not only what remained of King Stephen's treasure, but also 'the crown of the kingdom which she had always eagerly desired'.[28] By the late twelfth century, however, thanks to the pulling power of a great port and its international commerce, London and the nearby Palace of Westminster had replaced Winchester. A decisive stage in the emergence of a settled centre of English government occurred during the reigns of Henry II and Richard I, i.e. in that half-century when the household itself was most frequently abroad, often for years at a time, and when measures had to be taken to ensure that routine administration was carried on in its absence.

There were two spheres in which this really mattered to both ruler and subject: finance and justice. Although it was from the household offices of chamber and wardrobe that kings spent money to meet the daily needs of pleasure and politics, it was in their interest to have a fixed place where the accounts of the sheriffs were regularly examined. By the 1180s the Exchequer routinely did this at Westminster, no matter where the king himself was. Similarly a judicial committee, the embryonic Court of Common Pleas or Common Bench, met there when the judges returned from their circuits or 'eyres' (see p. 213). At this stage both central committees were presided over by the justiciar, the king's deputy, who had his own copy of the royal seal. From this time on there was in effect a government machine operated by two panels of specialists according to the rules of their profession as set out in the two earliest administrative handbooks in British history,

The Dialogue of the Exchequer written by Richard FitzNigel, the treasurer of the Exchequer, and *The treatise on the laws and customs of England*, written in the 1180s by an as yet unidentified author, though often attributed to Ranulf Glanvill, Henry II's justiciar. A secretariat permanently based at Westminster provided the routine documentation which the law courts and the Exchequer required. The Westminster model was then transferred to Ireland as an act of considered policy. John ordered that a fixed centre for routine government be set up in Dublin, an exchequer and a central court (Common Bench), while his deputy in Ireland, the justiciar, continued to itinerate like a king. The king himself began to use a privy seal (kept by a senior wardrobe clerk) when he wanted written authentication of his wishes. In thirteenth-century Scotland by contrast, as in Wales before the loss of independence, the ruler's itinerant (if increasingly institutionalised) household remained the only hub of government. Not until the later fifteenth century did Edinburgh begin to function as Scotland's capital.

In England the elaboration of central offices continued, and it became increasingly difficult for them to keep close to the king. During Edward I's Welsh wars, for example, the Chancery stayed at Chester; during his Scottish wars, at York. From Edward III's reign onwards, it stayed at Westminster, keeping about a hundred clerks in employment. The formerly itinerant King's Bench of judges (specialising in cases in which the king had an interest) sat increasingly at Westminster. In the later fourteenth century a Chancery court, also sitting in Westminster Hall (where it and the other central courts remained until 1884), developed as a court intended to provide justice where the common law failed. A Westminster council, presided over by the chancellor, began to meet daily during the law terms, usually in the Star Chamber, functioning as a supplement to the more informal counsel that the king had by him as and when he chose. When the council developed its own writing-office, employing privy-seal clerks for this, the king adopted a 'secret' seal; hence by 1399 the signet, headed by a secretary, was the new private office. By 1400 about 300 officials (many of whom had clerical staffs of their own) were employed in the central departments of state: the law courts, Chancery, Exchequer and privy seal. When Richard II was deposed in 1399, none of those who held office in these departments, like the menial servants of the domestic household, lost their jobs. Only the clerks of the signet, the king's private office, were dismissed. Except for brief periods during Edward I's and Edward III's wars against the Scots when it had moved to York, the whole governmental machine stayed at Westminster and was serviced by the city of London. The Inns of Court (see p. 218) were here. The main royal mint was in the Tower of London, as was its principal arms factory and arsenal, employing more than 300 engineers, armourers, gunners and carpenters. When the rebels of 1381 seized the Tower (see p. 165), they knew what they were doing.

But although English central administration had become firmly based in Westminster and London, the court in the itinerant household still remained at the heart of politics and fashion. Outside London there were almost no full-time paid officials. Local government was the preserve of part-time amateurs, the landed aristocracy and gentry. They were the king's servants, but their active co-operation, without which the king's commands were unenforceable, could not be taken for granted. It had to be won by the skilful exercise of patronage, and by drawing them into Parliament.

Counsel

Kingdoms were traditionally thought to belong not to the kings alone, but to the communities of their peoples. This old assumption was most stirringly stated at Arbroath in 1320, when the barons and freeholders of Scotland declared that should their king, Robert Bruce, 'give up what he has begun, we would at once drive him out as our enemy and a subverter both of his own right and ours'.[29] In practice, as well as in theory, all rulers depended upon the support and advice of their leading subjects, who were assumed to represent the rest. Thirteenth-century texts of Welsh law imagined their model king, the tenth-century Hywel Dda, summoning and taking advice from six men from each commote in Wales. Hence as a crucial supplement to the advice they received from 'privy counsellors' based in the royal households, kings everywhere regularly held assemblies of their greater subjects, their barons, both ecclesiastical and lay, to advise them on political and financial matters and to act as judges in their courts. The necessity for this was taken for granted on all sides – an assumption of which kings sometimes took advantage in order to refuse a request they did not like. Thus Henry I wrote to Pope Innocent II explaining that he had no choice but to resist papal demands because otherwise 'my barons and my men (whose counsel and help I cannot do without) will taunt and insult me . . . and will not allow me to enjoy this land any longer'. According to the late twelfth-century Battle Chronicle, no king could make a permanent change to the ancient laws without the common consent of the barons of the realm.[30]

Up to a point the need for wider consultation was met by the 'great courts' which all rulers held at the major festivals of the Christian year. According to the Anglo-Saxon Chronicle, when he was in England William I held court every Christmas, Easter and Whitsun for 'all the powerful men over all England, archbishops and bishops, abbots and earls, thegns and knights'. It was to provide a splendid setting for such assemblies that palaces and great halls such as William II's Westminster Hall (at that date the largest in Europe) were built. According to the twelfth-century account of his life, Gruffudd ap Cynan of Gwynedd 'built his courts and held his feasts honourably'.[31] Raymond of Perelhos reported that all O Neill's lords, bishops, abbots, clerks and knights, were present on Christmas day when he distributed beef to large numbers of poor.

'Great councils' were also summoned whenever rulers sensed a political need or opportunity such as those in 1164 when Henry II intended to deal with Thomas Becket. Particularly significant were those called when kings believed that special circumstances meant they were entitled to ask for more than their customary revenues. When Henry II took the cross in 1188 he persuaded great councils in France and England that he could levy a heavy tax, the Saladin Tithe, on all who did not go on crusade. In 1190 William the Lion levied a 'common aid' so that he could buy Scotland's release from servitude to England. Significantly it was on the matter of taxation that it was first felt necessary to define just what was meant by a 'great council'. Chapter 12 of Magna Carta stated that the king could not levy a tax 'except by the common counsel of the realm', and chapter 14 spelt out how that common counsel was to be obtained, i.e. prelates and barons were to receive individual letters of summons giving them at least forty days' notice of the meeting, and the rest of the tenants-in-chief were to be summoned via the sheriffs and bailiffs. In an assembly of tenants-in-chief, the greatest of them, prelates and barons, would inevitably dominate

– though no doubt sensible lords took note of the opinion of other members of the 'community of the realm', particularly when questions of taxation were being discussed. It was, after all, the others who bore the greater share of the burden of taxation. It was on this issue that the barons who previously had both agreed and refused taxation, for the first time, in 1254, announced that they unwilling to commit others. In times of crisis it made sense for hostile parties to bid for support from wider social groups; both John and his opponents did this in 1212–5. In the crisis of 1264, in a bid to shore up his shaky government, Simon de Montfort summoned representatives of the shires to a great council; in 1265 he added representatives of towns to the list of those summoned.

Parliaments

In twelfth- and thirteenth-century usage the French and Latin words *parlement* and *parliamentum* simply meant a conference, irrespective of who was there. But it has long been the convention of historians to reserve the term 'Parliament' for a national assembly summoned by a king and attended by the 'Commons', members of the 'Third Estate', as well as by members of the first two estates, nobles and clergy. This usage will be followed here. In this modern sense of the word, Parliaments first appear in England and Ireland in the later thirteenth century, in Scotland in the fourteenth century (see pp. 120, 122), but in Wales only very fleetingly, in 1404–5 during the brief period of Owain Glyndwr's rule. When compared with the representative institutions which developed in continental Europe during the later Middle Ages, the Parliament of England was odd in the sense that here the three estates did not sit separately, instead the nobles and upper clergy sat together with the king's council in one place, while the Commons met in another place. In this way it seemed as though the Commons came to represent the nation while the lords were part of the government.

From the later 1290s, when Edward I's wars (see pp. 200–2) led him to make massive financial demands, the presence of the Commons in Parliaments, hitherto only occasional, became increasingly frequent. The higher the level of taxation, the greater the need for mechanisms that ensured the community of the realm's consent. A realist might be tempted to scoff at so woolly a notion as the community of the realm – what, after all, could it actually do? – but in fact it was good at dragging its feet, at paying taxes slowly. The concern for effective consent meant that also in the 1290s Edward I's advisers drafted a formula for the writs of summons which emphasised the representatives' power to commit their constituents. By sending representatives to take part, local communities came explicitly to acknowledge this. The fiscal revolution (see p. 108) that took place in the years between 1275 and 1350 meant that the Commons became a fixture. From Edward III's reign onwards meetings which did not include shire knights were no longer referred to as parliaments in government records. At the same time another representative group summoned to some parliaments, the proctors of the clergy, now dropped out, since they had made it plain that they would do no more than assent to taxation conditional upon subsequent ratification in convocation, an entirely ecclesiastical assembly – though one which often met at the same time as Parliament. As the most formal occasion at which kings took counsel, in practice almost always seeking assent and publicity for decisions already made in council, Parliament became the setting in which new taxes were granted and new laws authorised.

In 1278 Edward I encouraged people to bring petitions to him in Parliament, when he had the best advice to hand. From then on one of the first events in every parliament was the appointment of people, called receivers and triers, to deal with the petitions that flooded in. In Edward II's reign the Commons as a body supplemented petitions from individuals by drawing up requests which they claimed to be in the 'common' interest. By the 1340s the common petitions and the replies given to them by the king and council were recorded in the official record, the Parliament roll. Before the end of the century it had become usual for the Commons to delay their answer to any request for a tax until the last day of a parliament when the king's answers to petitions were read out. Not surprisingly special interest groups lobbied the Commons in the hope, often justified, that their own requests would be 'avowed' and presented as common petitions. Complaints that statutes drawn up in response to petitions did not always accurately reflect their purpose led to petitions containing the form of the desired enactment, in which case they were known as 'bills'.

By the mid fifteenth century procedures for considering bills were well developed, involving them being read, considered and sometimes debated by both houses. In the Lords each peer present was asked to vote for or against a bill; in the Commons assent was normally by the noisy route of acclamation. Clearly it was the Commons' role as petitioners that meant that shires and towns valued the right that gave them an opportunity to press matters of local concern. It was also this role that reinforced the bicameral character of the English Parliament: the Commons sitting in one place while the lords, both temporal and spiritual, sat with the king and judges in another. The Commons petitioned, while the king took counsel with the lords and answered.

As petitioners MPs were valued by the communities that sent them to Parliament, but it was as answerers to royal requests for money that MPs came to wield some political clout, in, for instance, campaigning successfully that men of their own sort, the gentry of shire and town, should be given real local authority as JPs. Although the king's right to appoint his own ministers was not challenged, the gauntlet was thrown down in the 'Good Parliament' of 1376 when the Commons, led by their Speaker (the first in parliamentary history), Sir Peter de la Mare, for the first time used the device of impeachment to bring charges against unpopular ministers. This procedural device, which was employed again in 1386 and 1388, involved the whole body of Commons crowding into the lords' chamber in order to make their accusations in common and their noisy presence felt. Few phrases occur more often in the rolls of Parliament of this period than 'the clamour of the Commons'.

They demanded the right to exercise some control over the way in which the proceeds of taxation were spent, sometimes by securing the appointment of special treasurers, sometimes by insisting on the right to view and audit the treasurers' accounts. Between 1376 and 1406 the Commons enjoyed greater influence over central government than any time before the seventeenth century. But this was a consequence of awkward political circumstances which nobody liked. It was never intended as a trial run for a more permanent solution to the problems of governing a country. The businesslike co-operation of the Commons in Parliament with Henry V in the affairs of the nation, to the Crown's great profit, was on the whole more characteristic than the dramatic confrontations between 1376 and 1406, and was symbolised by the fact that subsequent Speakers, though formally elected by the

Commons, were in reality royal nominees. Indeed it was by frequently consenting to requests for taxes, not by refusing as in 1376, that the Commons won the right to consent.

It was in the justified expectation that they would continue to negotiate and consent that in England kings went on summoning them to Parliament. It was the place of Parliament in England which underlay the key distinction in Sir John Fortescue's patriotic political thought between a *regnum regale* (in his eyes typically France) and a *regnum politicum et regale* (typically England). By the end of this period the Commons had become a fully integrated part of Parliament, a process revealed even by the slowly changing terminology of the formal record. In the early fourteenth century Acts of Parliament were made 'by the king with the assent of the Lords'; a hundred years later 'by the king with the assent of the Lords and at the request of the Commons'; by Henry VII's reign, 'by the king with the advice and assent of the Lords and of the Commons, and by the authority of Parliament'. It was still accepted, however, that kings retained the right to modify or reject outright petitions and bills.

Taxes and customary revenues

The development of taxation has long been regarded as one of the ways in which medieval governments became more modern. Whereas traditional rulers relied on their domain, or 'demesne', revenues, whether paid in produce or in money, a defining mark of the modern state is taken to be its capacity to levy general taxes on the population at large. Domain revenues came from a king's own estates (which in England included nearly all the major towns) or were derived from their relationship with their tenants-in-chief, hence they include some tax-like levies such as scutages and the 'tallages' imposed on Jews and townspeople. Traditional kings, living on rents and the profits of lordship and jurisdiction, were in effect just higher-status versions of lords. Seen in this light, England, Ireland and Scotland (but not Wales) all underwent significant 'modernisation' during these centuries, though with striking regional differences in chronology and intensity. The relatively advanced English economy meant that the kings of England were in a position to make greater financial demands on their subjects than the other rulers in Britain and Ireland. Hence taxation, in the shape of the 'geld' (later known as Danegeld) assessed on hides of land, was already significant before 1066. William I may well have regarded it, in Maitland's phrase, as 'the most precious jewel in his English crown'.[32] It remained so after 1066 partly because the kings' possession of extensive territories in France involved them in continental politics and costly wars. A geld levied at six shillings a hide in 1083 provoked the Anglo-Saxon Chronicler to complain of a 'great and heavy' tax. The Scottish kings went to war less often than the English, and in consequence had less often cause to ask for taxes. They took a land tax equivalent to the geld, known as the 'common aid', from the later twelfth century on, but only very occasionally. In Ireland general taxation was first levied during the reign of King John, and might well have been developed by the native princes of Wales in the later thirteenth century, had they not been eliminated by Edward I. By contrast taxation remained as absent from Gaelic Ireland in the fifteenth century as it had been in the eleventh.

A significant difference between domain revenues and taxes was that the former were regarded as customary, while the latter – originally at least – were thought of as extraordinary, justified only in special circumstances. Rulers had to obtain the consent of their subjects before they taxed them. In 1204 King John, facing defeat in France, wrote to his 'faithful subjects of Ireland', asking them for financial aid 'not as a matter of custom but out of friendship'. Such requests implied that those who spoke for the king's subjects were entitled to negotiate about the amount and type of tax, or indeed to refuse it. Of course custom could be oppressive too. The fact that, apart from a few attempts $c.1300$, the English did not levy direct taxes in conquered Wales (in contrast to their regime within Ireland), but instead exploited customary ways of extracting revenue, led a modern Welsh historian to write of 'the systematic financial rape of the country'.[33] In the early history of the Parliaments of England, Ireland and Scotland – for, except during Glyndwr's rebellion (see p. 130), there was no Welsh Parliament – the shift from 'domain state' to 'tax state' turned out to be crucial. It was not, however, a one-way street. In both England and Scotland the old-fashioned 'domain state' made something of a comeback in the later fifteenth century.

The earliest documents enabling historians to estimate the relative importance of various types of royal revenue are accounts produced by the English exchequer, known as pipe rolls because the sheets of parchment were rolled up and stored in a pipe. These are a written record of orally presented accounts which were heard (hence the modern word 'audited') by Exchequer officials sitting at a table on which was laid a cloth patterned like a chess-board (in Latin *scaccarium*, hence the name Exchequer). On this they moved counters, abacus-fashion, in order to do their sums in full view of everyone sitting there. The pipe rolls show that for most of the twelfth and thirteenth centuries the kings relied principally upon domain revenues, of which the most important were the county 'farms', fixed sums paid into the treasury by the sheriffs responsible for managing the Crown estate in their sheriffdoms. Their predictable yield meant that for centuries they were the backbone of Crown finances. The earliest surviving near-complete pipe roll, for 1130, reveals that a total of about £23,000 was paid into Henry I's treasury. (Although this inevitably strikes the modern reader as a pitifully small sum, Henry was regarded by his neighbours, including the King of France, as a ruler whose coffers overflowed with silver.) Out of this total, less than £2,500 came from the geld. More than 80 per cent derived from domain. The county farms alone yielded nearly £10,000. Adding in the profits of estates that were temporarily in Henry's hands (as a result of confiscation, for example), revenue from land came to almost £13,000, more than half of the total for the year.

The other significant sources of customary income – the profits of justice, i.e. fines imposed in the king's courts, and the profits of his rights of lordship over tenants-in-chief, both ecclesiastical and lay – would have varied considerably from year to year. In 1130 they totalled about £7,000, of which approximately £2,400 came from the profits of justice, about £1,000 from church vacancies (see p. 171), and about £3,600 from wardship and marriage. This last alone brought in more than Henry obtained in taxes that year – and was even more important in non-fiscal terms (see pp. 172–3). The earliest equivalent Scottish record, a fragment of the chamberlain's account for part of 1264 suggests that in that year the Scottish king was entirely dependent upon domain; out of a total receipt of over £5,400, two thirds came from the farms of sheriffs and burghs and one third (£1,808) from reliefs and payments for grants of wardship and marriage. By this date the King of England's domain revenues had been considerably increased by the profits he was taking out of Ireland; receipts at the Dublin Exchequer at the end of Henry III's reign came to over £4,000 a year.

For all their importance, royal estates were, none the less, a declining asset. William I held both the old West Saxon royal lands and the Godwineson estates. Domesday Book indicates that they had been worth more in 1086, about £14,000 a year, than they would be in 1130. Kings needed to be generous, and particularly in political crises, it was natural that they would reward their key supporters with land, the most desirable of commodities. The county farms still produced no more than £10,000 a year in 1300; inflation over the previous 170 years means that in real terms they were far less lucrative than in 1130. As the stock of Crown lands shrank, it became more useful as an instrument of patronage, estates being leased on terms favourable to the lessee, than as an asset managed in order to maximise revenue. It was also prized as a means of endowing members of the family. Queens and unmarried daughters received life endowments; sons, brothers and uncles received land entailed upon them and their heirs male, with reversion to the king if the line failed.

Twelfth- and thirteenth-century Scottish kings were relatively successful in retaining the stock of royal lands. But then Robert Bruce's desperate need to win support in the long war he fought against both Scottish and English enemies forced him into donations which, in his own words to Parliament at Cambuskenneth in 1326, 'so diminished the lands and rents which used to belong to the crown . . . that he had not the maintenance becoming his status'.[34] For over 300 years in both England and Scotland the underlying trend was for there to be an outflow of royal estates into private hands. It was wiser not to attempt to reverse the flow. Those kings who did embark on a policy of wholesale confiscation of estates paid for it with their lives: in England, Edward II, Richard II and Richard III; in Scotland, James I and James III.

Kings were naturally tempted to exploit other sources of customary revenue. Nearly all could indeed be made to yield substantially more, but only at a high political cost. It was one thing to derive an income from judicial fines, quite another to give the impression that the king saw justice primarily as a money-raising operation. One area in which Henry II and his sons gave exactly that impression was in their administration of forest law; hence the prominence of the forest in Magna Carta and the promulgation of a separate Forest Charter in 1217. It was one thing to take church estates into protective custody during a vacancy, quite another deliberately to prolong vacancies in order to maximise revenue. In 1214 John promised that in future there would be no delays in the election of new bishops, but even a king as pious as his son Henry III was raising £6,000–7,000 a year from this source in the 1240s. It was only in the fourteenth century, when in formal terms bishops were appointed by papal provision – a method which in other ways kings found convenient (see p. 258) – that vacancies became significantly shorter. It was one thing to have many of the most powerful men in the realm in the king's debt, quite another to shape their indebtedness into a stick to beat them with, as King John did all too often. Indeed between 1208 and 1213 he exploited all his domain revenues to the full, imposing both frequent scutages and heavy tallages. In 1211 income from these sources alone as audited at the exchequer came to over £20,000. But as the Magna Carta rebellion demonstrated, all this was to offend contemporary notions of justice and good lordship. Later kings of England learned the lesson. After 1215 these customary sources of income rarely produced more than £5,000 a year, in real terms massively less than the £7,000 of 1130.

In the early twelfth century taxation too had been a dwindling asset. In 1130 Henry I took it at two shillings a hide. Next year he promised to levy no more gelds for seven years; it was a promise fairly easy to make because the geld's yield had been reduced by the many exemptions which had been granted as favours to individuals and religious communities. Indeed so little did the geld yield that Henry II phased it out altogether. But appeals for help from the crusader states (1166, 1184, 1188), and then the need to find a king's ransom for Richard I in 1193, gave the kings of England unassailably good causes which enabled them to experiment with a new kind of general tax, later known as the subsidy, which in the long run was to revolutionise the government's financial base. Assessed on a valuation of movable property, it could be remarkably lucrative. The first subsidy for which an official record of yield survives, the thirteenth of 1207, reveals that it brought in no less than £57,000, at least fifteen times as much as twelfth-century gelds and scutages! Despite – or because of – its massive yield, it was resorted to only occasionally. In 1207 John had wanted it to finance the recovery of the ancestral dominions lost in 1203–4, but after that date he was allowed no further subsidies, hence his ruthless exploitation of his domain. Henry III obtained three subsidies between 1225 and 1237, but his growing reputation as an incompetent ruler meant that he did not get another one until 1269, and that was to pay for his son Edward's crusade.

The fact that Henry failed to obtain consent to taxation for more than thirty years can be related to another crucial feature of the subsidy in its early stages. As taxes for the Holy Land and for the ransom of a crusader-king, no exemptions were allowed – except, in 1188, for those who went on crusade themselves. Even in 1207 it was explicitly affirmed that the thirteenth was to be paid 'by every layman of all England'. Because the rich and powerful paid the tax they also had powerful cause to refuse to consent if they thought a king failed to make a case for one. Whereas in many continental kingdoms the nobility secured exemption from taxation, in England they did not – a contrast of importance in a comparative history of parliaments.

A major turning point occurred in 1294 when Edward I found himself faced by war on three fronts, in Gascony, Scotland and Wales. In the first twenty-two years of his reign he had obtained three subsidies, but in the next eight then found ways of gaining consent to no fewer than five tax grants. From 1294 to the end of his reign he averaged £20,000 a year from this source alone. At the same time he raised about £18,000 a year by taxing the English clergy either directly or by persuading the pope to hand over to him the greater part of the yield of papal taxation, usually on the grounds that he was preparing a crusade, though in the event he never went. From then on the near permanent state of war against the Scots and/or the French meant that direct taxation, generally in the form of tenths from clergy and towns and fifteenths from shires, became a major part of English royal finances.

In 1334 to save the expense of a reassessment each time a tax was levied, the yield of a lay tenth and fifteenth was fixed at £37,800, lowered in 1433 and 1446 to about £31,000, with the costs of collection amounting to about £1,000. A known sum was laid upon each borough and village in England (except the palatinates of Durham and Chester) and local communities decided on who would pay. The outbreak of the Hundred Years War in the 1330s put an end to the pope's subsidies, but convocations of the English church, usually meeting at the same time as Parliaments, were persuaded to continue making grants, with each clerical tenth bringing in about £15,000. Although most of the fighting took place in France and Scotland, these taxes were almost always asked for in the name of 'defence of the realm'. Apart from periods such as the 1360s and 1420s when English taxpayers enjoyed a respite thanks to the recent triumphs enjoyed by Edward III and Henry V, this form of direct taxation remained central, if irregular, until after the English had been swept out of France in 1453, when it became more sporadic – even though by then the government had had some success in persuading the Commons that taxpayers should bear some of the costs of peacetime government.

In Scotland direct taxation became more important after 1326 when at Cambuskenneth the earls, barons, burgesses and all the rest of the freeholders of the realm responded to Robert Bruce's plight, by granting him an annual subsidy of a tenth, assessed on their lands and rents, in return for a promise to abandon excessive prises (purveyance, see p. 154). This precedent was occasionally followed, notably in the 1350s and 1360s, in order to raise the ransom for David II, but direct taxation never became as frequent as in England. There was, for example, a long gap from 1374 to 1399, and Robert of Albany – de facto ruler of Scotland until 1420 – liked to boast that in his time the poor had had no cause to curse him for levying taxes. By 1469 the 'contribution' (as the Scottish tax was known) had been levied just twenty-two times, and rarely raised as much as £2,000.

Edward I was also responsible for innovation in the sphere of indirect taxation. Britain's coastline had long enabled its rulers to profit from charges on seaborne trade. In Scotland David I imposed port dues known as cain and custom. In 1194 Richard I levied a 10 per cent duty on overseas trade, which lapsed in John's reign. By the late thirteenth century the rise of the international banking system combined with demand for English wool from the expanding Flemish and Italian woollen cloth industries had created a new situation. In 1275 Edward I obtained consent to a duty on the export of wool and hides (both bulky commodities not easy to smuggle profitably) from an assembly in which towns and merchants were strongly represented. The assumption that the cost of the duty would be borne by overseas customers in the shape of higher prices disarmed opposition. At the rate of 6s. 8d. on each sack of wool and every hundred hides, it was designed as a mechanism by which Edward I repaid loans made him by Italian bankers. Levied at Irish and Welsh ports as well as English, it fulfilled this function admirably, regularly bringing in about £10,000 a year. In 1282 Alexander III introduced a similar scheme to Scotland, adding some £2,000 a year to his income.

Although Edward had neither intended nor justified this duty as a war tax, in practice he was able to pay for his first Welsh war of 1277 by borrowing virtually the whole sum needed from the Ricciardi of Lucca, whose agents then collected what they were owed. By 1294 he had borrowed about £400,000 from them and repaid nearly all of it. In 1294 Edward I suddenly increased the rate sixfold to £2 a sack, and Edward III did the same thing again in 1337. On both occasions this was justified by a plea of military necessity. Political crisis in 1297 forced Edward I to back down, but the successes of Edward III's wars against France and Scotland in the 1340s and 1350s allowed him to turn the wool subsidy into a fixture. By 1370 revenue from overseas trade was averaging £70,000 a year (over 80 per cent of it from the export tax on wool). This was two thirds of his total income, collected by less than a hundred Crown agents, three quarters of them unpaid.

David II's capture (see p. 120) meant that once again the Scots followed suit, quadrupling the rate of duty in order to raise the king's ransom. By 1370 the Scottish wool subsidy yielded about £10,000 a year. During these decades British and Irish raw wool was in effect the crude oil of the Middle Ages. Granted for the lifetimes of kings this indirect tax became part of their customary revenue – which is why such charges are still called 'customs'. Royal finances had been transformed. Under Henry IV and Henry V 85–90 per cent of the King of England's annual income came from taxes, direct and indirect; the ratio between taxation and domain revenue was now almost exactly the reverse of what it had been in 1130.

After 1370 wool exports gradually declined, in part as a consequence of the high duty inducing buyers to look elsewhere. In terms of the national economy, the rising volume of exported textile manufactures more than compensated for the decline in raw wool exports, but the export duty on cloth was low and could not readily be increased without seriously damaging the ability of English cloth producers to compete in continental markets. Hence the changing pattern of international trade caused a long-term decline in the proceeds of indirect taxation; in England down to about £40,000 a year in the 1470s, in Scotland to about £3,000. The relatively weak tax base in Scotland led James I to create new officials both in localities and in the household to manage income from Crown estates. In 1486 Crown lands made up about two thirds of the Scottish king's revenue; tax about one fifth. In England the political turbulence of the Wars of the Roses meant that kings were reluctant to risk the unpopularity that taxes always caused. Thus Edward IV's proclamation in 1467: 'I intend to live upon mine own.'[35] The hope in both England and Scotland was that kings would live of their own, and at times they were authorised to revoke grants previously made so that they could do so. With lower yields from direct as well as indirect taxation, it is not surprising that kings of England from 1461 onwards, notably Henry VII, worked hard to make the royal estates almost as important in terms of cash income as they had been in the twelfth century.

Debtors and creditors

Kings of England before Edward I had certainly floated some of their schemes on borrowed money – Henry II's war against Stephen, Henry III's Sicilian venture are two examples, and the Norman Conquest itself may be another (see p. 250). But except in the possible case of 1066, it had never before been on a scale sufficient to transform the country's political structure. The rapid advance of the Italian-led international banking system combined with Edward's control of the wool export trade changed all that. When the king could borrow on this scale, as Edward had from the Ricciardi of Lucca, he no longer needed to build up large reserves of cash in the manner of predecessors such as Henry II or John. With the commercial revolution of the thirteenth century the financial system became more sophisticated. It was no longer necessary to pay the high transport and security costs of moving large weights of coin to and from a central treasury. Moving financial documents, small pieces of parchment or wooden tallies (which functioned as receipts), was much easier, safer and cheaper.

Both Edward II (from the Frescobaldi) and Edward III (from the Peruzzi and Bardi of Florence) continued to borrow large sums from Italian firms. In the early stages of the Hundred Years War the Bardi and Peruzzi lent about 1.5 million gold florins. In the 1340s Edward III's inability to repay them contributed to the first great banking crash in European history. In consequence his successors were never again able to borrow on this scale from foreign bankers. But by this time loans had become the essential lubricant of the machinery of government and English businessmen were in a position to step into the Italians' shoes. In the 1330s an English consortium headed by William de la Pole from (Kingston upon) Hull, the new town founded by Edward I, lent well over £100,000, and he was rewarded for his financial services to the crown by being made a banneret. In 1343 he set up the Company of the Staple, which was granted a monopoly of wool export in return for making loans to the crown and being repaid out of the revenues of the wool subsidy. Other kinds of Englishmen also lent large sums of money to their kings, Richard Fitzalan, Earl of Arundel, for example, in the later fourteenth century and Cardinal Henry Beaufort in the early fifteenth, but since London was both the principal port and from this time onwards the nation's political capital (see p. 186), its businessmen became and remained the Crown's chief creditors, the most celebrated being Richard Whittington (d.1423), three times lord mayor.

Because men had confidence in a fiscal system based upon the woolsack (hence, famously, its presence in the House of Lords), thousands agreed to serve the King of England, whether as soldiers or lawyers or political agents, in return for written documents setting out what they were owed and where they could get payment. This became politically more important when Edward III, also in the 1340s, changed the way soldiers were paid. Whereas previously the financial offices (chamber or wardrobe) of the royal household had been responsible for paying the wages of individual soldiers, the king now made contracts with army captains, agreeing to pay them large lump sums out of which they were to raise and pay troops. This contracting out of military organisation meant that in the event of a cash shortage, it was the senior officers, most of them nobles, who had to carry a significant part of the royal debt. In practice this meant that, at any one time, many of the Crown's most influential subjects, both merchants and war leaders, were also creditors. Since it was in their interest that the king should be able to pay his debts, it was only natural that Parliament, representing, as in effect it did, the creditors, should generally speaking agree to royal requests for taxation, in particular the wool subsidy. Indeed in 1398 and again in 1415 Parliament granted the wool customs for the king's life. The fact that the king was now normally in debt to his own subjects had created a community of interests which proved to be of enormous financial advantage to the Crown.

But it also meant that whenever there was opposition to a king, it was now almost invariably led by nobles to whom the king owed large sums of money, as when the Percys took up arms against Henry IV in 1403 (see p. 130). One thing that never changes is the fact that military setbacks seriously damage a government's prestige. In the circumstances of the later stages of the Hundred Years War, this meant army commanders such as Richard, Duke of York, were angered not only by Henry VI's military ineptitude but also by the slowness with which his government paid its debts (except, they alleged, the debts owed to stay-at-home courtiers). Thus whereas the 1215 rebellion against John has been described, by J. C. Holt, as a rebellion of the king's debtors, the Wars of the Roses began as a rebellion of his creditors. This reversal reflects the contrast between a political and fiscal system based on lordship and one based on taxation and credit, between a 'domain state' and a 'tax state'.

Crime and punishment

Law and order was maintained in broadly similar and very local ways throughout eleventh-century Britain and Ireland. Everywhere there were broadly similar assumptions. If anyone were insulted, injured or killed, it was the duty of their kin either to wreak vengeance or take the matter to court and exact compensation in the form of an appropriate honour-price (known variously as *wergild*, *galanas*, *cro*, *enech* and *éraic*). If sufficient compensation were offered then the threat of feud should be called off. In such societies, as in international law today, violent actions could in some circumstances be legitimately taken by people who were not officials acting on behalf of a central government. Here, then, there was no state monopoly of violence.

If an accusation were made against someone, he looked to kin and neighbours, his friends, to swear to his character and good standing and to be his oath-helpers (i.e. be prepared to add their word to his when he swore that he was innocent). This might happen at assemblies, such as meetings of the men of the shire or hundred, in which the role of any royal official present was supposed to be limited to summoning and chairing the meeting; judgements were made by 'law-worthy men', men of local eminence by virtue of their wealth, age or wisdom. This often amounted to arbitration of the dispute by a sworn panel (a jury) acceptable to both sides, making a decision in the light of generally accepted local custom, perhaps occasionally guided by the opinions of learned men such as those responsible for the production of written codes of law. In such a system the position of an outsider, the foreigner or 'friendless' man, was always awkward. Evidence from thirteenth-century England suggests that one in ten murder victims were unidentified strangers or vagabonds.

Kings everywhere were expected to do justice, keep good laws and abolish bad ones, but in practice what mattered most often was local influence and custom. In the localities peace was maintained more by the threat of feud, possibly even, in cases of homicide, of a blood feud, than by the power of central government and its servants. Greater royal power and Cnut's requirement that all men should take an oath not to engage in crime or harbour those who did, meant that kings of England were inclined to regard crime as infidelity. At the root of the word 'felony' lay the idea of disloyalty to a lord. The notion of a kingdom-wide king's peace already played a more prominent role in eleventh-century England than elsewhere in these islands. Even here though it would be another century before the idea was established that all serious offences were to be regarded not merely as offences against individuals but as offences against the whole community and hence as breaches of the king's peace. Except in one respect, the Norman Conquest of England made little difference to institutions which already had a long history behind them.

Regional variation in the survival of sources, itself the result of greater royal power, means that English practice is best known. In the first instance it was up to the victim of crime to raise the 'hue and cry'. On hearing it, every able-bodied man in the district was supposed to help form a posse, i.e. do everything in his power (*pro toto posse suo*) to chase and arrest the accused. A thief caught red-handed could – though need not – be executed on the spot after summary judgement. So too a man caught in the act of adultery could be lawfully killed by the husband, although an observer in early thirteenth-century England noted that times had changed and the law now only allowed husbands to castrate adulterers. In any case no feud was meant to follow the killing of a proven thief, whether hanged after trial in court or earlier.

Whenever possible, trials were decided on the basis of evidence and witnesses. But when alleged offences had been committed stealthily, as in cases of theft or murder (as opposed to the open killing of homicide), there was frequently suspicion but no witnesses, and – as at all times before this modern age of forensic science – no evidence either apart from the missing goods being in the suspect's possession, a fact which might be readily explicable in several different ways. In such cases, when only God could be depended upon to know the truth, an accused might be sent to trial by ordeal – either a unilateral ordeal such as the ordeal of hot iron and water, or the bilateral ordeal of a judicial duel (a continental practice introduced into England by William I). Duels were fought between accuser and accused, or between champions on their behalf (in cases where one or other party was too young, too old, too ill, a woman, a churchman or a Jew). They fought with clubs and shields, teeth and nails until one or other cried 'Craven', i.e. admitted defeat. In England champions were also supposed to have been witnesses to what had or had not happened, until 1275 when that requirement was abolished. But since it had long seemed obvious that sometimes the victor in a trial by battle was the one who was stronger rather than the one who fought for justice, there was more scepticism about the bilateral than about the unilateral ordeal. In 1179 Henry II granted defendants in disputes over property rights the privilege of being allowed to choose whether the case should be decided by battle or by a panel of twelve local knights, a privilege described at the time as 'a royal benefit granted to the people by the clemency of the prince on the advice of the magnates'.[36]

In cases of ordeal by hot iron, after the accused had formally sworn their innocence, they had to carry red-hot iron three paces; guilt or innocence was decided three days later depending upon whether those who inspected the burn judged that it was healing cleanly or not. In the case of ordeal by cold water, the accused was bound and lowered into a deep pit. If the water received him, he was deemed innocent and pulled out. If he appeared to stay on the surface, probably thrashing about, he was adjudged guilty. Although historians long regarded the ordeal as irrational and superstitious, in some cases it may have functioned much like the modern lie detector. For local communities the ordeal by iron or water was an orchestrated religious drama, signalled by their priest's blessing of pit or iron. Both forms of the ordeal made room for interpretation by those called upon to decide. The several hundred cases where the outcome is reported suggest that the accused had a better than 50/50 chance of being found not guilty.

Common law

In 1166 Henry II, deciding like many rulers before and after him, to be tough on crime, took a number of measures which, in hindsight, can be seen to mark the start of a transformation of the English judicial system. By instructing sheriffs to empanel a jury of twelve men in every hundred whose job it was to present (i.e. name) those of their neighbours that they believed to be guilty of serious offences, he launched a public prosecution service. Sheriffs were to arrest those named and hold them until they could be brought to trial before the king's judges on their next visit to the county. Beginning in the 1170s Henry II sent royal judges out on circuits known as eyres (derived from the Latin word *errantes* meaning 'travelling') to preside over sessions (assizes) of the county courts. In these courts judges dominated the process of making judgements and not – as before – the local 'law-worthy men'. Juries, forerunners of Grand Juries, were fined if the judges decided they had made frivolous or malicious presentments. Later evidence indicates that accusations were often made by local officials – bailiffs and constables – with the jury deciding whether it had been a 'true bill'. In every county, jails were to be built at public expense, evidence of the seriousness with which Henry launched this drive against crime. In 1194 the office of coroner was established to keep a record of serious offences (Crown pleas) in each county between eyres. Suspects who escaped and did not appear at four successive court sessions were outlawed.

The system offered an attractive alternative to the procedure of the 'appeal', in which an accuser might have to risk his own life and limb in a trial by battle. It also meant that should the accused be found guilty, there was no longer any question of compensation to the victim, only of punishment by the Crown, hanging, mutilation or a fine – not imprisonment, since one jail per county sufficed only for those awaiting trial. By Edward I's reign appeals were rare. Major crimes were now regarded as breaches of the king's peace punishable by mutilation or death; they could not be privately settled by the offer of compensation ('blood money'). Criminals belonging to families which were too poor to be able to pay compensation were now subjected to a public judicial system. A clear distinction between crime and what lawyers later called tort had emerged, between on the one hand those offences prosecuted by the state and resulting in punishment, and on the other those offences prosecuted by individuals and resulting in the payment of damages. In English eyes those legal systems which were still based on the old ways now seemed inferior, even morally wrong.

Henry II's reign also witnessed important developments in the sphere of disputes about possession of land. For many centuries, going back before the Norman Conquest, such quarrels had sometimes been settled when the parties agreed to abide by the decision of a panel of neighbours, who could give a verdict on the basis of their local knowledge. Henry II identified certain types of property dispute in which a jury was to be imposed on the parties, whether it suited them or not. Whatever the intention, one of the effects of this new procedure – which brought a large number of cases into the rapidly developing structures of the royal courts – was to undermine the traditional jurisdictions of lords. People who wished to start litigation in such cases were invited to buy standardised written orders (writs) from Chancery, ordering the appropriate sheriff to arrange for a jury to be in court to decide the case on the basis of their local knowledge when the king's judges next visited the county. With a branch of the Chancery settled permanently at Westminster by the 1170s, no matter where the king or his representative in England, the justiciar, happened to be, the new system proved to be very litigant-friendly. Previously complainants had been expected to draft their own writs and then deliver them to their opponent.

The system of sending royal appointees on judicial eyres expanded so rapidly that whereas royally appointed judges had previously been men likely to be employed in many different aspects of government, from now on they tended to specialise in legal business. In view of the common belief that in the Middle Ages only churchmen could read and write, it is worth noting that the overwhelming majority of these judges were laymen, working within a system which depended for its regular functioning upon documents drawn up in due form being sent to and fro between litigants, sheriffs' offices and Chancery, including documents initiating procedures for removing cases from other courts into the king's court. A machinery of justice dealing with both criminal and civil cases had been created which depended for its regular functioning upon correctly drafted writs, as can be seen in the text of the treatise known as *Glanvill*, composed in the 1180s. Judges' clerks kept brief records of court proceedings, and compiled lists of the fines they imposed. A timetable from the eyre that visited Devon in 1238 suggests they expected to deal with thirty cases a day. But as early as the mid 1190s they had so much civil business that on their return from the counties they continued to hear cases in Westminster Hall, creating, for the first time, a central court of justice at a fixed point (no matter where the king himself was), the embryonic court of Common Pleas or Common Bench. This was a court which heard litigation on a daily basis during the four law terms of the year – in contrast to local courts which usually met for a day every three or four weeks.

Rich landowners had long retained the services of legal advisers to look after their interests, but as early as 1200 the increasing volume of litigation, especially in and around Westminster, led to the emergence of a new class of professional lawyers, attorneys willing to advise any client in return for a fee. It may well be that as a result people were more inclined to resort to litigation. These developments combined to ensure that, so far as serious crime and property law were concerned, from now on there was a single framework of law common to the whole country: the common law. The suspicion grew that justice in England was a money-making operation: fees for clerks and lawyers, sweeteners for judges, fines for the Crown. In 1210 King John ordered that the main rules of English law were to be put into writing; the resulting document, the first official definition of the common law, was sent to Dublin to ensure its observance in Ireland.

Although it may then have been assumed that in time English law, and canon law as practised in England, would apply to all Ireland's inhabitants, the Irish preferred their own law. Outside the areas of English settlement, traditional Irish law continued to prevail for another four centuries, interpreted, taught and practised by a small number of lawyer families such as the MacEgans and the MacClancys. The differences in the ways the two laws dealt with crime, marriage and inheritance, persuaded the English that Irish ('Brehon') law was primitive and immoral. Welsh princes had already begun to move in the direction of anglicising Welsh law, but it was none the less in a spirit of confident virtue that Edward I insisted on the wholesale 'reform' of native law within the newly conquered Crown lands of north Wales (Anglesey, Caernarfon, Merioneth and Flint), imposing both English criminal law and English rules of inheritance, giving women greater rights than they had enjoyed under native custom. In the marcher lordships, however, even newly created ones such as Denbigh, marked differences remained between the traditional law allowed to the Welsh and the law extended to English colonists. Had Edward conquered Scotland, he might have been less interventionist than in north Wales, since by then a century of close relations between the two kingdoms had led to the Scots adopting and adapting a good deal of English law; much of *Regiam maiestatem*, a summary of Scottish law *c.*1300, was based on *Glanvill*. The 'laws and customs of the kingdom of Scotland' had been imposed on the inhabitants of the Western Isles and Man in 1266. Thus in Scotland, unlike Ireland and the Welsh marcher lordships, there was one law for both Gaelic- and English-speakers.

Trial by jury

During the thirteenth century trial by jury became a standard feature of both English and Scottish criminal law. Trial by ordeal had depended upon priests blessing the red-hot iron or the pits of water. But in chapter 18 of the 1215 Lateran Council, Pope Innocent III prohibited priests from taking part in ordeals on academic theological grounds. Theologians did not doubt that God could work a miracle such as causing a guilty man's body to stay on the water's surface. Yet the sense of the ordeal was that God had to work a miracle every time he was called upon to do so, which offended against the notion that a miracle had to be a free act of God. True, the church preached that in the Mass a miracle occurred every time a priest said *Hoc est corpus meum*. But the Mass was believed to be a sacrament. By contrast there was nothing about the ordeals of iron and water in the Bible, and the church had not instituted them. By 1215 most educated churchmen had decided that they were wrong. Yet even so Innocent III's decision was a remarkable one. Priests were paid fees for the work they did in making ordeals work. For many churches their possession of an ordeal pit and of consecrated irons was a privilege which gave them dignity and influence in the neighbourhood. In obeying the pope they surrendered an important and lucrative right.

In England the civil war of 1215–17 meant that it was some time before the government faced up to the problem posed by the papal prohibition. When a new judicial eyre was eventually dispatched in 1219 the council governing in the name of Henry III instructed the judges to 'proceed according to your good sense and conscience, ascertaining as far as you can the character of the individuals involved, the nature of the crime and the truth of the matter'.[37] After a few years of uncertainty the judges decided to transfer to criminal trials a procedure already used in some property disputes: allow the defendant to choose the 'benefit' of trial before a verdict-giving jury. In Scotland men followed suit. Here the defendant's alternative to jury trial ('visnet' in Scottish law) was trial by combat. For those who feared the verdict of their neighbours, this was a reasonable option. In England, however, although trial by battle was to remain in use in cases of criminal appeal until the late fifteenth century – and was not formally removed by statute until 1819 – the judges had no intention of extending that option to those who would previously have gone to the unilateral ordeal. In these cases the defendant's lot was to be imprisoned until he did choose to go before a verdict-giving jury. It was later laid down that a defendant who opted for jail should suffer *peine forte et dure* from heavy stones placed on his chest until he either chose to go to trial or was pressed to death. Later medieval evidence suggests that two thirds of all those indicted fled, preferring to suffer outlawry, liable to be killed if they resisted arrest. Not until 1722, i.e. thirty years after the Salem witch trials, was the Englishman's right to choose removed. Until then stubborn defendants could opt to be pressed to death, allowing them to die innocent and their family to inherit their property. Of those who chose to stand trial, despite the absence of any provision for defence counsel, a very high proportion, at times as high as 80 per cent, was acquitted. Some of the acquittals may have reflected a jury's dislike of the death penalty for anything other than homicide. Within the legal establishment juries were not surprisingly regarded with suspicion, on the grounds that they were susceptible to bribery and intimidation. None the less the system survived, and with it the notion that a jury verdict, being a substitute for God's decision, had to be unanimous and, once reached, irreversible.

It was by no means inevitable that ordeal would be replaced by trial by jury. Throughout continental Europe people faced the same dilemma as a result of Innocent's prohibition, and only in Denmark did men turn to a jury to fill the gap. What normally happened in those hard cases in which there was suspicion but no useful testimony or evidence, was that the authorities tried harder to get the accused to confess. They turned increasingly to torture – that is to say they went down the path of Roman law, for the law of Rome knew nothing of the ordeal but was very familiar with the torture of both suspects and witnesses as a way of getting at 'the truth', especially getting suspects to confess.

The professionalisation of law

In England torture was authorised in cases of alleged treason, but not otherwise.[38] No doubt there have been circumstances when British authorities have resorted to unofficial torture, also as a way of getting at 'the truth'. But throughout almost the entire continent of Europe torture became a normal judicial procedure throughout the later Middle Ages and early modern period. Since under prolonged torture the accused generally confessed, it is doubtful that this marked an advance on the ordeal.

While the Scottish version of English law remained relatively simple, in England the common law became increasingly complex and, to lay people, increasingly incomprehensible, not much mitigated by a slowly developing Chancery and equitable jurisdiction in the interests of fairness. Common-law specialists became indispensable: attorneys to advise litigants and serjeants to represent them in court. The training of all these experts was acquired chiefly through attendance at court and study of a highly technical literature, registers of writs, case reports and model pleadings, all written in jargon-ridden Law French (see p. 192). By the mid fourteenth century the Inns of Court (Inner Temple, Middle Temple, Gray's Inn and, by 1417, Lincoln's Inn) were serving not only as London hostels for law students, but also providing them with a fur-ther education based on lectures and disputations. In England and – on a much smaller scale – in English Ireland, a legal pro-fession, split into two branches (serjeants and attorneys), had emerged. By the end of Edward I's reign a small elite group of about thirty serjeants had become established as the main source of judges in the two central courts, Common Bench and King's Bench. Analysis of the social origins of these judges has shown that most came from obscure families, from the ranks of those who leave little trace in the records.

The eyre system suffered constant improvement over time, and in consequence became ever more elaborate, cumbersome and burdensome on the shires. Law, once a matter for local communities, had, it seemed, been handed over to professional judges who represented the disciplinary interests of central government. Not surprisingly local communities objected. Increasingly the county gentry pressed to have the power to decide some cases themselves, and in the fourteenth century, thanks to their voice in Parliament (see pp. 274–5), they obtained the right to sit as JPs deciding (without jury) and punishing minor offences at the peace sessions. Many such offences touched their own interests as masters and employers. More serious offences were held over for twice-yearly 'gaol-delivery' at the assizes heard before serjeants of the Common Bench dispatched to act as justices in the county courts. Accusations of criminal behaviour by members of the gentry class were reserved for King's Bench. This division of responsibility for law-keeping suited both Crown and gentry, and it, like the division between serjeants and attorneys – today's barristers and solicitors – was to prove remarkably durable.

In Scotland three high-status justiciars for Lothian, Galloway and Scotia (the land north of the Forth) were meant to visit each sheriffdom twice a year from the early thirteenth century onwards. But there was no central court until the fifteenth century and hence nothing approaching the complex English judicial structure. In the absence of a network linking centre and locality, theft continued to be dealt with in the courts of lords. Kings laid down guidelines for the procedures to be followed, but did not claim a monopoly of jurisdiction. The violence of the feud remained a part of this royally endorsed system until well into the sixteenth century when the legal profession began to develop and assert its own values.

Statehood?

Although there was no still state monopoly of legitimate force in England and especially not in Scotland, both kingdoms can be regarded as dynastic states – states in the sense of networks of governmental institutions exercising power over a territorially defined area and headed by a ruling family. Arguably England was already a state before the start of this period and Scotland would be before the end of it. In England, the fact that when Richard II was deposed in 1399, officials in the various departments of central government (the law courts, Chancery, Exchequer and privy seal) did not lose their jobs shows that they were thought of as serving 'the state' rather than the king (see p. 186). A few years later, a masterful dynastic ruler, Henry V, determined to ensure that his archers would be well equipped, reckoned that he could count on the servants of his state to pluck six feathers from every goose in England. On the whole, despite their routine distaste for red tape, English historians have applauded the growth of the state. Hence a great Welsh historian identified the 'informing principle' of English historiography as 'the belief that strong centralised government is a 'prerequisite of civilised life and human progress'.[39]

In Wales the embryonic Welsh state was finished off by English conquest under Edward I. In Ireland the events of the nineteenth and twentieth century meant that questions of statehood remained much more controversial than they have been in British history. G. H. Orpen claimed that the English invasion of Ireland marked 'the introduction of ideas of state-governance and organisation which, as developed in the British Isles, have become the model for all the free governments of the world'.[40] Reacting strongly against this condescension, Eoin MacNeill, one of the founders of the Gaelic League in the 1890s and the first minister for education in the Irish Free State in the 1920s, argued that a native Irish state was already in the process of formation during the eleventh and twelfth centuries. Although it is now widely accepted that the assumption both of them shared – that law and order are impossible without the state – may well be a mistaken assumption, there is still a tendency to look for signs of change in the nature of Irish politics before the arrival of the English, and to wonder whether or not these changes add up to some kind of progress.

Certainly not even in England was there a 'state' in the sense of an overarching disembodied network of institutions. A 'state' in this sense is a fiction, an ideological construct which may have its uses but has never existed anywhere. There was no word for such a construct in medieval Britain or Ireland. It is therefore unlikely that such a myth existed at the time.

PRINCIPAL CHURCHES AND CENTRES
OF LEARNING IN
BRITAIN AND IRELAND
1066–1485

N

THE ISLES
(The diocese of
Soder and Man
under Trondheim)

Aberdeen

St. Andrews
Dunfermline
Glasgow
Melrose

Raphoe
Clogher
Armagh
Kells
Ardagh
Tuam
Dublin
Mellifont
Killeloe
Raith
Bressail
Cashel
Lismore
Cork

Whithorn
Carlisle
MAN
Fountains
Rievaulx
York

Caergybi
St.
Asaph
Bangor
Glendalough
Chester
Lincoln

Llanbadarn
Fawr
Worcester
Northampton
Norwich
Stamford
Ely
Bury St
Edmonds
Cambridge
Hereford
Gloucester
St. David's
Tintern
Oxford
LONDON
Llandaff
Bristol
Rochester
Waverly
Sheen
Canterbury
Glastonbury
Salisbury
Winchester
Battle
Chichester
Exeter

0   100 miles
0   200 km

● Archbishoprics and bishoprics

Part IV:
Churches and Religion

By the eleventh century the people of Britain and Ireland had
been Christian for centuries; and they remained so throughout
this period. The Christian church had taken over the ancient
religious rituals of the farming year. From baptism to burial
the significant rites of passage through which everyone passed
were increasingly handled by Christian priests. Most people
went to church on Sundays and on the great feast days such as
Easter and Christmas; nearly all were buried in churchyards.
The only important exceptions were the communities of Jews
who came to England soon after the Norman Conquest,
settling in towns as far west as Exeter and as far north as
Newcastle upon Tyne. After their expulsion in 1290, England
became once again as uniformly Christian as Wales, Scotland
and Ireland. Virtually everyone recognised, at least nominally,
the authority of the Bishop of Rome in matters of religion. In
1215 the Fourth Lateran Council decreed that all were legally
bound to confess and receive Communion from their parish
priest once a year at Easter. The clergy – all male – were

everywhere. The evidence from England suggests that as many as one in every twenty adult males was a clerk (see p. 268). The major churches were wealthy corporations. Domesday Book demonstrates that in the England of 1086 the church held one seventh of the total assessed wealth of the kingdom. In 1410 it was calculated – by critics of ecclesiastical wealth and corruption – that the estates of English prelates, if confiscated, would fund the creation of fifteen earls, 1,500 knights, 6,200 esquires, 100 almshouses, fifteen universities and 1,500 more priests, and still leave the Crown with a tidy income from the proceeds.

But by comparison with much of continental Europe, in Britain and Ireland there was little open religious dissent. Very few heretics were found and persecuted: nearly all of them in England. In 1166 a group of twenty enthusiasts who reportedly denied the sacraments of baptism, Mass and marriage arrived in England, were branded (literally) as heretics and left to die. A few more arrived in 1210 and were burned. The royal government co-operated with the church in keeping the kingdom uncontaminated as they saw it by heresy. More were uncovered between 1380 and 1450, a tiny handful in Scotland and none in Ireland and Wales.

By the fifteenth century the official Christian religion was much more systematically taught and more thoroughly organised than it had been in the eleventh. Within Britain and Ireland the English church set the pace. The early twelfth-century life of Margaret, the English wife of King Malcolm of Scotland, represents her as insisting, against opposition, that all Scots should take Easter Communion. In 1170 the synod of Cashel, as part of a drive to 'anglicise' the Irish church, ordered that 'children should be baptised in the sacred font of the church' – as had long been obligatory in England.[1] In England

Sunday church attendance was a legal duty, enforceable in a court of law. No doubt most did their duty. A few did not, such as two women from Hungerford who failed to attend church or take Communion for five years, and were excommunicated and imprisoned in 1409. Whether or not in these centuries, any more than in any other age, people followed Christianity's rules of moral conduct, most accepted its code of ritual obligations.

An age of faith?

Whether this meant that virtually all the inhabitants of these islands believed in the God of the Christians is another question, and one to which no certain answer can be given. Pope Alexander IV was probably misinformed when in 1261 he instructed the Bishop of Raphoe (Donegal) to put a stop to the idol worship going on in his diocese. But, according to Peter of Cornwall, Prior of Holy Trinity, Aldgate (London), writing in about 1200:

> There are many people who do not believe that God exists, nor do they think that a human soul lives on after the death of the body. They consider that the universe has always been as it is now and ruled by chance rather than by Providence.[2]

We do not know whether Peter was right or wrong, nor what he meant by 'many people'. None of those 'many' unbelievers wrote anything that has survived the centuries. Nor indeed was anyone prosecuted for atheism, although fifteenth-century worries about heresy led to the uncovering of opinions such as John Brewer of Albourne's view that there was more good in a cask of ale than in the four gospels, and Thomas

Tailor of Newbury's belief that the soul died when the body died, snuffed out like the light of a candle. What does it say about attitudes to Christian dogma that John Tiptoft, Earl of Worcester, on being beheaded in 1470, was said to have asked the executioner to do it not in one stroke but in three 'in honour of the Trinity'?[3]

One of the paradoxes of a Christian and clerical culture is that throughout this period the standard primary schoolbook, a work read by all children who learned Latin, was pagan and secular in tone. This was the *Distichs* attributed to Cato (but composed by an unknown author, probably in the third century AD), a work of practical morality in the Stoic tradition, based on a cynical and calculating view of human motives. It taught that certain personal qualities were worth cultivating in order to obtain not salvation in a next world but public esteem in this. The religious-minded were particularly troubled by those distichs in which 'Cato' advised dissimulation on grounds of self-interest (see p. 284). None the less throughout the entire Middle Ages it remained the first full-length literary piece the student read, and from the twelfth century on was translated into vernaculars.

The deathbed scene in the early thirteenth-century biography, *L'histoire de Guillaume le maréchal*, is revealing for what it says about the extent and limits of the piety of a man held up as a model knight. During his final illness William confessed his sins every week and obtained a plenary indulgence from the papal legate. Even when preparing for death, however, he knew his own mind. When told that he could go to heaven only if he returned all his tournament winnings to the men from whom he had taken them, William's answer was that:

churchmen shave us too closely. If the kingdom of heaven is closed to me just because I've captured 500 knights and kept their arms, horses and equipment, then there's nothing I can do about it. Either their argument is false or no man can be saved.

Later a clerk advised him to sell eighty fine robes and spend the money for the salvation of his soul. William rounded on him. 'Be quiet you wretch. It will soon be Whitsun when I always hand out new robes to my knights, and this will be my last chance to do so.'[4] His determination to leave behind a reputation as a good knight and an honourable lord counted for more than anything else.

Inevitably many of the church's rules caused resentment. The requirement that every year all farmers should hand over a tithe (in Scotland, a teind) – one tenth of their produce – meant that the richer churches collected tithes on such a scale that special barns had to be built, some of which still survive. Churchmen had to work hard to overcome both tithe avoidance and tithe evasion, especially in Ireland and Scotland. According to the Melrose chronicle, Bishop Adam of Caithness was murdered (and then roasted in his own kitchen) in 1225 because he had insisted on people saving their souls by paying tithes. Many people were undoubtedly angered by the rule against working on Sundays and holy days. When a man working on the feast day of St Erkenwald (London's saint) was rebuked for doing so, he 'belched out his poisonous brew of insults':

You clerics have so much time on your hands that you meddle with what's none of your business. You lot grow fat and soft with idleness, you don't have a real job, your life is just a game or a play. You clerics with your everlasting useless dirges despise us, though we are the ones who do all the real work. And then you go and bring in some Erkenwald or other to justify your idleness and to try to stop me doing the job that I need to stay alive. You might just as well tell me I can live without eating as tell me to stop working. Why should I pray alongside drones like you? When we've made a bit of money, enough so we can eat – and a bit more too, so we can drink – then we have a holiday, and a good time dancing and singing. You keep your festivals, your mouldy old tunes and your Erkenwald to yourselves. Leave us alone[5].

Their insistence that all farmers should pay them a tithe of their produce made churchmen vulnerable to the suspicion that they were motivated by greed. The saintly Gilbert of Sempringham countered this by setting fire to the tithe of grain he collected from a reluctant farmer. Most churchmen preferred to store it in their barns – though it is unlikely that most so-called tithe barns were built for that purpose only.

According to the author (a twelfth-century canon of St Paul's, London), the critic had no sooner finished his diatribe than he staggered under the heavy weight of timber he was carrying, tripped over a half-buried skull in St Paul's churchyard and was fatally injured. Our author was delighted by the swiftness of God's justice, but even he acknowledged that not every bystander felt the way he did.

The fact that for our sense of what a hard-pressed working man might have said, we have to rely on words written by an ecclesiastic, illustrates the historian's problem. It is not just that clerics did most of the writing. Not all clerics, after all, were particularly pious. The main problem is that those writings which have survived the centuries best are those which were kept in the libraries or archives of bodies which came to enjoy a long institutional life, that is to say the English and Scottish monarchies, a few towns and hundreds of churches. Inevitably we know much more about the thoughts of ecclesiastics than we do about the thoughts of laymen and women. Similarly church buildings survive better than any other sort of building, as do the artefacts kept within them. For those who love medieval cathedrals and parish churches it cannot but seem that this was, as it is often called, an 'Age of Faith'. Why else would people have spent such huge sums in erecting and furnishing churches? Yet the rich and the powerful spent far more money on building and decorating houses to live in than on churches to pray in. It is just that thousands of medieval churches still survive today while very few great houses do except as ruins. The surviving evidence unavoidably exaggerates the role played by religion in the life and culture of the people – but by how much? How many believed in a steady-state godless universe? We cannot tell.

Gregorian 'Reform'

What is, however, certain is that the beginning of this period witnessed a Europe-wide campaign aiming at far-reaching changes in church and society in which the Bishop of Rome took the leading role. Conventionally known as Gregorians (from Gregory VII, pope 1073–85), these radicals set out to abolish both secular control of the church (see p. 171) and the family life of the clergy. This was a wildly ambitious project. Throughout Christian Europe churches had owed, and continued to owe, their existence to the piety and generosity of those wealthy landowners, usually laymen, who had endowed them. In these circumstances it was not at all surprising that kings and secular lords chose the bishops, abbots and priests who headed their churches. Despite the fact that canon law had long held that priests could not marry, churchmen everywhere had partners and families. Celibacy was the preserve of monks, and in eleventh-century Britain and Ireland there were few of them – fewer than was once believed (see p. 244). The Gregorians, most of them monks themselves, saw in sexual and familial ties a threat to the moral and spiritual life of the clergy.

In William the Conqueror, reform-minded popes found an immensely powerful king who was sympathetic to some parts of their programme. He chose Lanfranc, the Italian-born abbot of the monastery of St Stephen's at Caen, as his Archbishop of Canterbury and lent his support to Lanfranc's attempts to drive through those parts of the papal and monastic reform agenda that posed no threat to their own authority as king and archbishop. The clergy were not to participate in activities such as hunting, carrying arms, nor – for the upper clergy, i.e. subdeacons, deacons and priests

– sex and marriage. The intention was to make plain their difference from – and moral superiority over – ordinary men and women. Yet in many ways parish priests shared the lifestyle of the ordinary villager, and the 'reform' campaign inevitably caused a great deal of distress in many families. Often a priest had inherited his church from his father. Given the shortage of schools at the time, learning at home was a sensible way of training priests. Over subsequent centuries the growing number of schools, when combined with the pro-celibacy campaign, gradually led to the disappearance of the married priest in England. Elsewhere the campaign was less successful. Later medieval church court records give the impression that Welsh bishops tolerated married priests, allowing them, for example, to provide for their children in their wills. Critics alleged that in the bishops' eyes the fines they took for licensing priests' 'concubines' were too useful a source of regular income to lose. Within Gaelic Ireland even less stigma attached to clerical marriage or concubinage, so the priesthood remained hereditary, as indeed in the absence of educational institutions did the professions, medicine, poetry and Irish law (see p. 214). Familial succession to bishoprics such as Ardagh or Killaloe remained as common in the later Middle Ages as earlier. Eoin O'Grady, Archbishop of Tuam (1364–71), graduate in canon law at Oxford, was son of an Archbishop of Cashel of the same name. Canon law permitted such men to obtain the papal dispensations which allowed them to be bishops despite their canonical illegitimacy.

Although the material realities of church life meant that the achievement fell far short of Gregorian ideals, the reformers' drive did much to put in place three fundamental building blocks through which Christian life in Britain and

Ireland was to be organised well into modern times. These were dioceses, parishes and church courts.

Dioceses

Christian doctrine had long given overall responsibility for pastoral care to bishops, and bishops could be found through eleventh-century Britain and Ireland. But only in England were there archbishops and a network of dioceses (fifteen of them) with defined borders and cathedrals as their centres. Each cathedral had its own chapter, either of monks as at Canterbury and Winchester or – more commonly – of canons each holding a portion of the cathedral's revenues as his own individual stipend, his prebend. Valuable prebends became highly desirable objects of patronage and were often held by men who preferred to remain close to centres of power and who certainly had no intention of performing cathedral services themselves. The usual arrangement was for non-resident canons to employ vicars choral to do their singing for them. In eleventh-century Ireland, Scotland and Wales, by contrast, there were bishops but as yet no cathedral cities, no clearly demarcated dioceses, and no archbishops – a situation which allowed York to claim authority over Scotland, and Canterbury over the whole of Britain and Ireland. (The two archbishops were already locked into a long-running dispute over precedence which was not settled until 1353, in the latter's favour.) There was some movement in England after 1066. A few bishops moved their sees to more populous cities, notably to Norwich, Lincoln and Chester. Two new bishoprics were established, at Ely in 1108 and at Carlisle in 1133, bringing the total up to seventeen. After that no more dioceses were created until after the Reformation.

The changes in Ireland, Scotland and Wales were much greater. By 1200 ecclesiastical organisation had been transformed, putting in place the diocesan structures that were to frame church life through all subsequent centuries. In Wales four dioceses, more or less corresponding to the kingdoms of Deheubarth, Glamorgan, Gwynedd and Powys, emerged at St David's, Llandaff, Bangor and St Asaph during the first half of the twelfth century. Here Canterbury, effectively supported by English political and military power, succeeded in defeating attempts to make St David's an independent archbishopric for Wales. After the completion of the conquest of Wales in the 1280s, Welsh bishoprics were increasingly used as stepping stones for men who were to rise higher in the English church. The failure of Owain Glyndwr's rebellion (see p. 130) meant that this was to remain the diocesan structure of Wales until the twentieth century.

In Scotland ten dioceses had been established on the mainland by the early thirteenth century, nine of them within the area more or less controlled by the kings of Scots. Several, such as Glasgow, Moray and Ross, reflected older political territories. The rulers of Galloway managed, with English support, to retain a degree of independence from the Scottish kings until 1235; in consequence their bishopric, Whithorn, accepted the authority of the Archbishop of York. Not until after the Great Schism (1378–1419) during which Scotland and England supported opposing popes, did Galloway's subjection to York finally end. From David I on several kings tried to persuade the pope to make Scotland an ecclesiastical province with its own archbishop, but in vain. What saved the other nine sees from ecclesiastical subjection to York was a papal declaration, made by 1192, that the Scottish church was the pope's 'special daughter'. In the absence of an archbishop, the nine bishops took it in turns to summon provincial church councils. Beyond the mainland two dioceses (the Isles and Orkney) owed formal ecclesiastical obedience to the Norwegian Archbishop of Nidaros (Trondheim), although after the thirteenth century their bishops tended to be Scotsmen. When in 1472 St Andrews was at last made an archbishopric, both Galloway and the 'Norwegian' dioceses were formally added to its province. Scottish ecclesiastical unity under a single archbishop did not last long; Glasgow became an archbishopric in 1492.

In Ireland where there were lots of kings, there were also plenty of bishops, but the territorial extent of their responsibilities fluctuated according to the rise and fall of kingships until two twelfth-century councils, both chaired by papal legates, systematically restructured the Irish church. At Raith Bresail in 1111 two provinces were established under the archbishops of Cashel and Armagh; at Kells in 1152 better account was taken of Irish political divisions with the creation of two more provinces under the archbishops of Dublin and Tuam. All of this was a bitter pill for Canterbury which had been claiming authority over Irish churches since Lanfranc's time. After a few minor adjustments early thirteenth-century Ireland was left with four archbishoprics and no less than thirty-three dioceses; hardly surprising that with the exception of Dublin, Irish bishops were much poorer than their English counterparts. But the theoretical stability of this structure was always complicated by ethnic divisions. After the death of Laurence O'Toole in 1180, one of Henry II's English clerks, John Cumin, was made Archbishop of Dublin, and for more than a century after that the gradual extension of English control over the island was reflected in the increasing numbers of English or Anglo-Irish bishops. Then the Gaelic revival halted and reversed the process. Throughout the fourteenth and fifteenth centuries the eight dioceses of Tuam (Connacht) were ruled by Gaelic bishops, while the bishops of the five sees in the province of Dublin were all English. Difficulties were greatest for bishops based in the 'land of war' on the moving frontier between Gaels and Anglo-Irish.

Parishes and their priests

At the beginning of this period nearly all the major churches in Britain and Ireland were minsters, collegiate churches staffed by groups of priests who provided both services and burial in consecrated ground, and who in return received renders and/or tithes from the people living within the large area, the parish, which they served. In the more populous south and east of England many of these large parishes had already fragmented by 1066 as lesser churches acquired both burial rights and a portion (usually a third) of the tithes, creating a network of smaller parishes. Over the next 200 years the process of small parish formation continued, and spread north and west. In Scotland David I ordered his sheriffs to ensure that all parishioners paid the teind (tithe) due to the local kirk. When the English invaded Ireland, they took the English pattern of small parishes with them. By 1300 there were about 9,500 parishes in England and 1,000 in Scotland and the Isles. At this point the territorial organisation of the church, for so long in flux, froze in the state it had then reached. The development of canon law and the increased influence of the lawyer tended to protect innumerable vested interests (see p. 241). Hence the thirteenth-century parochial grid survived until the nineteenth century.

From the eleventh century on, many of these small English parish churches, even some of the tiniest, were built in stone rather than timber. Hence they achieved an enduring presence in the landscape, creating the archetypal village scene: manor house and nearby church, squire and parson. The pattern of small parishes never reached the less densely populated parts – upland Wales, the far south-west and north of England, the west of Scotland, Gaelic Ireland. In such regions other centres of pastoral care and preaching such as oratories, standing crosses and holy wells played a greater role.

A conscientious parish priest was a busy man, even when helped, as commonly, by two or three assistant clergy. He recited the daily office, or at least matins and vespers. Although his parishioners were expected to attend only on Sundays, he was meant to celebrate Mass daily. Every parish church had to have a font and a graveyard. The priest baptised babies, received the confession of the dying and administered the last rites. Official doctrine was that no fee could be charged for the services of baptism, marriage and burial, but that it was acceptable for priests to receive gifts at such ceremonies. Priests counted on these customary offerings and consequently regarded hospital clergy and, especially, friars as threats to their standard of living. Complaints about their low standard of education led to more systematic attempts to educate them in their duties, including their role as confessors. In 1281 John Pecham, Archbishop of Canterbury, published a manual of instruction in Latin, requiring each parish priest four times a year to explain the rudiments of the Christian religion. These were the creed, the Ten Commandments, the two precepts (to love God and one's neighbour), the seven sins and the seven virtues, the seven works of mercy, and the seven sacraments (baptism, confirmation, penance, the Eucharist, marriage, extreme unction and ordination). He was to do this in his mother tongue and without any 'fancifully woven subtleties'. The manual was translated into English in the mid-fourteenth century. Later that century John Mirk composed *Festial*, a collection of English sermons intended for use by parish priests. As Mirk put it, 'It is much more useful and of greater merit for you to say your paternoster in English than in such Latin as you do. For when you speak in English, then you know and understand well what you say.'[6]

Yet the words of the Eucharistic sacrament itself, the miracle by which the bread and wine were turned into Christ's body and blood, while still appearing – by another miracle – to remain just bread and wine, were not translated. The priest performed this double miracle at the altar, partly hidden by a rood screen, inaudible to the Sunday congregation and, in Latin, incomprehensible. Despite the Fourth Lateran Council issuing an authoritative statement of the doctrine of transubstantiation in 1215, it too remained incomprehensible to many. A contemporary, Alexander of Ashby, complained that it was at this most solemn moment that a hubbub of gossiping and joking commonly broke out among the congregation. When during the interdict (see p. 257) parish priests, in obedience to Pope Innocent III's command, stopped celebrating Sunday Mass, no member of the laity is known to have complained. By 1300 the laity could bring complaints to local church courts. These provide a useful sense of what parishioners expected of their priests. Most complaints related to a failure to carry out their duties, though the most common single charge was of sexual misconduct. Priests had been brought to renounce marriage, but many found chastity impossible.

Because most parish churches owed their existence to the power and generosity of the local lord, the founder's descendants tended to take it for granted that they should have the right to choose (in technical language 'present') a priest, even if they allowed that he could not enter into his duties until approved and ordained by the bishop. In societies such as Wales where property rights were partible among males, the right to present was also partitioned. Thus by the fifteenth century no less than thirty-six people shared the right to present to the church of Caergybi (Holyhead). Parish churches which had some glebe land as well as tithes from more than ten householders generated more than enough revenue to support a village priest who was expected to live among his parishioners almost like one of them. In many cases this led to a division of the tithes revenue, the greater part going to an absentee rector, and the remainder to a vicar who did the work. Thirteenth-century synodal and diocesan legislation made more explicit the responsibilities of the laity for the fabric and furnishings of their parish church. Hence the provision of pulpits (more than 200 pre-Reformation examples survive in English parish churches) and, from the fifteenth century, fixed seating in the form of pews. Before then people sat on benches or stood – so they could leave quickly, some said, if they did not like what they heard. Organising these responsibilities led to the development of the office of churchwarden and the further proliferation at parish level of guilds and fraternities, voluntary associations of pious laymen (and sometimes women) for the mutual benefit of members and usually funded by their subscriptions.

Church courts

During the two centuries after the Norman Conquest a system of ecclesiastical law was developed which, in addition to dealing with the internal business of the church, touched the lives of laymen at many critical points: the legitimacy of their birth, their sexual conduct, their marriages and divorces, the distribution of their property after death. This law – canon law – came to be defined with increasing precision and subtlety as a result of the systematic study of law, initially at Bologna in the twelfth century and then at law faculties in universities throughout Europe. It was administered separately from the law of the land by a network of ecclesiastical courts in which the papal court had the last word. As a result of the Reformation the papacy was shut out, but in other respects the system survived.

The beginnings of this system in England can be traced back to the 1070s when William I issued a writ setting out the principle of separate spiritual and temporal jurisdictions in conscious departure from the previous practice of churchmen and laymen acting in joint sessions. 'Before my time,' ran the words of William's writ, 'episcopal laws were not properly administered in England according to the precepts of the holy canons.'[7] By announcing that he and his sheriffs would help bishops and archdeacons enforce ecclesiastical discipline in England, William I ushered in a long period of unusually close co-operation between 'church' and 'state'. Remarkably little resistance came from the king's judges as thirteenth-century church courts extended their jurisdiction to cover not just pious and charitable bequests but all bequests of movable property. Not until the later nineteenth century did church courts in England lose their jurisdiction over probate and testaments.

Although rulers throughout Europe proved to be ready to accept the principle that there should be separate courts, there were inevitably disputes as to where the boundary between ecclesiastical and secular jurisdiction should be drawn. In order to demarcate the boundary Henry II had the sixteen chapters of the Constitutions of Clarendon drawn up in 1164. Pope Alexander III rejected most of them, including chapter 3, which dealt with benefit of clergy. Since church courts could not impose the death penalty, it appeared to Henry and many others that allowing the clergy freedom from secular judicial process was tantamount to encouraging criminal behaviour. But Thomas Becket fiercely defended the right of the church to have exclusive jurisdiction over 'criminous clerks'. The damage to Henry's reputation caused by Thomas's murder in his own cathedral in 1170 forced the king to give way. In modified form benefit of the clergy was to last in England until 1827.[8] Henry also gave ground on the question of allowing appeals to Rome, but he and his successors retained jurisdiction over disputes concerning the patronage of churches, which they regarded as part of their jurisdiction over land. Later kings used writs of prohibition to order church courts not to hear cases that in their view belonged to them. Despite Edward I's writ *circumspecte agatis* (issued in 1286) ordering his judges to 'act circumspectly' and recognising tithes, mortuaries and parochial dues, defamation, and attacks on clergy as matters for the church courts, the clergy consistently and continually complained to king and Parliament about what they regarded as infringements of their jurisdiction.

Archdeacons were given the job of enforcing the church's law at the local level. Although outstanding prelates such as Archbishop Wulfstan of York had appointed archdeacons long before 1066, there is little to suggest that most bishops were much concerned to supervise local clergy and parish life. At the Council of Windsor in 1070 Lanfranc ordered bishops to appoint archdeacons. Very quickly all English dioceses were divided into archdeaconries and their subdivisions, rural deaneries. With the power to impose fines as well as penances, archdeacons were able to make a good living out of the failures of both clergy and laity to live up to the standards, especially in sexual matters, being set by canon law. The earliest surviving records of archdeacons' courts show that 90 per cent of offences detected were sexual, mostly fornication. In time both the continuing development of ecclesiastical organisation and the volume of complaints against the venality of archdeacons led to the establishment of episcopal courts meeting regularly to which appeals could be made. In the hope of creating safeguards for the accused, increasingly complex rules were devised. Things now had to be done by the book. The informality of earlier centuries was no longer acceptable. All this helped to transform the church into a structure in which clerical officials and lawyers counted for as much as – and inevitably many said more than – priests. In practice the expense of going to appeal meant that the greater part of the population continued to remain at the mercy of 'rural chapters', i.e. the courts of archdeacons and deans which operated an inquisitorial system developed from Roman law and designed to detect offences.

The laws of marriage

Even when dealing with property and inheritance disputes, the king's judges took for granted the notion that disputes over the validity of a marriage or legitimacy of birth were properly decided by canon law. In earlier centuries rules on marriage and divorce had been promulgated by both secular and ecclesiastical authorities. But reformers such as Lanfranc were keen to take control of marriage. He prohibited marriages within seven degrees of kinship – i.e. couples who had great-great-great-great-grandparents in common could not enter into a valid marriage – and decreed that no marriage should take place without a priest's blessing. By the end of the twelfth century when questions of the validity of a marriage came up in the king of England's courts, the judges routinely passed them over for churchmen to settle. Until the nineteenth century matrimonial litigation remained exclusively a matter for the church courts. One consequence was that marriage became a contract for life, unless one or other proved to be incapable of consummating the marriage, in which case it could be dissolved. Judicial separation was possible for adultery, cruelty or heresy, but in this case neither was permitted to remarry. If it turned out that a couple had entered into an invalid marriage, then it was annulled. This was relatively common on grounds of consanguinity before 1215, but much harder after the Lateran Council of that year reduced the 'forbidden degrees' from seven to four. Until their conquest by the English, Wales and Ireland were different. The Irish *Cain Lanama* (the law of couples) took polygyny and divorce for granted, including 'no fault' divorce and the corresponding property arrangements. It seemed to Henry II's clerk, Roger of Howden, that the Irish could have as many wives as they liked. Welsh law as reflected in thirteenth-century lawbooks was similarly open to divorce.

By this time theologians and canon lawyers were working out a set of rules to define and regulate marriage based on the unworldly proposition that it was a sacrament which symbolised the union between Christ and the church which was made through the freedom of love. This was interpreted to mean that if two people who were free to marry and were old enough (fourteen for boys, twelve for girls), freely exchanged words of consent spoken in the present tense (*verba de presenti*) – 'I, John, take thee, Agnes', for example – then they were married. Couples did not need the consent of their parents, guardians or lords. No witnesses or public ceremony were necessary, not even the presence of a priest. In earlier legal traditions – Roman, Germanic, Jewish, Christian – the consent of parents or guardians and a public ceremony had been two basic criteria for testing the validity of a marriage. Not any longer. The church taught that marriage was one of the seven sacraments, but allowed it to become the one significant rite of passage which the clergy did not control. This idealistic law made clandestine marriages easy, and this in turn meant that collusive or fraudulent claims of a prior marriage were not difficult to make. This opened a back door to divorce, and could be manipulated in other ways. In 1483 Richard of Gloucester exploited the assertion that Edward IV had made a clandestine marriage in order to bastardise the 'princes in the Tower'. This extraordinary law of marriage survived in England until the eighteenth century and in Scotland for longer, most visibly, though in modified form, at Gretna Green. In practice most marriage partners were chosen by family and friends with, in the absence of strong protest, the consent of the couple assumed. Sensible people realised that marriage, with all its consequences for the descent of property, was too serious a business to be left in the hands of lovers. But in the earliest extant substantial collection of private letters, the Paston letters, the case of Margery Paston and Richard Calle in the fifteenth century shows that there were some able to take advantage of the church's law in order to make their choice in defiance of the well-meaning pressure of both family and disapproving church.

Monasteries

Although on the eve of the Norman invasion nearly all major churches Britain and Ireland were 'minsters' – in Latin *monasteria* – there was little that was 'monastic' about most of them. Even though many of these collegiate churches were headed by a man bearing the title 'abbot', the clergy attached to them, often members of the founding family, did not generally eat together in a refectory or – since many of them were married – sleep in a dormitory as required in those communities which followed the Benedictine rule (*regula*). Only in England, and then only in the Midlands, East Anglia and the south, as a result of the 'tenth-century Reformation', were 'regular' monasteries to be found, less than fifty in all, including ten for women. Reform-minded twelfth-century commentators, drawing a sharp distinction between cleric and layman, found the traditional lifestyle of the members of such family churches (*clasau* in Wales) shockingly secular. A decree of the 1101 Council of Cashel, the first Irish council to be presided over by a papal legate, ordered that in future no laymen should be chosen as head (*erenagh*) of a minster.

The monastic impulse so prominent among eleventh-century ecclesiastical activists contributed to a massive increase in the number of monks and nuns in the 150 years after 1066 – at a much faster rate than overall population growth. By the 1220s there were about 550 regular abbeys and priories for men in England, about 200 in Ireland, forty-six in Scotland and thirty-three in Wales. In England there were also about 150 religious houses for women. Some – not all – male monastic leaders saw nuns either as a threat to sexual purity or, partly because there were no women priests, as a tiresome burden. Hence in England, as everywhere, women's houses were both fewer in number and poorer than male communities. Women were even less well provided for in Ireland and Wales – which may reflect inheritance customs which provided less well for daughters and widows.

Monks and nuns were there, as they and others saw it, not just to save their own souls, but also to fight for the spiritual welfare of the whole kingdom, and especially for those who had founded or endowed their community. Their role as trained and dedicated soldiers of Christ was to wage strenuous warfare against the Devil. To this end each day they chanted the full cycle of prayer: matins, lauds, prime, terce, sext, nones, vespers and compline. The great expansion began in Norman England. The extraordinary and violent success of the Norman Conquest meant that there were many from the king downwards who felt in dire need of prayer, and who suddenly had the wealth to be generous. They turned to the long-established Benedictine model of a religious house, sometimes in the style of the fashionable Burgundian monastery of Cluny. During the reigns of William I and II, thirty abbeys and priories were founded in England; an additional forty-five priories (later to be known as alien priories) were established as daughter houses of French abbeys. When the Normans invaded Wales, they 'reformed' *clasau* by turning out the natives and bringing in monks from outside. By 1100 the Benedictine model had also been adopted in Ireland (at Dublin) and in Scotland (Queen Margaret's priory at Dunfermline).

Monks and nuns may have given up sex – though, inevitably, there were a few notorious exceptions – but it sometimes seemed as though they had given up few other pleasures or comforts. Although their vow of poverty meant that they were supposed to have no property of their own, they lived in property-owning communities, some of them – such as

Glastonbury, Ely, Bury St Edmunds, St Augustine's at Canterbury, as well as the cathedral monasteries of Winchester and Christ Church, Canterbury – very rich indeed. The sheer scale of the abbey churches built after 1066, whether in ruins or still standing, impresses even today's visitor. In these ancient houses monks were poor in name only. The Rule of St Benedict banned eating meat (defined as the flesh of quadrupeds) in the refectory, but reading the letter of the text suggested that just so long as there were enough monks eating in the refectory to maintain the sense of a community observing the Rule, then it would be permissible to eat whatever you liked so long as it was in some other room. Special dining rooms known as misericords were provided. Moreover by defining 'meat' as something freshly cooked, they came to see that pre-cooked was merely meat-ish. Not surprisingly Benedictines acquired a reputation for gluttony. Gerald de Barri claimed that lunch (the main meal of the day) at Christ Church, Canterbury, consisted of no less than sixteen dishes, leaving no one with an appetite for vegetables.

But in the twelfth century shortcomings such as these – used in the sixteenth century to justify the dissolution of monasteries – provoked instead the creation of new orders: Cistercians, Augustinians, Templars, Hospitallers, Premonstratensians, Carthusians and Gilbertines. In all of them rather greater importance was given to the individual monk's own spirituality and salvation, but each had its own distinctive style and ethos. The most high-profile was the Cistercian, brought to England (Waverley) in 1128, to Wales (Tintern) in 1131, Scotland (Melrose) by King David I in 1136, and to Ireland (Mellifont) by Bernard of Clairvaux's friend, Archbishop Malachy of Armagh, in 1142. Cistercians explicitly aimed at returning to what they saw as the simplicity and humility of the original Benedictine rule, giving up the linen underwear and black woollen top garment of the Benedictines (the Black Monks) of their own day, and wearing nothing but an undyed woollen habit, hence coming to be known as White Monks. If their austerity, and their ability to win exemption from payment of tithes, impressed, inspiring other religious communities to seek incorporation into the Cistercian order, so also did the spirituality of authors such as Abbot Ailred of Rievaulx. Whereas Benedictine houses recruited largely children (oblates), given by their aristocratic parents to be brought up in the cloister, the Cistercians prohibited entry for anyone under sixteen (later eighteen), and insisted upon a year's novitiate. The sheer size of houses such as Fountains Abbey bore witness to their success. At the end of the twelfth century even the Benedictines felt compelled to follow the Cistercian example. From now on the new model army of monks and nuns consisted of adult volunteers not child conscripts. And since the army was increasing in size, it offered places to people from a wider social range than previously. Indeed for a while the Cistercians took further the Carthusian practice of offering a half-share in the religious life to the poor, allowing both lay brothers and, occasionally, lay sisters to take the vow and wear the habit in return for doing the manual labour on their estates.

A significant aspect of the reform movement was a concern, consciously modelled on the life of Christ, for the sick. Lanfranc's foundation of a leper hospital outside Canterbury was the first of nearly 350 hospitals founded in medieval England, most during the great expansion before 1250. As religious establishments endowed with one or more priests, hospitals offered the sick, who were themselves expected to follow a quasi-monastic life, a full range of pastoral care:

preaching, hearing confession, burial in the hospital cemetery. Founders often brought in Augustinian regular canons, a monastic order which valued pastoral work unusually highly, to run their hospitals, as, for example, London's St Bartholomew's. Their readiness to undertake pastoral duties led to the Augustinians taking over the properties and functions of many minsters throughout Britain and Ireland (expelling those 'secular' canons who refused to give up their families). In Ireland, for example, well-known minsters such as Armagh, Clogher and Cork were turned into Augustinian houses. This practice made founding them relatively cheap so, although not the most celebrated of religious orders, the Augustinian became the most numerous. At its height there were no less than 274 houses of Austin canons in England, more than the combined total of 219 Benedictine and Cistercian.

Of the new orders only one, the Gilbertines, founded by Gilbert of Sempringham, was made in Britain. The fact that all the others had their origins in France illustrates the extent to which religious life in Britain was bound into a single, largely francophone, Latin Christendom. The most consciously international of the new orders was the Cistercian. All Cistercian houses were dedicated to the same saint, Mary, the mother of Christ. Abbots were obliged to travel to an annual general chapter at Citeaux, although Irish and Scottish abbots had to do this only one year in four. According to St Bernard's Life of the Irish reformer, the slogan adopted by Malachy's local enemies was 'We are Irish, not French.' When stories of violence and sexual scandal in some Irish Cistercian houses reached the general chapter in the 1220s, Stephen, Abbot of Stanley in Wiltshire, was authorised to carry out a visitation, at the end of which he laid down that 'no one, no matter what his nation, is to be received as a monk unless he knows how to confess in French or Latin'.[9] It was also a militant Christendom, with two of the new orders keyed into the crusading movement. All the houses of the military orders, the Templars and Hospitallers, no matter where they were in Europe, were parts of two great networks of assistance for the crusader states in Palestine and Syria.

Yet the very success of the new orders in obtaining endowments as well as recruits meant that they too tended to slip into the comfortable ways that had provoked their founders to turn away from the Benedictines. Fresh inspiration came in the shape of two radically different new orders, both originating in southern Europe in the early thirteenth century: the Franciscans and Dominicans. They were like the Austin canons in their emphasis on pastoral work, but unlike them and every other order in being determined to own nothing. Their mission was to preach penance and sustain themselves by begging. They concentrated on towns, where their preaching was badly needed and where begging was easier. Such idealism and dedication was impressive, and they attracted thousands of recruits, often to the dismay of well-off parents who were shocked to see their children begging.

Dominicans and Franciscans came to England in the 1220s. Two more mendicant orders, the Carmelites and the Austin friars, arrived in the 1240s. By the 1340s there were about 5,000 friars in England (housed in 190 friaries); in Ireland eighty-five friaries, more than twenty in Scotland and eight in Wales. The friars had been absorbed into the ecclesiastical establishment. Although they never became great property-owners, they attracted many small gifts in money, often in the form of bequests (as is clear from the evidence of wills, which survive in increasing numbers from the late thirteenth century on). They built bigger churches. They attracted criticism as hypocrites, and suspicion on the grounds that they were always to be found in people's houses when the husband was out. As has famously been said, in the field of religious enthusiasm nothing fails like success. None the less the success of the mendicant orders marked the culmination of two centuries of astonishing creativity in the development of religious institutions, catering for almost every conceivable variety of religious life: contemplative, ascetic, active, rural, urban.

Jews

Throughout most of the twelfth and thirteenth centuries there was one small non-Christian religious community in England: the Jews. So far as is known none lived in England before 1066, but in Normandy the flourishing community of French-speaking Jews at Rouen supplied the aristocracy with luxury goods, and it is possible that they had helped to finance Duke William's invasion. By the end of his reign there was a Jewish community in London, and by 1130 it was able to call upon very substantial cash reserves. In practice Jews were restricted to one sphere of economic activity, banking and moneylending. With interest rates set at one, two or occasionally three pence per pound per week (i.e. 22 per cent, 44 per cent or 66 per cent per annum) this was an occupation which brought them great profits. The financial services they offered were widely welcomed. Hugh of Bury St Edmunds (abbot 1160–80), for instance, borrowed large sums, and the abbey's chronicler, Jocelin of Brakelond, paints a vivid picture of Jewish families taking sanctuary within the precinct during a time of unrest. By the later twelfth century there were small Jewish communities in more than twenty English towns, the most important being in York, Lincoln, Canterbury, Gloucester, Northampton, Cambridge and Winchester. In 1177 Henry II gave permission for Jews to have a cemetery outside the walls of every city in England; before then the bodies of all of them, no matter where they had lived, had to be brought to London (to the cemetery outside Cripplegate) for burial.

In time the Jews in England were to pay dearly for being cultural outsiders who were thought, especially by those religious who felt they were living through an age of greed, to be making excessive profits through alarmingly clever financial manipulations and thanks to an excessive influence at the centres of power. In the 1140s a Norwich monk, Thomas of Monmouth, accused them of the ritual murder of a young boy called William. Thomas's book on the subject launched the anti-Jewish 'blood libel' which was to scar subsequent European history.

Crusades, with their reminders of Christ's crucifixion, tended to stimulate anti-Jewish sentiment; a crusading vow was an expensive commitment and plundering Jews sometimes seemed an all too appropriate way of raising the cash, or of liquidating debt. Anti-Jewish riots and killings broke out in 1189–90 in London, King's Lynn, Stamford, Norwich and Bury St Edmunds. The killings of 1190 reached a climax at York. Jews, as they often did, took refuge in the royal castle, Clifford's Tower. A mob led by some of the local gentry, crusaders among them, and urged on by a fanatical hermit, mounted an assault on the castle. When they realised they could hold out no longer, most of the Jewish men killed their wives and children, then committed suicide. Those families which did not opt for the ancient Jewish tradition of self-martyrdom surrendered when promised that their lives would be spared if they accepted Christian baptism. But on leaving the castle they were killed. The mob then rushed to York Minster where the records of debts owed to Jews were stored and there, in the nave, they made a bonfire of them. So far as it could – which wasn't very far – the government punished those responsible for the massacre of York, and over the next few decades Jews returned to the city until it, once again, contained one of the richest communities in England.

As a small, wealthy, exclusive and culturally distinctive minority faced by increasing anti-Semitism and religious discrimination, Jews needed the protection of the secular power. In return kings exacted a heavy price, regulating their business dealings closely and at times taxing them very harshly. 'Jews are the sponges of kings,' wrote the theologian William de Montibus.[10] In 1210 John demanded the staggering sum of £44,000 from the Jews, employing mass arrests and brutal measures to enforce payment. According to one author, he extracted £6,666 from a rich Jew of Bristol by removing one of his teeth every day until he paid up. Since Jews were in no position to enforce payment of debts owed to them, this was done by royal officials. Debts owed to Jews who died intestate were simply taken over by the Crown – an obvious cause of friction between king and landowning families in debt to Jews that left its mark on Magna Carta. In chapters 10 and 11, John was forced to promise that he would deal sympathetically with the widows and children of any landowner who died in debt to the Jews.

In 1215 Pope Innocent III decreed that Jews and Muslims were 'to be publicly distinguished from other people by their dress'.[11] In 1218 the English regency council ordered 'all Jews to wear on the outer part of their clothing two strips on their breast made of white linen or parchment so that Jews may be distinguished from Christians by this visible badge'.[12] This, it was stated, was to stop a person of one faith from unwittingly having sex with someone of another. A 'certain deacon' (name unknown), however, certainly knew what he was doing when he fell in love with a Jewish woman, for he circumcised himself for her sake. On the orders of a church council chaired by Archbishop Stephen Langton of Canterbury in 1222, he was defrocked and burned. Generally the church's rules about distinctive dress for Jews were set aside in England; in return for money the king was happy to exempt individuals or communities from the obligation to wear the Jewish badge. On this and related matters the king's view was that ecclesiastical authorities were not to interfere with 'our Jews'.

The Jews enjoyed a period of prosperity until Henry III's shortage of money led him to tax them aggressively from the 1240s onwards. Before the end of the century royal financial demands had pressed their Jewish sponges so hard that increasing numbers decided to convert to Christianity, while little more could be squeezed out of those who remained true to the faith of their fathers. Jews had always been a tiny minority, at most little more 5,000, counting men, women and children, and by the later thirteenth century were as few as 2,000. Fundamentalist Christians such as Robert Grosseteste, Bishop of Lincoln, and John Pecham, Archbishop of Canterbury, taking as literally as possible the 'perpetual servitude' said to have been imposed upon the Jews as punishment for their share in the death of Jesus, argued that their property should be confiscated and they should be compelled to work at menial tasks. Whereas in the 1140s King Stephen had protected the Jews of Norwich, Henry III and Edward I promoted the cult of 'Little St Hugh of Lincoln'. In

1275 the Statute of Jewry banned usury. Money lenders had to look for other ways to make a living. In 1278–9 Edward I had no fewer than 300 Jews hanged on charges of clipping coins. In 1290 he expelled them, to general English applause, and was rewarded with the most generous grant of taxation in the history of the medieval kingdom.

The Bishops of Rome

In all these twelfth- and thirteenth-century developments papal leadership was central. This was the time when papal influence was at its height, when the western church as a whole was being turned into an elaborately organised structure administered from the Curia. From the twelfth century onwards churchmen throughout Europe looked to the pope to settle local quarrels. When John of Salisbury entered the service of the Archbishop of Canterbury in 1147 his job was to represent the interests of Canterbury and, to some extent, the interests of the whole English church, at the papal court. This involved him in frequent journeys to the Curia. Gerald de Barri went to Rome three times between 1199 and 1203 in the forlorn hope of persuading Innocent III that St David's should be freed from its subordination to Canterbury and become an independent archbishopric of Wales. The more systematic study of canon law meant that decisions taken at the Curia became in effect legislation for the whole church. Papal councils, often held in the Lateran Palace in Rome, became councils for the whole church. In the twelfth century papal legates visited Scotland and Ireland for the first time. In 1125, 1139, 1237 and 1268 papal legates presided over councils of the English church. The churches in Britain and Ireland became, in more ways than ever before, parts of a single whole, everywhere moved by the same commands and obeying – more or less – the same rules. The theory of papal plenitude of power justified papal provision, the pope's right to make appointments to all benefices throughout Christendom. Churchmen became accustomed to doing what the pope advised or told them to do.

In imitation of papal practice, for example, pastorally active twelfth-century English bishops issued indulgences, remitting part of the penance imposed on a contrite sinner. Since indulgences were sometimes offered to the dying, it is clear that they were already expected to have an effect in the afterlife. Although doctrinally controversial, in practice even bishops with qualms of conscience were unable to resist offering them, going so far as to employ travelling salesmen for the purpose – two centuries before Chaucer's pardoner, with his 'wallet brimful of pardons hot from Rome' – as a way of encouraging pious acts such as church attendance on saints' days, alms-giving, or making financial contributions to causes such as the crusades or church, hospital- and bridge-building. Since to obtain an indulgence it was necessary to have confessed first, one effect of the increasingly attractive offers of indulgences was to encourage lay people not to wait, as previously nearly everyone had, until they were dying before confessing their sins. In this religious climate Pope Innocent III decreed that everyone should confess once a year. Initially no more than a few days of the penance were remitted, but the law of com-petitive generosity gradually took its toll. Not even the attempt by the 1215 Lateran Council to limit indulgences to forty days was to stem the tide. Once embarked on this road, it was prob-ably inevitable that popes, who ever since Urban II preached the First Crusade (1095–6) were believed to possess the power to grant plenary indulgences, would continue to set the bishops an example in supplying indulgences in response to an insatiable demand from those who hoped they were truly contrite.

But there were limits to papal authority, most clearly exposed by the Gregorian belief that if the moral and spiritual life of the clergy were to be, as they saw it, purified, then the church must be free. It ought not to submit to the commands of the laity, be subject to their jurisdiction, or pay taxes to them. By exploiting more systematically an income stream from the wider population, i.e. tithes, it was hoped to free the church from dependence on secular lords. Bishops and abbots should not be chosen by lords, but freely elected, the former by the cathedral canons, the latter by the monks of the abbey. In Gregorian eyes the ceremonies of lay investiture and homage by which a new bishop or abbot received the ring and staff of office from the hands of the secular ruler and then did homage for his church were hated symbols of dependence. It took time for pronouncements made at Rome to reach the north-western corner of Christendom, but in 1099 Anselm, Lanfranc's successor as Archbishop of Canterbury, attended a papal council in Italy and there heard these ceremonies condemned. On his return to England he would neither do homage to King Henry I nor consecrate those bishops whom Henry invested. In 1106 a compromise was reached. Henry renounced investiture, but prelates continued to do homage.

Both parties saw this as a temporary concession, but it endured. Churchmen could not bring themselves to renounce those rich landed estates which, they claimed, were held not by them but by the saints to whom their church was dedicated. This enabled rulers to make life miserably uncomfortable for those canons or monks who did not elect the king's candidate, while at the same time so long as bishops and the richer abbots held so much land, they were too powerful for kings to permit them to be freely elected. Only in those cases where the king had no strongly held view, was free election more than a facade. Hence the allegation that Henry II sent a writ to Winchester ordering the monks of the cathedral priory to hold a free election and to 'elect no one except Richard my clerk'.

Unfortunately for the reformers' theory that even the humblest priest counted for more than a king, on the grounds that priests cared for souls while kings ruled only over bodies, most men did not see it that way. When Pope Gregory VII asked William I to swear fealty to him, the vicar of Christ on St Peter's throne, he was given a dusty answer. When Pope Innocent III, with the intention of bringing pressure to bear on King John, imposed an interdict on England in 1208, banning the holding of church services and burials in consecrated ground, his instructions were obeyed to the letter. The interdict suited John well enough. He confiscated the assets of the clergy on the grounds that they were doing nothing to earn them, then allowed them to buy back the privilege of managing their own lands. He arrested the partners and mistresses kept by many, then released them back into the custody of their 'husbands', once again for cash. In 1209 Innocent III excommunicated John in the hope of increasing the pressure on him, but in vain. Excommunication and interdict, the strongest weapons in the church's armoury, were effective only against truly pious laymen, and most were not.

Kings of England regularly promised that the church should be free – as in chapter 1 of Magna Carta – but the occasions when they did not get the bishops they wanted, no matter how unsuitable, remained very few. Like Thomas Becket, Henry II's all too worldly chancellor, most bishops earned their promotion by working in the king's administrative or diplomatic service, and many continued to do so after their promotion. This remained the case even after the system of papal provision to benefices had developed to the point of ensuring that all bishops were in formal terms provided not elected. It was rare that the pope provided a man the king did not like. In 1278 Edward I reluctantly acquiesced in the provision of the Franciscan John Pecham to Canterbury, after which both archbishop and bishops were made to feel the weight of royal displeasure. Subsequent popes took greater care to provide men who were keen to continue working with kings. By this date, moreover, in yet another indication of the increasing centralisation of the western church, the development of papal taxation of the church had created a situation in which popes depended upon the active co-operation of kings in collecting this revenue. In 1326, 1381 and 1450 Bishop Walter Stapledon of Exeter, Archbishop Simon Sudbury of Canterbury, Bishop William Ayscough of Salisbury and Bishop Adam Moleyns of Chichester, all papally provided, were lynched for the offence of being too closely involved with unpopular royal governments. Not just in England, but throughout Britain and Ireland appointment to major ecclesiastical offices was generally controlled by the ruler. The kings of Scotland, for example, saw their bishops as a means by which royal influence could be extended throughout their realm.

In these later centuries the limits of papal authority were more clearly exposed. It never recovered from the battering it took during the Great Schism from 1378 to 1417 (when there were always at least two popes at the same time, one who came to be based at Avignon and was regarded by the English as a French puppet), but even before then it had been significantly weakened. From the 1290s onwards the kings of

England were able to impose direct taxation on the clergy without first obtaining papal permission. Edward III raised some £500,000 from this source alone. Parliamentary statutes in 1351 and 1353 banned first provisions and then, by the Statute of Praemunire, appeals to the papal court. Despite this the kings of England continued to exploit the papal 'plenitude of power' as and when it suited them, above all to reward their clerical servants by getting popes to provide them with lucrative benefices.

Religious decline?

The Black Death struck religious communities hard. Throughout Britain and Ireland there were smaller houses which never recovered. The generally less well-resourced Irish monasteries suffered particularly badly. Within Anglo-Irish areas the number of Benedictine houses went down from eighteen to three at the dissolution; Cistercians to only two (St Mary's, Dublin and Mellifont). Beyond the Pale, Gaelic recovery led to a revival of traditional religious culture in which family values counted for more than strict observance of the rule. In several Cistercian houses son succeeded father as abbot. In England anti-French sentiments, stirred up by the Hundred Years War, led to the suppression of alien priories. By Henry VIII's reign there were fewer than 600 religious houses of England, as opposed to about 1,000 before the Black Death. The monasteries that had the greatest staying power were the richest ones, almost always the oldest. Of the twenty-four houses assessed at the time of the dissolution as having a net annual income of over £1,000, twenty-three had been founded by the mid twelfth century, and seventeen had a history going back to before 1066. These were precisely the houses in which standards had always tended to be relaxed, and often still were. The earliest surviving Westminster Abbey kitchen accounts, from the fifteenth century, indicate that each monk had a daily ration of two pounds of meat or fish, two pounds of bread and a gallon of ale. Wine was reserved for the sick and for feast days – of which there were about a hundred a year.

The greater survival of records from the later Middle Ages, including records of visitations – a main point of which was to discover and eradicate abuses and shortcomings – inevitably provided ammunition for those who argued that Catholic Christianity was in decline well before the Reformation. Such records have to be treated with caution. None the less there were genuine changes. Whereas in the twelfth and thirteenth centuries a surge of new religious orders catered for those who wanted greater austerity and dedication, there was little of this in the later centuries. This may have been because the authorities took the view that a saturation point had been reached. In 1215 the Fourth Lateran Council decreed that no more new orders should be founded, and none were. Great landowners had long been unhappy at the loss of future reliefs and profits of wardship (see p. 176), when their tenants gave estates to institutions which did not die. In 1279 Edward I issued the Statute of Mortmain forbidding grants of land into the 'dead hand' of the church. In fact grants continued, but only with the king's licence, which had to be paid for. Not surprisingly the flow of land into ecclesiastical hands slowed down. In the fourteenth century the number of religious houses founded in England dropped to sixty, mostly friaries, and declined still further in the fifteenth. In the 200 years after 1300 only ten monasteries with an income of more than £100 a year were founded, in sharp contrast to the 220 founded in the previous 200 years.

In England only one order witnessed an increase in its

numbers. The Carthusian brand of austerity, in which the monks lived as solitaries in cells grouped around a cloister, observing a strict rule of silence, found admirers at the highest level when kings such as Henry V (who founded Sheen in 1415) and James I (Perth in 1429) followed the example set by Sir Walter Manny, who founded the London Charterhouse in 1371. But Carthusian houses were always few; these late foundations brought the total in Britain up to only nine. In terms of numbers the one significant exception to this picture of late medieval 'stagnation' is the success of the Observant branches of the mendicant orders in Ireland. The movement for stricter observance of their original rules, which began in fourteenth-century Italy, had little impact in Britain, apart from a dozen Observant Franciscan houses set up in Scotland. In Ireland, however, no less than ninety Observant friaries were established. They did particularly well among the Gaels, offering a degree of independence from the control of Franciscan and Dominican minister provincials who were nearly all Anglo-Irish. When a Gael was appointed Franciscan minister provincial in 1445 a group of Anglo-Irish Franciscans persuaded the English government to withdraw its recognition of him and to order friaries not to receive those 'born among the rebels'. In the next century the Observant friaries of rural Ireland doubtless stiffened Gaelic resistance to Protestant Reformation.

A long Protestant tradition has read the declining number of religious houses, including hospitals, in Britain as an indicator of an overall decline in religion. Others have disagreed, pointing out that from the mid thirteenth century on chantries (chaplainries in Scotland) and almshouses became the principal beneficiaries of lay endowment. Because the inmates of almshouses (the poor and old rather than the sick) were expected to attend the parish church, they caused less parochial tension than hospitals. Almshouses were correspondingly a more attractive proposition for would-be benefactors who wished to see the vulnerable cared for. Chantries, which first appear in the historical record in the twelfth century, could be separate chapels, but were often just 'private' altars in existing churches, each altar endowed to employ priests to say daily Masses on behalf of the dead. The Christian church had long emphasised the idea of judgement on people's lives, both immediately after their death and, ultimately, at the end of the world. The torments of hell were a favourite theme for wall paintings or stained-glass windows.

Arguably Christianity became a less demanding religion to live by in this period thanks to developments in the doctrine of Purgatory, clearly visible by the twelfth century but not formally defined until 1274. Purgatory was believed to be where the dead were chastised for their sins and purified by fire in preparation for heaven. The length of time spent in Purgatory – potentially tens of thousands of years – could be reduced by the intercession of saints, especially the Virgin Mary, by the prayers of the living, and by offerings of Christ's sacrifice in the Mass. The development of indulgences to the point at which they could be bought by the living on behalf of the souls of the dead facilitated further reductions in the length of time spent in Purgatory. As always the pious and wealthy made the most of their purchasing power. William Courtenay, Archbishop of Canterbury (1381–96) bought 10,000 masses for his soul.

That was on the grand scale but testamentary endowment of temporary chantries for the celebration of a trental – thirty Masses on thirty consecutive days after death – became common form. The proliferation of such chantries meant that in many churches the divine office was virtually continuously celebrated. By the time they were suppressed by Henry VIII there were at least 2,000 chantries in England. The survival of wills from the late thirteenth century onwards shows that testators from an increasingly wide social range were able to secure this kind of spiritual comfort for themselves, their families and often also for the souls of 'all the faithful departed'. Together testaments and chantries made it significantly easier for those who wanted neither to be monks themselves nor make large donations to the church during their lifetime, to believe that they could make a monetary contribution to their own salvation. Such practices suggest that the waning of support for monasteries was far from representing a late medieval failure to create new institutional forms for the expression of piety. Increasing numbers of lay people from a wider social range were able to secure burial for themselves inside monastic churches. If the secular world was no longer so strictly kept out, should that be regarded as a symptom of decline?

A growing number of religious works written in English for clerks to read to a lay audience suggests that religious enthusiasm was far from declining. Some of the most popular, judged by the number of surviving manuscripts, reinforced traditional confessional and penitential discipline. *The Prick of Conscience*, composed *c*.1360, for example, encouraged self-examination in terms of the four last things: death, judgement, hell and heaven. Other works, such as those written by Richard Rolle (d. 1349), and Walter Hilton (d. 1396), developed the idea of a 'mixed life', combining life in secular society with periods of intense contemplation, even direct and mystical communion with God. This offered a way as open to women as to men, as the lives and writings of Juliana of Norwich (d. *c*.1416) and Margery Kempe (d. *c*.1440) demonstrate.

Heresy

In the fifteenth century the mystic's claim to direct communion with God worried the authorities in England more than it had earlier. The Oxford theologian John Wyclif was largely responsible for this heightened nervousness. Whereas a few isolated incidents in the twelfth and thirteenth centuries had demonstrated the capacity of the English church and government to deal swiftly with groups of heretics who came from the Continent, it proved harder to suppress a home-grown movement. Employed in the 1370s by Edward III's government when it wanted to justify taxing the church in order to pay for war with France, Wyclif took the opportunity to argue that in the present state of ecclesiastical corruption, kings as stewards of the nation's wealth, were entitled to seize church property. The argument was condemned as erroneous and subversive by Pope Gregory XI in 1377. At this point, instead of turning to safer academic questions, Wyclif launched fundamental attacks on the structure and doctrine of the Catholic church. In 1378 he argued that because all people were predestined to either salvation or damnation, priests were superfluous as channels of grace. All they could usefully do was preach God's word as it appeared in the Bible – where, as he pointed out, there was no mention of popes, bishops or property-owning prelates. In 1379 in his treatise *On the Eucharist* he denied transubstantiation – the ritual which, above all others, was held to express priestly authority. Condemned as a heretic in 1380, in May 1381 he defiantly reaffirmed his beliefs in his *Confession*.

The outbreak of the great rebellion of 1381 (see p. 165) a month later made him an easy target for those who looked for someone to blame. He was driven out of Oxford, but continued to write until his death in 1384. Meanwhile some of his Oxford followers had begun to take his ideas to a wider audience, both going on preaching tours and composing – in English – Wycliffite sermons, treatises and broadsheets such as the satirical *Letter from Satan*, praising the clergy of the day. Above all they translated the Bible into English. They rapidly won adherents in a few towns such as Leicester, Coventry and Bristol. A few of the gentry were persuaded, most prominent among them the soldier and courtier Sir John Oldcastle. Sober-minded Lollards, as Wycliffites came to be called, tended to associate pilgrimages and the veneration of relics and images with greed and noisy excess. In pointed contrast to the worldliness of many of the higher clergy, the simple lifestyle adopted by the Lollards was attractive. They concealed, as their enemies put it, 'the perversity of their doctrines under a veil of sanctity'.

In fact their numbers were always few, but the orthodox could not be sure; energetically led by Archbishop Thomas Arundel of Canterbury, they exaggerated the danger. In 1401 the death penalty for relapsed heretics was introduced into English law (bringing England into line with continental practice). In 1407 Arundel ordered that all preaching had to be licensed, and all translations of the scripture approved by the diocesan. In 1413 the last Oxford Wycliffite, Peter Payne, principal of St Edmund Hall, was driven out. Pressed by Arundel, Henry V failed to persuade Oldcastle to recant. In consequence Oldcastle was sent to the Tower in 1413, but soon escaped. He avoided capture until 1417 but his alleged leadership of a pathetically small rising at St Giles' Fields, just outside London, in January 1414 was exploited by the government in order to tar Lollardy with the brush of sedition. Oldcastle's 'rebellion' put an end to any lingering support for

Lollardy among the elite. From now on all those rounded up and put on trial for heresy were poor and illiterate. By the middle of the century dissent had been all but eradicated. The lack of much overt opposition suggests that the great majority were content with what the church offered. They accepted a set of values that bound together not only communities of the living but also, through the doctrine of purgatory and the value placed on intercession, those of the living with the dead.

Part V:

Education and Culture

Schools

In the eleventh century and earlier very few children received any schooling in the sense of entering the world of letters. Those with a parent or parents who could read were expected to follow suit. A few bright children were taught the Latin alphabet and prayers such as the paternoster and the Ave Maria by their parish priest using one of his service books. Christianity being a religion of a book, a bookish education was available in major churches throughout Britain and Ireland, and not just for children who were going to stay on there as priests, monks or nuns. According to a poem written by Ieuean ap Sulien, his father Sulien, Bishop of St David's, spent five years learning in Scotland, then ten years in Ireland, before returning to Wales to teach at Llanbadarn Fawr. Such is the absence of evidence from Scotland that we don't know where he might have found scholars there, whereas in Ireland churches such as Armagh, Glendalough and Lismore enjoyed a reputation as centres of learning.

Hitherto educational provision, no matter how good, had

always been ancillary to the main business of the institutions which offered it, whether cathedrals, religious houses or the households of prelates, nobles and kings (see p. 284). But in twelfth-century England the growth of towns made it possible for a man to make a living by charging fees for teaching reading and writing. 'Are not teachers,' one mid-twelfth century commentator complained, 'now as common as royal tax-collectors?'[1] There was evidently a growing demand for education, not fully met by the 1179 papal decree requiring all cathedrals to maintain a schoolmaster to teach poor scholars for nothing. By the late twelfth century one very learned clerk, Walter Map, was asserting that rustics sent their sons to school so that they could become clerics and get rich.

The campaign against simony meant that it was not so easy to buy church offices, but there was no ban on buying an education, and although younger sons of barons and knights possessed some social advantages over sons of burgesses, primogeniture meant that greater wealth was not always one of them. Most clerks had no intention of becoming priests. Many were not 'ordained' at all, and many others took only 'minor orders', which meant that they stayed on the lower rungs of the clerical hierarchy, as cantors, doorkeepers, and lectors. A clerk was a man – there were no women clerks – with a tonsure: i.e. the crown of his head had been shaved. He was also expected to renounce beard and moustache, colourful clothes, weapons and visits to taverns. Their clerical education meant that clerks could act as administrators and secretaries, which is what most of them did. The increasing output of documents implies a growing number of clerical staff; William FitzStephen asserted that as chancellor Becket employed fifty-two clerks.

As, through the centuries, the volume of surviving

documents increases, so also the number of known schools increases, rising from about forty in twelfth-century England to about 300 in the fifteenth. The establishment of public elementary schools – 'public' in the sense of being open to anyone whose parents or patrons could afford the fees – was the educational environment out of which the universities of Oxford and Cambridge evolved *c*.1200. By this date too the pattern of the modern school year was set: three terms starting in September and ending in June. In the fourteenth century charitable benefactors founded grammar schools where boys could be taught free of charge. Although endowed schools were for boys only, by this date in towns such as London and Oxford there were also schoolmistresses teaching girls how to read. The widespread use of bureaucratic Latin in government and manorial administration implies that the gentry could cope well enough with that language. Writing was another matter – for the most part that could be left to clerks, as to typists and secretaries in the twentieth century. Once pupils had mastered Latin, many switched to reading and writing in their vernaculars: English and French. The ideal for ladies and gentlemen from the later twelfth century onwards was to be able to read in all three languages.

In Ireland and the less urbanised parts of Britain few such grammar schools were founded. Education remained in the hands of either the church, in particular Dominican and Franciscan friaries in the later centuries, or was left to those hereditary learned classes such as the O'Dalys of Ireland or the Mhuirichs of the Western Isles which flourished in Welsh Wales, Gaelic Ireland and Scotland – but did not exist in England – and which kept alive a vibrant vernacular culture (see pp. 277–8).

Universities

In 1188 Gerald de Barri put on a one-man literary festival at Oxford. Over three days he staged readings of his new work, *The Topography of Ireland*, and paid for three book-launch parties, to which he invited teachers, students, citizens. It was, he boasted, a magnificent and expensive achievement, the like of which had not been seen since antiquity. He chose Oxford, he explained, because that was 'the place in England where the clergy were the most numerous and most learned'.[2] At this date there were other towns where well-known teachers congregated: Exeter, Lincoln, London and Northampton. Nowhere in England, however, was as celebrated as Paris, and many English flocked there either as teachers or as students. Between 1179 and 1215 one third of all students in Paris whose origins are known were English – and already celebrated for their drinking and womanising (or so an English monk claimed).

At this stage there were just informal gatherings of teachers and learners, living in lodgings or rented houses, with no university in the sense of a corporation. At Oxford a quarrel between the scholars and the town authorities over the hanging of three allegedly innocent clerks in 1209 eventually led, in 1214, to the formation of a union of masters and students, the university. The quarrel also led to the beginnings of Cambridge University since many clerks migrated there, withdrawing their purchasing power as a way of putting economic pressure on Oxford. By the mid fifteenth century both English universities were venerable institutions, their colleges and halls containing about 1,700 (teachers and students) at Oxford, and 1,300 at Cambridge. The arts degree took seven years (four for the BA, and three more for the MA).

The baccalaureate consisted mainly of the three arts of the trivium: grammar, logic and rhetoric (in practice an intensive training in linguistic analysis, logic and the techniques of presenting an argument). For the master's degree they used these techniques to debate questions arising from the three philosophies: natural, moral and metaphysical. This was a formidable training in transferable skills which made its products desirable commodities in the upper reaches of the labour market, since both secular and ecclesiastical princes wanted men who could present a good case, or demolish a competitor's, as well as act as administrators, managers and consultants. Not many students stayed on to work for higher (doctoral) degrees in the three faculties of law, medicine or theology. Theology was recognised, principally by theologians, as the 'queen of sciences', but law and medicine were the 'lucrative sciences'. At Oxford and Cambridge more than two thirds of the few who stayed on chose law. These remained the only two universities in Britain and Ireland until 1412, when St Andrews was founded, soon followed by Glasgow (1451) and Aberdeen (1495). In the 1160s Rory O'Connor gave his support to an attempt to establish Armagh as the centre for higher education for Ireland and Scotland, but neither this, nor an early fourteenth-century scheme for a university at Dublin, got off the ground. Owain Glyndwr's vision of an independent Wales included universities in both north and south, but it remained a vision.

Languages

In every part of north-western Europe in the eleventh century at least two languages were in use: the regional vernacular for everyday speech, and Latin, the language written as well as spoken by clerks. In some regions the absence of written records means that hypotheses about the spoken languages have to be based on the fragile evidence of later place names, though the survival of Norn in Orkney and Shetland until the eighteenth century leaves little room for doubt about the vernacular of the far north. In some regions there may well have been two vernaculars – Gaelic and Norse in the Western Isles and in some Irish ports, for example, or Cornish and English in the far south-west. No more than a handful of words attest to the existence of written Cornish in Cornwall and written Gaelic in early Scotland, but Ireland and Wales were, in European terms, unusual in having a developed vernacular literature, though it survives only in later manuscripts. The fact that in the early fourteenth century the Bruces, when looking for alliances with Irish chiefs, appealed to their common language and way of life shows that the Scottish Highlands and islands, despite the lack of extant manuscripts written there, were part of Gaeldom, sharing the same legends and mythical heroes such as Finn McCool.

Pre-Norman England was even more unusual since English was used not only for verse and religious writing but had become the predominant language of law, historical writing and government. The Norman Conquest had a huge impact. It brought over thousands of French settlers who called their own language 'romanz' and who looked upon English as a barbarous language, not to be used in polite society. Hence English as the written language of law and government was rapidly ousted by Latin, and died out gradually as a language of record, though surviving in the shape of the Anglo-Saxon Chronicle kept at Peterborough Abbey until the 1150s. For a few generations after 1066 the distinction between the language of the rulers and the language of the ruled was sharper in England than anywhere else in Europe. Yet by the mid twelfth century the descendants of the conquerors, or at any rate those who did not also possess great estates in Normandy, had come to think of themselves as English, and could speak English as well as French. No doubt this was the consequence of ordinary day and night contact between a ruling minority and the English-speaking majority, and perhaps above all through intermarriage with English women. The Anglo-Norman chronicler Orderic Vitalis, a Shropshire lad born *c.*1075, tells us that his French father Odelerius of Orleans, 'gave me a weeping child into the care of monks . . . And so, a boy of ten I crossed the Channel and came to Normandy . . . where I heard a language which I did not understand.'[3] Orderic never mentioned his mother, yet when he arrived in Normandy his mother's was the only language he could speak.

Although men and women of French descent came to acquire English as a class-inclusive vernacular, they continued to identify themselves as a social elite by using Anglo-Norman French as their preferred language. Religious works and verse continued to be composed in English, but the pre-eminence of French culture in literature, music and architecture made French the lingua franca of the princely courts of Europe. In many different genres the oldest surviving works of French literature were written in multilingual twelfth-century England. When francophone settlers went to Scotland by invitation of the Scottish kings, and to Ireland in the slipstream of invasion, they took their culture with them. Hence the composition of a narrative of the English conquest of Ireland written in French, and the *Roman de Fergus de Galloway* whose hero swears by St Mungo. French was, one author writing in French explained, the language '*de gentil home*'. Those who were comfortable in French belonged to a cosmopolitan world which stretched as far as the crusader states in Outremer, 'the land beyond the sea'. French remained par excellence the language of international communication and diplomacy. This was, for instance, the language chosen when in 1352 a German duke, Otto of Brunswick, challenged an English one, Henry of Lancaster, to a duel.[4]

In fact the ability to speak French offered so many advantages that it did not remain exclusive to the ruling class. Some knowledge of it was indispensable for those involved in the workings of the king's courts of justice. Hence the syntax and vocabulary of the English language was dramatically altered by French influence in a way that is explicable only in terms of widespread bilingualism. In some fields such as law, administration and war, a whole new vocabulary was created. Hundreds of Old English words were lost; *leod*, for example, was replaced by 'people', and *stow*, meaning 'place', survives only in place names. But the acquisition of over 10,000 French words in the centuries after the Conquest meant not only a doubling of the size of the English lexicon, it also created a language more receptive to further borrowings from French and Latin in subsequent centuries. At the same time and partly as a result of English emigration into Scottish towns, English (first called 'Scots' in 1494) came to be more widely spoken north of the Forth. Not until the later fourteenth century, the age of Chaucer and John Barbour, did English become a high status language in England and Scotland, and not until the fifteenth was it routinely used in the business of government, in Scotland as well as in England. In 1483 the King of England took the coronation oath in English instead of French. The language of the first printed statute book was Law French; the next one, William Caxton's edition, and all subsequent ones, were in English. In his *Book of Courtesy*, Caxton recommended reading authors writing in English rather than French: Gower, Chaucer, John Lydgate and Thomas Hoccleve. The use of French went into a steep decline, although Law French survived until 1731; indeed it still survives in the phrases of the royal assent to Acts of Parliament: *La reyne le veult*.

In the west, in Scotland, Wales and Ireland, although the old vernaculars – Gaelic in the Gaeldom of western Scotland and Ireland, Welsh in Wales – were not immune to the influence of other languages, none of them went through anything approaching the transformation that was to help English to become a global language. But this was many centuries later. The immediate impact of the Chaucerian revolution was to cut English literature off from the mainstream of European culture, in effect to return authors to the relative isolation of the time before the Norman Conquest when readers on the Continent knew nothing of the works of authors who wrote in Irish, Welsh and English. The Celtic stories of King Arthur or Tristan and Isolde entered world literature only in the twelfth century and through the medium of Latin and French. The triumph of the language of Chaucer marked a return to insularity, modified principally by the fact that throughout Europe Latin remained the language of the church and of the learned. Not until the rise of the British Empire in the eighteenth century did people outside England want to read Shakespeare. Within England, however, the proliferation of schools and wider distribution of wealth created the demand which William Caxton met when he began printing books in English, in the process contributing, for good or ill, to the standardisation of a written language which had hitherto always been characterised by marked regional differences. Spoken English, naturally, continued to give rise to comments such as that made by William of Malmesbury: 'Of course, the language of the Northumbrians, particularly in York, is so inharmonious and uncouth that we southerners can make nothing of it.'[5]

Leisure pursuits

The limitations of the surviving evidence means that for what little we know about the leisure pursuits and cultural interests of those men, women and children who did not belong to the elite, we depend chiefly upon comments made by people who wanted to curb them: churchmen who disapproved of the pleasure taken in 'lascivious' music and dance, or complained that too many people preferred watching wrestling matches to listening to sermons; secular authorities who wanted to see free time used for archery practice rather than on football or golf (see p. 121). Richard III added tennis, bowls and quoits as well as dice to the games he disapproved of. Such spoilsport voices are at least sufficiently numerous to indicate that early versions of most modern games in which players use bats, clubs or their feet in order to knock a ball about were widespread. Archaeological evidence – items such as musical instruments, toys, dice or pieces for board games – allows us to 'see' the objects and make replicas, but otherwise adds little to what written sources tell us about the social milieux in which they were used. Chess, for example, a game which came to Europe via the Arab world, seems to have reached England soon after 1066. A fashionable game of pure skill, played by women as well as men, it offered men opportunities, in the words of the *Romance of Alexander*, 'to speak courteously of love to ladies'. Music-making was no doubt found at all social levels, but since it was the elite who commissioned, patronised and rewarded artists and writers, the surviving written sources inevitably focus on their accomplishments and tastes. Descriptions of evening entertainment reveal that the well-brought-up aristocrat, male as well as female, was expected not only to appreciate music but to be able to play an instrument.

Stories

What appear to be the oldest stories to represent secular values from the 'inside' are the vernacular tales of the violent deeds of long-dead heroes such as Beowulf, Cú Chulainn and Roland. A few such works, *Beowulf* for example, survive in eleventh-century form, but most are known only from manuscripts written in the twelfth century, such as the Irish *Book of Leinster* and the Oxford *Chanson de Roland*, or from even later, such as the fourteenth-century Welsh books containing the Arthurian tale *Culhwch and Olwen*. After the Norman Conquest, *Beowulf* was forgotten until exhumed in the nineteenth century. But in Wales, thanks to the patronage from Welsh lords such as Hopcyn ap Tomas ab Einion, traditional literary forms survived the English conquest. Indeed in Dafydd ap Gwilym (*c.*1320–80) a fourteenth-century Welsh literary revival produced the poet generally thought of as Wales's wittiest and most innovative.

Ireland's more or less contemporary literary revival was given added impetus both by the political resurgence of Gaelic chiefs and by the attractions of Gaelic culture and music to some among the English of Ireland – for, as the fourteenth-century poet Goffraidh Fionn Ó Dálaigh wryly observed, in poems for them we promise that the Irish will be driven from Ireland, while in poems for the Irish we promise that the foreigners will be routed across the sea.[6] In praise poems commissioned by such chiefs, including the MacDonald lords of the Isles, the immediate and contemporary was blended with a self-conscious harking back to the heroic old days. When Niall Óg Ó Néill built a house for bards within the old hill-fort of Emain Macha in 1387, he was duly rewarded by being hailed as successor to Conchobhar mac Neasa and Cú Chulainn. On both sides of the North Channel the Irish heroes lived on in the literature of Gaeldom. But outside Ireland and Gaelic Scotland the tales of these heroes had little impact until the invention of an imaginary Celtic world in the nineteenth century. By contrast, thanks to Geoffrey of Monmouth's *History of the Kings of Britain*, probably composed at Oxford in the 1130s, the court of King Arthur rapidly became the setting for some of the finest works of European secular literature.

Geoffrey took the traditional Welsh themes of resistance to the Romans, loss of sovereignty over Britain to the Saxons and the hope of future recovery, and converted them into a history which covered the reigns of no less than ninety-nine kings of Britain, beginning with the great-grandson of Aeneas of Troy, Brutus, the king from whom the island was said to take its name, and ending with Cadwalader who died in 689. To present almost 2,000 years of British history, including within it such memorable figures as the magician-prophet Merlin and the all-conquering King Arthur, was a stunning imaginative feat, the greatest work ever produced by a historian working at Oxford. Because it was written in Latin, it entered the wider world of learning; indeed in number of extant manuscripts it far outstrips any other history written anywhere in Europe during the twelfth century. Whether its readers believed it to be true or not – and some sceptics did dismiss it as a tissue of lies – most were bowled over by a history that celebrated successful kings, both pagan and Christian, and measured their success by non-religious criteria: victory in war, lawmaking, road building, town founding, and the holding of magnificent courts. Indeed just at a time when the Anglo-Norman world of learning had come to look upon the Welsh as barbarous, Geoffrey's history proved that they were people with a splendid and highly civilised past.

Such was its impact that it was immediately turned into French verse by Geoffrey Gaimar. This has been lost, but Gaimar's continuation of it, a history of the English (*Estoire des Engleis*), does still survive. Composed in the late 1130s (earlier than any known history of the French written in French), it was commissioned by Constance FitzGilbert, a woman whose family held estates in Lincolnshire and Hampshire. For the most part a verse translation of the Anglo-Saxon Chronicle, it is also, like Geoffrey of Monmouth's work, a king-centred and court-centred history, a 'celebration of the world's delights, values and activities'.[7] Kings and magnates such as William Rufus, Robert Curthose and Earl Hugh of Chester, condemned as wicked or feckless by contemporary ecclesiastical authors writing in Latin, were here represented as models of good lordship by an author writing in the vernacular of the secular elite. In all the surviving manuscripts of Gaimar's *Estoire des Engleis* it is preceded by the version of Geoffrey of Monmouth's *History* which superseded his own. This was the *Roman de Brut* composed by Wace, a Canon of Bayeux, and completed by 1154. Wace not only added the Round Table to the court of King Arthur, he also had Sir Gawain proclaim that 'it's for love and for their beloved that knights do knightly deeds' – words unlike any heard in earlier European literature, and which in their coupling of love and action were to have a great future.[8]

The imagined world of rulers such as King Arthur or Mark

of Cornwall was the setting in which a new kind of literature emerged: the prose romance. The earliest extant romances were written in French, but in subsequent centuries the form was taken up in many European languages, including English. By implication writers such as Chrétien of Troyes and Thomas, author of the *Romance of Horn* (both more or less speculatively linked with the court of Henry II), set out a code of noble conduct for women and men, models of behaviour in peace as well as war. In the courtly setting of French romances such as the *Prose Lancelot*, the central themes were not politics, war and conquest, but the individual's search for personal fulfilment through prowess, courtesy, loyalty and love – values which could be, and sometimes were, in tension, as in the famous case of Lancelot and Guinevere. In exploring the effects of passion on men and women the romances took a generally relaxed attitude to sex. None the less, sexual relationships as presented in them were models of decorum and restraint when compared with the exuberantly down-to-earth bawdiness in the *fabliaux* surviving in thirteenth- and fourteenth-century English manuscripts. These give us, as few other surviving sources do, some idea of what less earnest people liked to laugh about. Most twentieth-century readers preferred to avert their eyes. Chaucer's *Miller's Tale* looks very tame indeed when compared with the abandon with which the 'crude' French equivalents for words such as 'fuck', 'prick' and 'balls' were thrown about in stories such as *Le chevalier qui fist parler les cons*.

However many clerks there were, they were never more than a tiny minority of the total population. Moreover many, perhaps most, clerks were more interested in secular culture than in religion. One of the priests in William Langland's *Piers Plowman* (late fourteenth century) confesses:

> I don't even know the paternoster perfectly, not as a
> priest should really sing it. I know plenty of ballads
> about Robin Hood and Randolph Earl of Chester, but I
> don't know a verse about our Lord or our Lady.[9]

But no ballads of Randolph Earl of Chester survive, and none of Robin Hood pre-date the fifteenth century. Indeed although works written in English survive from every century in this period, more survive from the fifteenth than from all the previous centuries added together. In part this was due to the achievement of late fourteenth-century poets such as Langland, John Gower, the unknown author of *Sir Gawain and the Green Knight* and, above all, Geoffrey Chaucer in demonstrating to what sophisticated uses the English language could now be put. Chaucer, born into a family of wealthy London wine merchants with court connections, spent the greater part of his life in royal service, and it was for this, not for his poetry, that he was buried in Westminster Abbey. Diplomatic missions took him to France, Navarre and Italy, helping him to attain an unprecedented familiarity with contemporary French poets as well as with Dante, Petrarch and Boccaccio. Their influence on him was considerable, but into everything he read and took from them, he breathed a new life of his own which often made his models look stilted. The immediate popularity of Chaucer's masterpiece, *The Canterbury Tales*, unsurpassed in fluency and wit, helped to establish English as the main language of the nation's literature. Not long after his death, the poet Thomas Hoccleve described him as 'the first finder of our fair language'.

John Barbour's romance biography *The Bruce* (completed in 1375) suggests that in Scotland too the late fourteenth century was a critical period of breakthrough for the English vernacular. But other works attributed to Barbour have been lost; indeed very little literature survives from Scotland, though *The Kingis Quair* (attributed to King James I) is notable for its acknowledgement of the influence of Chaucer and Gower, while Blind Harry's *The Wallace* (c.1470) is equally notable for its influence on the film *Braveheart*. Even more influential was Sir Thomas Malory's *Morte d'Arthur* (c.1470), the brilliant reworking of the tales of the knights of the Round Table and of the search for the Holy Grail which inspired both Victorian poets and modern TV producers and film-makers. Another essential ingredient in the mix of modern literary culture was provided by the earliest known English cookery book, *Forme of Cury,* compiled in about 1390.

Courtesy

One consequence of the triumph of English is that the pleasures and values of the secular world appear more in evidence in the fifteenth century than earlier – which fits only too readily into a scheme of a 'decline' in religious vitality before the Reformation. It is, however, likely that even in periods of active religious reform such as the early twelfth century, elite secular culture was both dominant and self-confident. Eadmer, Anselm of Canterbury's young friend and biographer, remarked that the long-haired and courtly aristocrats of his day mocked those who cut their hair short, calling them peasants (*rustici*) or priests, both evidently terms of abuse.

Words such as *rustici* and *rusticitas* (boorishness) are key terms in the earliest extant courtesy books. 'Do not grab the tastiest morsels,' wrote one author, 'or you will be reproached for your *rusticitas.*'[10] Table manners were particularly important in an age when food was served in units, known as messes, shared between two, three or four people, and when in addition to spoons and in the absence of forks – which only gradually came into use from the late fourteenth century onward – diners used their fingers to help themselves. Bodily functions too were to be kept under control. Hence the advice given by Daniel of Beccles, author of the longest of all courtesy poems, the twelfth-century *Liber urbani*, 'The Book of the Civilised Man', on when, where and how to belch, defecate, fart, spit and urinate politely; only the head of household, for example, was entitled to urinate in the hall.

But courtesy books, in Latin from the twelfth century, Anglo-Norman from the thirteenth, and English from the fourteenth, were much more than books of etiquette. Often in the fictional guise of advice from father to son, or in the case of one fourteenth-century work, from an equally fictional mother to daughter, they instructed their readers in deportment, dress and on a wide range of social relationships (between men and women, master and servant, host and guest), on how, in Daniel's phrase, to lead a civilised life (*urbanam ducere vitam*). The much shorter twelfth-century Latin poem 'Facetus' ('The man of refinement'), which became a standard text in English schools until ousted by Erasmus's *De civilitate morum puerilium*, contains the dictum: 'he who speaks badly of women is a boor (*rusticus*), for truly we are all born of women'.[11] Such language reflects courtesy literature's claim to teach a code of conduct assumed to be appropriate to people of rank. The image of a gentleman as someone who looks after his estates, lives on friendly terms with neighbours with whom he exchanges visits, and who acts as local magistrate can be found as far back as the *Liber Urbani* – and may well be older than that. Erasmus's *De civilitate* put medieval commonplaces into classicising schoolbook Latin seasoned with occasional phrases in Greek, but in substance had nothing new to say.

Moderation and restraint were the watchwords in this literature. The most basic rule in courtesy books was: do not do or say anything that might offend or humiliate others, because if you do in the end you will pay for it. Do not always insist on your rights – if you do you will have few friends. If you hear unkind words about yourself, pretend not to have noticed. The emphasis on elegance of manner and charm of speech, an emphasis which led to the creation of new words – *curialitas / courtoisie* – especially when accompanied by the recommendation, as in the *Distichs of Cato* (see p. 226), that it was often better to dissimulate than to tell the truth, meant that men who took a monk's view of Christianity were disturbed by the values taught by the courtesy books. So far as we can tell, however, these were the values which were taught in the schools and great houses of England and Lowland Scotland. Throughout this period the households of the elite remained, in a wider sense, the principal schools. In them, future heads of households served as pages, in this way experiencing what lordship and service meant. But they were expected to learn more than how to give orders. According to the *Black Book of the Household* of Edward IV, the master of the boys brought up at court was to teach them to ride, to joust, 'to have all courtesy in words, deeds and degrees, the rules of goings and sittings, various languages and other virtuous learning, to play the harp, pipe, sing and dance, and with other honest and temperate behaving and patience'.[12]

Of course even the domesticated peace-loving gentleman of medieval England, bending the law to his own advantage, continued to listen to the old stories of epic violence.

Occasionally, as in the 1320s or during the Wars of the Roses, he would himself have lived through periods of bloodshed. Most of the time, however, he lived in a society in which less blood was shed in the pursuit of rights claimed or in the defence of honour impugned than in sixteenth- or seventeenth-century England. Hence the astonishment expressed by a Stuart historian, Samuel Daniel, at how little blood was spilled during the so-called 'Anarchy' of King Stephen's reign. The evidence of inventories makes it plain that in medieval England nobles and gentry spent far more money on comfortable living and on the arts of peace than on preparation for war.[13] Hunting parties, banquets and other forms of lavish entertaining contributed quite as much to an aristocratic host's reputation as did time spent on campaign. The image of the gentleman as officer and swordsman survived, of course, but except on the Scottish border, castles were more about image and display, powerhouses in that sense, than they were places primarily designed to withstand siege.

In England half the population may have been able to read by the later fifteenth century, at least in the sense of being able to recognise the words of familiar prayers, even though many fewer could write, since that was then, much like typing, a separate skill. As demand for books increased so it became possible to turn book production into a commercial proposition centred on London, where lived people who listed their occupations as scriveners, parchment-makers, bookbinders. This happened on such a scale as to lead to the closing down of book production in religious houses; increasingly monks and nuns bought the volumes they wanted from the book trade. The fact that printing's staggering increase in productivity did not lead to Caxton going bankrupt as a consequence of overproduction suggests that a literate public already existed. In the short run one effect of the print revolution was to concentrate English book production in London and Westminster even more than before. This would facilitate the capture of the commanding heights of the new medium by an ambitious new intellectual elite, the humanists whose insistence on seeking their own models of good style and good conduct in classical antiquity led them and their disciples to ignore or dismiss as of no interest virtually every- thing that had happened in the previous thousand years.

Chivalry and war

In 1484 at Westminster Caxton printed a book which he presented to the reigning king, Richard III, 'to the end that he command this book to be had and read unto other young lords knights and gentlemen within this realm that the noble order of chivalry be hereafter better used and honoured than in late days past'.[14] This was a familiar theme. Commentators had been lamenting the decline of chivalry ever since the twelfth century, the century during which the word 'chevalerie' is first recorded in the sense of a code of knightly conduct. One of the hallmarks of this code was the knight's readiness to spare the lives of those of his defeated enemies who were of a similar status to his own, i.e. could afford to pay a ransom. According to Jordan Fantosme, when Bernard de Balliol brought down William Mortimer in the fight at Alnwick in 1174, he not only spared his life, he granted William parole 'as is customary with a knight'.[15] In France these knightly con- ventions of ransom and parole can be traced back to the eleventh century, long before the first (late twelfth century) treatises on the code of chivalry. After all, the first known treatises on dancing were composed in the mid fifteenth century, but it would be rash to argue that dancing was little practised before then. The diffusion of new knightly conventions in England was evidently related to the presence of the new French elite after 1066 – even though at the Battle of Hastings itself the victors had chosen to follow the older conventions of mass slaughter. Indeed in Anglo-Saxon England men of high rank had been at great risk of being killed in battle or of being summarily executed afterwards. But from 1067 onwards King William dealt with high-status English opponents in the noticeably more merciful manner he had already adopted towards rebels in Normandy. The changes consequent upon the Norman Conquest meant that Hastings was the last old-style battle to be fought on English soil for 200 years. At the battles of the Standard in 1138, Lincoln in 1141, Alnwick in 1174, Lincoln in 1217 and Lewes in 1264 almost no 'noble knights' were killed. Simon de Montfort and his friends expected to make a tidy profit from the release of the prisoners they took at Lewes. In Ireland, by contrast, battles continued to be bloody. According to the Annals of Tigernach, at Móin Mor in 1151 'until sand of sea and stars of heaven are numbered, no one will reckon all the sons of kings and chiefs and great lords of the men of Munster that were killed there'.[16]

In 1264 the royalists at Lewes flew the dragon banner that signalled the intention of fighting to the death, taking no prisoners. They lost, but had they won – as they expected to – then the battle might have marked a reversion to old-style bloodshed. In the event it was the Battle of Evesham in 1265, when about thirty knights of aristocratic birth were killed and Earl Simon's dead body was mutilated, that marked a deliberate breach of the conventions which had held sway for almost 200 years. Contemporaries were shocked. Robert of Gloucester wrote 'such was the murder of Evesham, for battle it was

The knight from the prologue of Caxton's edition of *The Canterbury Tales* in 1485.

not'.[17] Subsequent battles on English soil in the fourteenth and fifteenth centuries followed the pattern set at Evesham. Aristocrats on the losing side were in serious danger of being killed in battle, and if not killed there, then of being summarily executed immediately afterwards (see pp. 161–2). For the elite, political life in England once more became just as dangerous as it had been before 1066.

But other forms of chivalry in wars between Christians proved to be more lasting. A new custom of war granting a degree of immunity to non-combatants, notably women and children, came to be accepted in early twelfth-century England. That women and children did not yet enjoy that same immunity in Wales is suggested by the laudatory mid-twelfth-century biography of Gruffudd ap Cynan (ruler of Gwynedd 1095–1137). In this we are told that Gruffudd, after defeating and killing Trahaearn and his men, invaded their cantref of Arwystli, 'where raging with slaughter and fire, he dragged their wives and daughters into captivity'.[18] In Ireland the annals are full of laconic references to raids and the carrying off of cattle and captives in the wars between kings up until the mid twelfth century. In 1111, for example, the Annals of Inisfallen report the King of Munster's raid on Bréifne: he 'plundered them and carried off their women and cattle'.[19] Just what could be concealed under such brief phrases can be judged from Richard of Hexham's description of a Scottish invasion of England in 1138:

> So that hateful army, more savage than any heathen, respecting neither god nor man, harried the whole province and slaughtered everywhere people of both sexes, of every age and condition, destroying, pillaging and burning vills, churches and houses. By sword's edge and spear point they slaughtered the sick on their beds, women who were pregnant or in labour, babies in their cradles or at their mothers' breasts, and sometimes they killed the mothers too. They slaughtered worn-out old men, feeble old women, anyone who was disabled . . . They killed husbands in front of their wives. Then they carried off their plunder and the women, both widows and maidens, stripped, bound and roped together they drove them off, goading them with spears on the way. This is how they behaved in other wars, but even more so in this. Then, after their captives had been shared out with the rest of the spoil, some of them were moved to pity and freed some of them, giving them to the church

of St Mary in Carlisle. But the Galwegians and many others took their share away with them, for these bestial men who think nothing of adultery, incest and other crimes, after they had tired of abusing them in the manner of brute beasts, either kept them as slave girls or sold them on to other barbarians in exchange for cattle.[20]

There is so powerful a propagandistic strain here that it is tempting to dismiss Richard's account, but other evidence from other parts of Europe indicates that for as long as societies found slavery acceptable, so they also accepted the slave raid, and the terrifying military logic of a type of warfare in which human beings were regarded as desirable items of plunder. For in practice if women and children were to be seized and rapidly removed to places where they could be held securely, it was necessary to kill not only everyone who put up a fight, hence the slaughter of men, but also anyone who got in the way – those categories of persons whom it was uneconomic to put to work in domestic service but whose lamenting, clinging presence would have slowed down and endangered the whole operation.

Whatever happened to these captives later – and some no doubt were assimilated into the society which took them – they had been violently carried off and their families had suffered the slaughter that went hand in hand with enslavement. As men fought to save their wives, sisters and children there were very few who were prepared to surrender. In this kind of warfare battles were desperately fought, and casualties were correspondingly high. Disturbing as the thought may be, it appears that in Wales and Ireland, just as in ancient Greece, people could combine a sense of belonging to a common culture (whether Welsh, Irish or Greek) with a readiness to fight fiercely against different polities within that same culture: adult male captives being killed and women and children dragged off as slaves. This appears to be the pattern of war characteristic of many – perhaps all – early societies, the *Iliad* and the Old Testament providing the most famous examples.

As recently as the eleventh century the English had themselves been a slave-owning, slave-trading, slave-raiding people, and they had taken this kind of thing for granted. But by the 1130s, having abandoned slavery, they regarded such practices as barbarous and wrote passionately about them. Importantly Richard of Hexham's narrative of the 1138 invasion also reveals that the Scots were themselves coming under pressure to adopt the new European morality of war. Alberic, a French monk and Cardinal Bishop of Ostia, appointed papal legate to England and Scotland by Pope Innocent II, met King David I and the Scottish magnates at Carlisle. There the Galwegians promised him that they would free the women and children they had captured, and all the Scots promised that in the future they would spare women, children, the infirm and elderly; they would kill only those who fought against them.[21] There is indeed some evidence that the promise was kept since in equally propagandistic narratives of later Scottish raids on the north there is no mention of slaving. Similarly slave raiding within internecine Irish warfare seems to have withered away in the mid twelfth century. The capture and enslavement of women and children was not mentioned in the long catalogue of Irish vices which Gerald de Barri composed in the 1180s.

Although ordinary soldiers gained very little, arguably nothing, from the new conventions of warfare, the lives of the civilian population at large were massively more secure.

Women and children were among the principal beneficiaries of this change. This is at the core of the rise of chivalry, including its much-mocked concern for damsels in distress. Of course, violence against women remained, and remains, a phenomenon of war. In war women continued to be raped, or seized and threatened in order to extort money from their husbands or fathers. But in Europe ever since the age of chivalry that sort of conduct has been regarded as reprehensible, as damaging to military discipline, by those men who wrote about war or who held high military command. When Richard II invaded Scotland in 1385 the disciplinary ordinances drawn up for his army laid down hanging as punishment for anyone who killed cleric, hermit or woman, raped a woman or who took unarmed civilians prisoner. These guidelines were, within well-disciplined armies, observed, as when, for example, Henry V captured Harfleur in 1415.

After this transition – and for the first time in history – non-combatant immunity existed in the sense that although enemy soldiers might intend to ruin civilians economically by destroying or taking their wealth, they no longer risked going out of their way in order to capture and enslave ordinary people – the sort of people who could not afford to pay a worthwhile ransom. In pre-chivalric warfare the capture and enslavement of women and children had been a source of pride.[22] After this the sufferings of women and children were mostly 'collateral damage'. Historians have tended to regard chivalry rather cynically, seeing it as 'a sham, a tinsel covering disguising the ugliness of war'.[23] But had they measured the treatment of women, children and the poor in the 'age of chivalry' not against some ideal standard, but against the standards that had been regarded as acceptable, indeed honourable, in all previous ages, they might have taken a different view.

Ideas of progress?

William of Malmesbury, looking back over the previous 700 years, believed that the English people of his own day were more humane, more civilised and more capable of great artistic achievement in literature and architecture than their pre-Conquest ancestors had been. He put this down to the influence of Christianity and the example of French models. He particularly applauded the end of enslavement and the slave trade – aspects of English society on the eve of the Norman Conquest which he detested. 'The common people were oppressed by the powerful, some were even sold abroad. One particularly unnatural practice was that many of them got their female slaves pregnant and then, having sated their lust, sold them into prostitution or slavery abroad.'[24]

William also looked upon towns and commerce as central components of a good society; praised kings such as Alfred and Athelstan whom he regarded as promoters of towns and markets, though this did not, of course, prevent him from simultaneously lamenting the rampant greed which, in sombre mood, he saw as the curse of his own age. He regarded societies without towns as inferior.

> In Ireland the cultivators of the soil are so poor, or rather so unskilful, that the land produces only a ragged mob of rustics, while by contrast the English and the French, with their more cultivated way of life, live in towns and carry on trade and commerce.[25]

Gerald de Barri took up and developed this train of thought. According to him, the first mode of living was the pastoral, and the Irish were barbarous people who still inhabited the pastoral mode and made little use of money.

> Mankind usually proceeds from the woods to the fields, and then from fields to settlements and communities of citizens in which it can enjoy the rights and privileges of urban civil life.[26]

The tone of condescension towards the Irish is not the only striking thing about William's and Gerald's remarks. Both evidently shared a concept of progress through various stages of economic and material life, without feeling any need to claim that they were saying anything remarkable or revolutionary. For them the idea of societies advancing through economic stages of development, an idea more usually associated with eighteenth- and nineteenth-century thought, was commonplace – as it was still in the 1530s when the pamphleteer Thomas Starkey wrote that 'men were brought by little and little from the rude life in fields and woods to this civility which you now see stablished and set in all well-ruled cities and towns'.[27]

According to a panegyric composed in the 1150s by the English Cistercian Ailred of Rievaulx, King David had transformed Scotland:

> He adorned you with castles and towns . . . He filled your ports with foreign goods and added to your own delights the riches of other kingdoms. He refined your barbarous customs with Christian piety . . . He knew how to bring a whole people, once rough and rustic, to manners which were refined and gentle . . . The barbarity of that people was completely overcome by his benevolence

and by the laws which his royal gentleness imposed.[28]

Given this English view of how the Scots were improved, it is not surprising to find the English justifying their invasion of Ireland in the 1170s in similar terms. Thus Gerald de Barri asserted that if the barbarous Irish could be compelled to obey the King of England, then they would enjoy the benefits of peace and be introduced to 'a better form of life from England'.[29]

It became commonplace to note the relative lack of towns, commerce and agriculture in Ireland and Wales, to regard their marriage customs as immoral and their way of making war as primitive and savage. Gerald drew a sharp contrast between what he portrayed as the Irish and Welsh practice of killing their captives and what he called French chivalry (*gallica militia*). Indeed in Book 1 chapters 8 and 9 of his ethnographic monograph *The Description of Wales* he worked out the structural links between economic conditions and ferocity in war. Similarly the mid-twelfth-century author of the *Gesta Stephani* based his views of the warlike and fierce nature of Welsh and Scots on their pastoral mode of subsistence. This same author believed that these neighbouring Celtic regions, barbarous and backward could be improved, even were being improved, being made to look like a 'second England'.[30] Such beliefs made sense at a time when thousands of English settlers were muscling their way into lands where they were rarely welcome.

In contrast to their image of their Celtic neighbours, the English saw themselves as prosperous, urbanised, enterprising, peaceful, law-abiding and with higher standards of sexual morality. English assumptions of superiority were to have a very long life, even if they were not always expressed with as much force and clarity as in the twelfth century. But twelfth-century authors such as William of Malmesbury and Gerald de Barri were to exert a powerful influence over subsequent generations. For centuries William of Malmesbury's English history remained a standard work of reference. Gerald's comment on the stages of mankind's development appeared in *The Topography of Ireland*, a work which long remained widely read. As one seventeenth-century Irishman put it: 'I find the calumnies of which he is the author published in the language and writings of every nation; no new geography, no history of the world, no work on the manners and customs of different nations appearing in which his calumnious charges against the Irish are not chronicled as undoubted facts . . . and all these repeated again and again until the heart sickens at the sight.'[31]

Most, perhaps all, peoples think they are better than others, just as the Irish whom Raymond of Perelhos visited *c*.1400 reckoned that their customs were the best in the world. The English, of course, continued to think equally highly of their own customs. After the loss of Normandy during King John's reign and during subsequent cross-Channel wars against the French, English pride became deeply imbued with a patriotic francophobia. That would long remain one strand in the English sense of superiority; another was a perception of Celtic peoples which was felt to justify institutional dis-crimination by those who ran the increasingly bureaucratic English dynastic state.

Part VI:
Counterfactuals

It is hard to imagine Britain and Ireland not sharing in the great economic, social and religious changes common to the whole of western Europe: the end of slavery, population growth, the proliferation of towns and schools, markets and monasteries, the Black Death and its consequences. Historians of religion have often observed that, compared with the Continent, Britain was relatively free of heresy. But it might have been different. After all, the Hussite revolution in Bohemia was inspired by the heretical ideas of the Oxford academic John Wyclif. If his attacks on ecclesiastical authority had not happened, in England, to coincide with the Peasants' Revolt, the holders of secular power might have seen their attractive side, given the prelates' huge wealth and their reputation for corruption.

Alternative political histories are easy to imagine. Whereas the long, if intermittent, history of English pressure on Wales, both conquest and migration, suggests that Wales was ultimately bound to succumb to the wealth and military power of its eastern neighbour, the process might well have lasted much longer. It was far from inevitable that the first Prince of Wales, Llywelyn ap Gruffudd, would also be 'Llywelyn the Last'. The policy choices which Llywelyn made after 1272 provoked Edward I, the new and uncompromising King of England, but although they proved to be disastrous for the Welsh and their prince, they were at least understandable in the light of previous centuries of Anglo-Welsh relations. Other rulers made much more surprising choices. If in 1171 Henry II had not decided to invade Ireland – an island to which he had no hereditary claim and over which none of his predecessors had ever ruled – it might well have been many centuries before any subsequent English government, given the low priority they generally gave to Ireland, took a similarly fateful decision.

At a more structural level, because the kingdoms in Britain and Ireland were family firms, hereditary monarchies of one sort or another, they were always subject to biological accident. Two of the most famous examples suggest that the political map of Britain in 1485 was far from inevitable. If, for example, David I's adult son Henry, Earl of Northumbria, had not predeceased his father in 1152, then Britain might have long remained divided at the Humber with a northern kingdom almost as rich as the southern one. Alternatively a union of the royal houses might have occurred 300 years before it eventually happened, had Margaret, the 'Maid of Norway', survived and married, as planned, Edward (later Edward II of England). Had Henry V not been succeeded by so sad a figure as Henry VI, might a dual Anglo-French monarchy have thrown a permanent political bridge across the Channel? Others, even meticulous scholars, have conjured up wider vistas. According to K. B. McFarlane, had Henry V still 'been living in 1450 there is no reason why he should not have rolled up the map of Europe as in nine years he had rolled up that of France'.[1]

Not that hereditary monarchy was itself a foregone conclusion. The English crisis of 1215–16 that generated a document as unprecedented as Magna Carta might also have shifted the balance between inheritance and election as the theoretical basis of monarchy. Louis of France's supporters argued that he was rightfully king because he had been chosen by the people. Had he successfully dethroned John – as he might well have done if John hadn't died first (allegedly as a result of gorging himself on peaches and new cider) – then kingship in thirteenth-century England might have become as elective as it was in contemporary Germany. Among the probable consequences of such a shift is the avoidance of minorities such as those of Richard II, Henry VI and Edward V. It would not have been necessary for Edward IV's sons to be eliminated in order for Edward IV's brother, Richard of Gloucester, to ascend the throne. If this new English custom had, like many others, been adopted in Scotland, the political history of that kingdom would have looked very different indeed (see p. 146).

Finally, the most well known of counterfactuals should not be omitted. If it had been Duke William who died at Hastings – and, according to his chaplain, he had three horses killed under him – there would have been no Norman Conquest. Although as a consequence of a wider process of Europeanisation many of the changes often attributed to the Conquest would probably have happened anyway, there can be little doubt that an entirely different, and much less rich, English language would have developed.

Endnotes

Introduction

1 Cited in D. Cannadine, J. Keating and N. Sheldon, *The Right Kind of History. Teaching the Past in Twentieth-Century England* (Basingstoke, 2011), 24.

2 David Hume, *History of England* (3 vols., London, 1871; a reprint of 1786 edition), i, 704.

3 W. C. Sellar and R. J. Yeatman, *And Now All This* (London, 1932), 82.

Part I

1. The *Gesta Guillelmi* of William of Poitiers, ed. and trans. R.H.C. Davis and M. Chibnall (Oxford, 1998), 175.

2. *Anglo-Saxon Chronicle*, 1085

3. William of Malmesbury, *The Deeds of the Bishops of England*, trans. D. Preest (Woodbridge, 2002), 197.

4. *Food in Medieval England. Diet and Nutrition*, eds. C. M. Woolgar, D. Serjeantson and T. Waldron (Oxford, 2006), 34.

5. Gerald of Wales, *The History and Topography of Ireland*, trans. J. J. O'Meara (Harmondsworth, 1982), 34; *The Journey through Wales / The Description of Wales*, trans. L. Thorpe (Harmondsworth, 1978), 233.

6. Cited by Richard Britnell, *Britain and Ireland 1050–1530. Economy and Society* (Oxford, 2004), 510.

7. Patrick Gautier Dalché, *Du Yorkshire à l'Inde* (Geneva, 2005).

8. Henry of Huntingdon, *Historia Anglorum: The History of the English People*, ed. and trans. Diana Greenway (Oxford, 1996), 19.

9. *Waterways and Canal-Building in Medieval England*, ed. John Blair (Oxford, 2007), 53, 250.

10. Hugh Candidus, *The Peterborough Chronicle*, ed. W. T. Mellows (Oxford, 1949), 204.

11. *Food in Medieval England*, 102–130.

12. *A Relation of the Island of England*, trans. C. A. Sneyd (London, 1847), 9.

13. *Chronicle of the Kings of Man and the Isles*, ed. George Broderick (Edinburgh, 1973), 71.

14. Cited Britnell, *Britain and Ireland*, 99.

15. Walter Bower, *Scoticronicon*, ed. D. E. R. Watt (Aberdeen, 1987), vol. 8, 259–61.

16. John of Fordun, *Chronicle of the Scottish Nation*, ed. W. F. Skene (Edinburgh, 1872), 38.

17. *Memoirs of a Renaissance Pope. The Commentaries of Pius II*, trans. Florence A. Gragg and Leona C. Gabel (London, 1960), 35–6.

18. J. P. Mahaffy, 'Two Early Tours in Ireland', *Hermathena*, xviii, no. 40 (1914), 1–9.

19. Katharine Simms, *From Kings to Warlords* (Woodbridge, 1987), 4.

20. *Anglo-Saxon Chronicle*, 1085.

21. *Symeonis Monachi Opera Omnia*, ed. T. Arnold (London, 1885), vol. 2, 221.

22. William of Malmesbury, *Saints' Lives*, ed. and trans. M. Winterbottom and R. M. Thomson (Oxford, 2002), 101–3.

23. T. M. Charles-Edwards, *Early Christian Ireland* (Cambridge, 2000), pp. 69–70.

24. William of Malmesbury, *The History of the English Kings Gesta regum Anglorum* (Oxford, 1998), 497–9.

25. *Eadmer's History of Recent Events in England*, trans. G. Bosanquet (London, 1964), 152. Though here the Latin 'homines' is mistakenly translated as 'men'.

26. Lawrence of Durham, *Life of St Brigid* in Vitae Sanctorum Hibernie, ed. W. W. Heist (Brussels, 1965), 1.

27. *The Letters of John of Salisbury*, vol. 1, ed. and trans. W. J. Millor et al. (London, 1955), 135–6.

28. *Leges Henrici Primi*, ed. L. J. Downer (Oxford, 1972), 235.

29. Entry for 1258 from Matthew Paris, *Chronica majora*, ed. H. R. Luard, translated in *English Historical Documents*, ed. David Douglas, vol. 3 (London, 1975), 103–42.

30. R. R. Davies, *Domination and Conquest. The Experience of Ireland, Scotland and Wales 1100–1300* (Cambridge, 1990), 12.

31. Christopher Dyer, *An Age of Transition? Economy and Society in England in the Later Middle Ages* (Oxford, 2000), 193.

32. Gerald, *Journey through Wales*, 233, 251.

33. 'The Scots hate them, so they killed as many of the English as they could', William of Newburgh, *The History of England*, trans. *EHD*, vol. 2, (London, 1981), 379.

34. *The Chronicle of Richard of Devizes*, ed. and trans. John T. Appleby (Edinburgh, 1963), 65.

35. Description of London in William FitzStephen, *Life of Thomas Becket*, translated in *English Historical Documents*, vol. 2, 1042–1189, 1024–30.

36. Huntingdon, *Historia Anglorum*, 11.

37. Prose translation in *EHD*, vol. 2, 1027.

38. *EHD*, vol. 3, 472.

39. G. Clark, 'The long march of history: Farm wages, population and economic growth, England 1209–1869', *Economic History Review* 60 (2007).

40. M. Murphy, 'Feeding medieval cities: some historical approaches', in M. Carlin and J. T. Rosenthal, *Food and Eating in Medieval Europe* (London and Rio Grande, 1998).

41. Jocelin of Brakelond, *Chronicle of the Abbey of Bury St Edmunds*, trans. Diana Greenway and Jane Sayers (Oxford, 1989).

42. *Walter of Henley's Husbandry*, ed. and trans. Elizabeth Lamond (London, 1890), 11–13, 75–7.

43. 'Song of the Husbandman' in ed. Peter Coss, *Thomas Wright's Political Songs of England* (Cambridge, 1996).

44. This and the following quotations on the impact of the Black Death in Britain and Ireland are taken from *The Black Death*, trans. and ed. Rosemary Horrox (Manchester, 1994), 70–84.

45. Horrox, *Black Death*, 312–16.

46. William Langland, *Piers the Ploughman*, trans. into modern English by J. F. Goodridge (Harmondsworth, 1959), 89.

47. Sir John Fortescue, *De Laudibus Legum Anglie*, ed. and trans. S. B. Chrimes (Cambridge, 1942), 67–9.

48. *Prologue* from Geoffrey Chaucer, *The Canterbury Tales*, trans. Nevill Coghill (Penguin Classics), 22.

49. *Memoirs of a Renaissance Pope. The Commentaries of Pius II*, 33.

50. Britnell, *Britain and Ireland*, 361.

51. *Italian Relation*, 42–3.

52. *EHD*, vol. 4, (London, 1969), 1212–13.

53. Sylvia Thrupp, 'The Problem of Replacement-Rates in Late Medieval English Population', *Economic History Review* 18 (1965) 101–119.

54. Charlotte Roberts and Margaret Cox, *Health and Disease in Britain. From*

Prehistory to the Present Day (Stroud, 2003), 221–287. The debates surrounding the late medieval demographic problem are discussed in eds. Mark Bailey and Stephen Rigby, *Town and Countryside in the Age of the Black Death* (Turnhout, 2012), xx–xxii, 3–41.

55. *A Relation of the Island of England*, 24–7.

56. Peter Biller, *The Measure of Multitude. Population in Medieval Thought* (Oxford, 2000), 20. 57. Robert Bartlett, 'Heartland and Border: the Mental and Physical Geography of Medieval Europe', in eds. Huw Pryce and John Watts, *Power and Identity in the Middle Ages* (Oxford, 2007), 25.

58. Eric Fernie, *The Architecture of Norman England* (Oxford, 2000), 19.

59. Gerald, *Journey through Wales*, 252.

60. Trans. and ed. P. J. P. Goldberg, *Women in England c.1275–1525* (Manchester, 1995), 169–70.

Part II

1. Huntingdon, *Historia*, 13.

2. *Brut y Tywysogyon or The Chronicle of the Princes Peniarth* Ms 20 Version, ed. and trans. Thomas Jones (Cardiff, 1952), 13.

3. Pierre de Langtoft, *Chronicle*, ed. and trans. T. Wright, 2 vols. (London, 1866-8), vol. 2, 265–7; *EHD*, 230.

4. Fordun, *Chronicle*, 38.

5. Huntingdon, 393–5.

6. According to a contemporary annalist at Angers, William won the kingdom of the English *in bello publico* with great and heartrending cruel slaughter (*magna ac miserabili cede cruento*). See Elisabeth Van Houts, 'The Norman Conquest through European Eyes', *English Historical Review* 110 (1995), 832–53.

7. *Gesta Guillelmi*, 175–81.

8. *Anglo-Saxon Chronicle*, D version, 1066.

9. *Gesta Guillelmi*, 109, 159.

10. *Gesta Guillelmi*, 183.

11. Huntingdon, 403.

12. *Gesta Pontificum*, 327 (Preest, 139).

13. Walter Map, *Courtiers' Trifles*, ed. and trans. M. R. James et al. (Oxford, 1983), 451.

14. *History of William Marshal*, ed. A. J. Holden, trans. S. Gregory, 3 vols. (London, 2002–6), vol. 2, 233.

15. J. C. Holt, *The Northerners*, (Oxford, 1961), 100.

16. Ralph of Coggeshall, *Chronicon Anglicanum*, ed. J. Stevenson (London, 1875), 183.

17. *Chronique français des rois de France par un anonyme de Béthune* (Paris, 1904), 771.

18. Alexander Grant, 'Foreign Affairs under Richard III', in ed. John Gillingham, *Richard III. A Medieval Kingship* (London, 1993),113–32.

19. Symeon, *Historia Regum*, 192, trans. 1858 (Felinfach, 1987), 140; Life of St Margaret in Lois Huneycutt, *Matilda of Scotland* (Woodbridge, 2003), 169.

20. *Anglo-Saxon Chronicle*, 1093.

21. William of Malmesbury, *Gesta Regum*, 727.

22. *The Nation of the Scots and the Declaration of Arbroath*, ed. A. A. M. Duncan (London, 1970), 36.

23. Walter Bower, *Scotichronicon*, ed. D. E. R. Watt, vol. 8 (Aberdeen, 1987), 65.

24. M. Lapidge; 'The Welsh-Latin Poetry', *Studia Celtica*, 8-9 (1973–4); cited Davies, 88.

25. *Gesta Stephani*, ed. and trans. K. R. Potter (Oxford, 1976), 17; *Brut Y Tywysogyon*, 19.

26. Lesley Johnson and Alexander Bell, 'The Anglo-Norman Description of England', *Anglo-Norman Anniversary Studies*, ed. Ian Short (London, 1993), 11–47.

27. Cited in R. R. Davies, *The Age of Conquest. Wales 1063–1415* (Oxford, 2000), 239.

28. *Chronica Majora*, ed. H. R. Ward, vol. 4, (London, 1877), 647.

29. *Brut Y Tywysogion*, ed. Thomas Jones (Cardiff, 1955), 247–19.

30. Cited in Davies, *Age of Conquest*, 447.

31. Cited in J. Beverley Smith and Llinos Beverley Smith, 'Wales: Politics, Government and Law', in ed. S. H. Rigby, *A Companion to Britain in the Later Middle Ages* (Oxford, 2003), 326.

32. Davies, *Conquest*, 447

33. *La Geste des Engleis en Yrlande*, ed. Evelyn Mullally (Dublin, 2002), 64.

34. The Pope's letters translated in Edmund Curtis and R. B. McDowell, *Irish Historical Documents* (London, 1943), 19–22.

35. William of Newburgh, *Historia Rerum Anglicarum*, ed. R. Howlett (London, 1884), 165–8; *EHD*, (vol. 2), 367–8.

36. Gerald, *Topography and History*, 52, 65, 74, 85; *The Conquest of Ireland*, 140.

37. Cited by James Lydon in *A New History of Ireland*, vol II, ed. A. Cosgrove (Oxford, 1987), 245.

Part III

1. Huntingdon, 605

2. Sir John Fortescue, *The Governance of England*, ed. Charles Plummer (Oxford, 1885), 139.

3. Richard FitzNigel, *Dialogus de Scaccario*, ed. and trans. Charles Johnson (Oxford, 1983), 1–2.

4. Thomas Hoccleve, *The Regement of Princes*, ed. F. J. Furnivall (London, 1897), 145.

5. Gerald, *The Journey*, 137.

6. *The Historical Collections of a Citizen of London*, ed. J. Gairdner (London, 1876), 226.

7. Cited in K. Simms, *From Kings to Warlords*, 51–2.

8. David Carpenter, 'The Household Rolls of King Henry III', *Historical Research* 78 (2005), 20–1.

9. A. R. Myers, *The Household of Edward IV* (Manchester, 1959), 127–9.

10. Huntingdon, 589.

11. N. Vincent, 'King Henry and the Poitevins', in ed. M. Aurell, *La cour Plantagenêt (1154–1204)*, (Poitiers, 2000), 107.

12. Richard FitzNigel, *Dialogue*, 40–1.

13. Walter Map, *Courtiers' Trifles*, ed. M. R. James (Oxford, 1983), 439.

14. John Speed, *Historie of Great Britaine*, 1611, 725.

15. In 1138 Arnulf of Hesdin was hanged by the custom of war because by refusing to surrender when summoned to do so, he caused Stephen to risk the lives of his men in an assault on the castle of Shrewsbury. In 1242 William Marsh was hanged, drawn and quartered for an attempted assassination of Henry III.

16. *The Brut, A Chronicle of England*, ed. F. W. Brie (London, 1906), 224–5.

17. Andrew of Wyntoun, *The Orygynale Cronykil of Scotland*, ed. D. Laing (1879), vol. III, 55.

18. David Carpenter, *The Struggle for Mastery* (Oxford, 2003), 409.

19. Julie Mumby, 'The descent of family land in later Anglo-Saxon England', *Historical Research*, 84 (2011), 399–415.

20. Cnut II, chapters 70, 71, 73, 77, 78, *EHD*, vol. 1, second edn. (London, 1979), 465–6.

21. David Crouch, 'The Complaint of King John against William de Briouze', in ed. Janet Loengard, *Magna Carta and the England of King John* (Woodbridge, 2010), 173.

22. Cited in Susan Reynolds, 'Did all the land belong to the king?' in *Studies in Crusades and Medieval Culture in honour of Benjamin Z. Kedar*, ed. Iris Shagrir (Aldershot, 2007), 269.

23. For example David Crouch, *The English Aristocracy 1070–1272* (New Haven and London, 2011), 20–1.

24. For knights in the following of Æthelnoth Archbishop of Canterbury (1020–38) see Nicholas Brooks, 'The Archbishopric of Canterbury and the So-called Introduction of Knight Service into England', *Anglo-Norman Studies 34*,

2011/12, 41–62. For the range of services which knights were expected to provide see John Gillingham, 'Thegns and Knights in 11th century England', *Transactions of the Royal Historical Society* 6, 5 (1995), reprinted in Gillingham, *The English in the Twelfth Century* (Woodbridge, 2000), 163–85.

25. Michael Prestwich, *Armies and Warfare in The Middle Ages. The English Experience* (New Haven, 1996), 58–62.

26. F. Pollock and F. W. Maitland, *The History of English Law*, 2nd edn, (1898,) 24.

27. K. B. MacFarlane, *The Nobility of Later Medieval England* (Oxford, 1973), 2–3.

28. *Gesta Stephani*, ed. K. R. Potter and R. H. C. Davies (Oxford, 1976), 119.

29. *Nation of the Scots and Declaration of Arbroath*, ed. Duncan, 36.

30. *Patrologia Latina*, vol. 179, 669–70, translated D. J. A. Matthew, *The Norman Conquest* (London, 1966), 231; *The Chronicle of Battle Abbey*, ed. Eleanor Searle (Oxford, 1980), 144–5.

31. *A Medieval Prince of Wales. The Life of Gruffudd ap Cynan*, ed. and trans. D. Simon Evans (Felinfach, 1990).

32. F. W. Maitland, *Domesday Book and Beyond* (Cambridge, 1897, repr. 1997), 26.

33. Davies, *Age of Conquest*, 403.

34. *Acts of the Parliaments of Scotland*, vol. 1, 475.

35. *EHD*, vol. 4, 525.

36. *The treatise on the laws and customs of the realm of England commonly called Glanvill*, ed. G. D. G. Hall (London, 1965), 28.

37. *Patent Rolls of the Reign of Henry III (1216–1232)*, vol. 1, 186.

38. Although at papal insistence Edward II allowed torture in the questioning of Templars accused of heresy.

39. R. R. Davies, *Historical Perception: Celts and Saxons* (Cardiff, 1979).

40. G. H. Orpen, *Ireland under the Normans*, vol. IV (Oxford, 1920), 298.

Part IV

1. Giraldus Cambrensis, *The Conquest of Ireland*, ed. and trans. F. X. Martin and A. B. Scott (Dublin, 1978), 99–101.

2. Cited in Bartlett, *England under the Norman and Angevin Kings* (Oxford, 2000), 478.

3. Vespasiano de Bisticci, *Vite di Uomini illustri*, ed. L. Frati (1892), i, 325–6.

4. *History of William Marshal*, ed. A. J. Holden, 3 vols. (London, 2002–6), 2, 427, 437–9.

5. *The Saint of London*, ed. E. G. Whatley (Binghamton, 1989), 108–14.

6. Cited in John Arnold, *Belief and Unbelief in Medieval Europe* (London, 2005), 38.

7. *EHD*, vol. 2, 647.

8. In 1274 at the Council of Lyons one group of married clerks in minor orders were deprived of their clerical status. These were those whom the church defined as 'bigamous' on the grounds that they had either remarried or married a widow. Thus John of Worcester, a notorious burglar who pleaded benefit of clergy, was none the less hanged in Edward II's reign; had he not married a widow, he would have escaped the death penalty.

9. Stephen of Lexington, *Letters from Ireland 1228–1229*, trans. Barry O'Dwyer (Kalamazoo, 1982), 210.

10. Cited in Bartlett, *England under the Norman and Angevin Kings*, 353.

11. Lateran Council (1215), c. 68.

12. Cited in Bartlett, *England*, 354.

Part V

1. Cited in R. W. Southern, 'Master Vacarius and the Beginning of an English Academic Tradition', in eds. J. J. G. Alexander and M. T. Gibson, *Medieval Learning and Literature*, (Oxford, 1976), 268.

2. *The Autobiography of Giraldus Cambrensis*, ed. and trans. H. E. Butler (London, 1937), 97.

3. Orderic Vitalis, *The Ecclesiastical History*, ed. Marjorie Chibnall, 6 vols. (Oxford, 1968–80), VI, 553–5.

4. *Knighton's Chronicle*, ed. and trans. G. H. Martin (Oxford, 1995), 112–15.

5. William of Malmesbury, *Deeds of the Bishop*, 139.

6. Quoted by James Carney in 'Literature in Irish', in *New History of Ireland*, vol. 2, ed. Art Cosgrove (Dublin, 1987), 696.

7. A. R. Press, 'The Precocious Courtesy of Geoffrey Gaimar', in ed. G. S. Burgess, *Court and Poet* (Liverpool, 1981), 273.

8. Wace, *Roman de Brut. A History of the British*, trans. Judith Weiss (Exeter, 1999), 271.

9. Langland, *Piers the Ploughman*, 73.

10. The 'Disciplina Clericalis' of Petrus Alfonsi, ed. E. Hermes (London, 1977), 150.

11. *Le Facet en françoys*, ed. J. Morawski (Poznan, 1923), 73–4.

12. Myers, *Household of Edward IV*, 126–7.

13. Christopher Dyer, *Standards of Living in the Later Middle Ages* (Cambridge, 1989), 53, 76–7.

14. Cited in ed. John Gillingham, *Richard III. A Medieval Kingship* (London, 1993), 106–7.

15. Jordan Fantosme's *Chronicle*, ed. R. C. Johnston (Oxford, 1981), 138.

16. *The Annals of Tigernach*, trans. Whitley Stokes, 2 vols. (Felinfach, 1993), 174.

17. *The Metrical Chronicle of Robert of Gloucester*, ed. W. A. Wright, 2 vols. (London, 1887), 765.

18. *A Medieval Prince of Wales. The Life of Gruffudd ap Cynan*, ed. and trans. D. Simon Evans (Felinfach, 1990), 69.

19. *Annals of Inisfallen*, ed. S. Mac Airt (Dublin, 1977), 269.

20. *Scottish Annals from English Chroniclers*, trans. Alan O. Anderson (London, 1908), 187.

21. Ibid., 211–12

22. Robert Bartlett, *The Making of Europe* (London, 1993), 303.

23. Maurice Keen, *Chivalry* (New Haven and London, 1984), 232.

24. William of Malmesbury, *Gesta Regum*, 459.

25. Ibid., 739–41.

26. Gerald, *History and Topography of Ireland*, 101–2.

27. Thomas Starkey, *A Dialogue between Reginald Pole and Thomas Lupset*, ed. K. M. Burton (London, 1948), 60.

28. *Lives of Scottish Saints*, ed. W. M. Metcalfe (Paisley, 1889), 279.

29. Giraldus, *Conquest of Ireland*, 101.

30. *Gesta Stephani*, 17.

31. John Lynch, *Cambrensis Eversus*, ed. M. Kelly, (Dublin, 1842), 103, 107

Part VI

1. K. B. McFarlane, *Lancastrian Kings and Lollard Knights* (Oxford, 1972), 125.

Bibliography

Since this has to be limited to a tiny fraction of the scholarship devoted to this period, I have chosen to list books rather than articles in journals to which many readers will not have access, and have in general given preference to recently published or re-printed works in which guidance to earlier studies can readily be found. I have divided it into four parts, the second listing some outline surveys of single countries, the third suggesting some primary sources available in translation, and the fourth listing secondary works under a range of headings.

PART ONE
A feature of the historical writing of recent decades has been the more systematic adoption of a comparative approach to the histories of Britain and Ireland. No one did more to encourage this movement than Rees Davies.

R. R. Davies, *Domination and Conquest: the experience of Ireland, Scotland and Wales 1100–1300* (Cambridge, 1990)

R. R. Davies, *The First English Empire: power and identities on the British Isles 1093–1343* (Oxford, 2000)

R. R. Davies, *Lords and Lordship in the British Isles in the Late Middle Ages* (ed. Brendan Smith, Oxford, 2009).

Other studies along similar lines are:

Richard Britnell, *Britain and Ireland 1050–1530: economy and society* (Oxford, 2004) is indispensable for the economic history of these islands.

Michael Brown, *Disunited Kingdoms. Peoples and Politics in the British Isles 1280–1460* (Harlow, 2013)

David Carpenter, *The Struggle for Mastery. Britain 1066–1284* (London, 2003)

Robin Frame, *The Political Development of the British Isles 1100–1400* (Oxford, 1990)

John Gillingham and Ralph A. Griffiths, *Medieval Britain: a very short introduction* (Oxford, 2000)

Also useful are some multi-author works:

Wendy Davies (ed.), *From the Vikings to the Normans* (Oxford, 2003)

Seán Duffy and Susan Foran (eds.), *The English Isles: cultural transmission and political conflict in Britain and Ireland, 1100–1500* (Dublin, 2013)

Ralph Griffiths (ed.), *The Fourteenth and Fifteenth Centuries* (Oxford, 2003)

Barbara Harvey (ed.), *The Twelfth and Thirteenth Centuries* (Oxford, 2001)

S. H. Rigby (ed.), *A Companion to Britain in the Later Middle Ages* (Oxford, 2003)

Brendan Smith (ed.), *Britain and Ireland, 900–1300: insular responses to medieval European change* (Cambridge, 1999)

Brendan Smith (ed.), *Ireland and the English World in the Late Middle Ages* (Basingstoke, 2009)

Pauline Stafford (ed.), *A Companion to the Early Middle Ages: Britain and Ireland c.500–1100* (Oxford, 2009)

PART TWO: SINGLE COUNTRY OUTLINE SURVEYS
ENGLAND

Robert Bartlett, *England under the Norman and Angevin Kings 1075–1225* (Oxford, 2000)

Michael Clanchy, *England and its Rulers 1066–1307* (third edn., Oxford, 2006)

Gerald Harriss, *Shaping the Nation 1360–1461* (Oxford, 2005)

Maurice Keen, *England in the Later Middle Ages* (second edn., London, 2003)

Edmund King, *Medieval England. From Hastings to Bosworth* (Stroud, 2005)

Michael Prestwich, *Plantagenet England 1225–1360* (Oxford, 2005)

Nicholas Vincent, *A Brief History of Britain 1066–1485* (London, 2011). Of England, despite its title.

And, with past politics taken out:

Julia Crick and Elisabeth van Houts (eds.), *A Social History of England 900–1200* (Cambridge, 2011)

P. J. P. Goldberg, *Medieval England: A Social History 1250–1550* (London, 2004)

Rosemary Horrox and W. Mark Ormrod (eds.), *A Social History of England 1200–1500* (Cambridge, 2006)

SCOTLAND

A. D. M. Barrell, *Medieval Scotland* (Cambridge, 2000)

G. W. S. Barrow, *Kingship and Unity: Scotland 1000–1306* (second edn., Edinburgh, 2003)

Michael Brown, *The Wars of Scotland 1214–1371* (Edinburgh, 2004)

A. A. M. Duncan, *Scotland. The Making of the Kingdom* (Edinburgh, 1975)

Alan MacQuarrie, *Medieval Scotland: kingship and nation* (Stroud, 2004)

Richard Oram, *Domination and Lordship: Scotland 1070–1230* (Edinburgh, 2011)

Katie Stevenson, *Power and Propaganda: Scotland 1306–1488* (Edinburgh, 2014)

WALES

A. D. Carr, *Medieval Wales* (Cardiff, 1995)

R. R. Davies, *The Age of Conquest. Wales 1063–1415* (Oxford, 2000)

David Walker, *Medieval Wales* (Cambridge, 1990)

IRELAND

Seán Duffy, *Ireland in the Middle Ages* (Dublin, 1997)

Seán Duffy (ed.), *Medieval Ireland: an encyclopedia* (London and New York, 2005)

Robin Frame, *Colonial Ireland 1169–1369* (second edn., Dublin, 2012)

James Lydon, *The Lordship of Ireland in the Middle Ages* (second edn., Dublin, 2003)

K. W. Nicholls, *Gaelic and Gaelicised Ireland in the Middle Ages* (second edn., Dublin, 2003)

PART THREE: PRIMARY SOURCES IN TRANSLATION

Unless otherwise stated all these are available in Penguin Classics.

Works of literature well worth reading in modern English versions include Geoffrey Chaucer's masterpiece, *The Canterbury Tales*, an entertaining commentary on late fourteenth-century English society composed by one of the makers of our language, and a man right at the centre of affairs. From the same period, but from very different milieux come two other great poems, William Langland's 'Piers the Ploughman', and the anonymous *Sir Gawain and the Green Knight*, a verse translation by Simon Armitage (London and New York,

2007). Sir Thomas Malory's prose *Le Morte d'Arthur*, 2 vols., edited by Janet Cowen (1969), was to have a massive impact on later Arthurian imaginings. The earliest ballads of the English outlaw are edited in R. B. Dobson and J. Taylor, *Rymes of Robyn Hood* (London, 1989). The first great work of Scottish literature, John Barbour's *The Bruce*, the rousing tale of a fight for freedom has been edited and rendered in modern English by A. A. M. Duncan (Canongate, Edinburgh, 1997). The ethos of honour-centred societies is vividly recaptured in *The Mabinogion*, translated from the Welsh by Sioned Davies (Oxford University Press, Oxford, 2007), and in *The Táin*, translated by Thomas Kinsella (Oxford University Press, Oxford, 1970). *Early Irish Myths and Sagas*, translated by Jeffrey Gantz (London, 1981), contains selections from this and other tales. It is also apparent in an English translation of a thirteenth-century Welsh translation of a twelfth-century Latin text, *A Medieval Prince of Wales: The Life of Gruffudd ap Cynan*, trans. D. Simon Evans (Llanerch Press, Felinfach, 1990).

For the greater part of this period, the most distinguished literature produced in these islands was in French and Latin, part of a culture that was international rather than insular. French can be sampled in collections such as *The Birth of Romance*, translated by Judith Weiss (Everyman, London and Vermont, 1992), and in re-workings of Celtic tales such *The Lais of Marie de France* (London, 1986). Other works composed in French include Guillaume le Clerc, *Fergus of Galloway*, trans. D. D. R. Owen (London, 1991) and 'The Romance of Eustace the Monk' and 'Fouke Fitz Waryn' in *Two Medieval Outlaws* trans. Glyn Burgess (D. S. Brewer, Woodbridge, 1997).

There are some accessible translations from the Latin, notably the works of Gerald de Barri (still more commonly known as Gerald of Wales), an Anglo-Welsh author torn by his own ambiguous loyalties, for example, *The Journey through Wales/The Description of Wales* (London, 1978), *The Autobiography of Gerald of Wales*, trans. H. E. Butler (Boydell Press, Woodbridge, 2005), as well as his more one-sided books on Ireland: *The History and Topography of Ireland* (London, 1982) and *The Conquest of Ireland*, ed. and trans. F. X. Martin and A. B. Scott (Royal Irish Academy, Dublin, 1978). In terms of the number of surviving manuscripts by far the most successful fiction of this period was Geoffrey of Monmouth's *History of the Kings of Britain* (London, 1966).

More genuinely historical works readily available in translation include the Old English *Anglo-Saxon Chronicle* (in various translations) for the period up to 1154 and, in part based upon it, Henry of Huntingdon's *History of the English People*

1000–1154, translated from the Latin by Diana Greenway (Oxford University Press, Oxford, 2002). The Chronicle was turned into French verse in Geffrei Gaimar, *Estoire des Engleis History of the English*, trans. Ian Short (Oxford University Press, New York, 2009). Other narratives in French include Guernes de Pont-Sainte-Maxence's *Life of Thomas Becket in Verse,* trans. Ian Short (Political Institute of Mediaeval Studies, Toronto, 2013) and a near contemporary account of the invasion of Ireland, *La Geste des Engleis en Yrlande* ed. Eveyln Mullally (Portland Four Courts, Dublin, 2002). One of William of Malmesbury's great Latin histories is in paperback: *The Deeds of the Bishops of England,* trans. David Preest (Boydell Press, Woodbridge, 2002). The same translator has provided *The Chronica Maiora of Thomas Walsingham 1376–1422* (Boydell Press, Woodbridge, 2005)

Jocelin of Brakelond's *Chronicle of the Abbey of Bury St Edmunds*, translated by Diana Greenway and Jane Sayers (Oxford World Classics, Oxford, 1989) offers insights into the daily reality of monastic life. For remarkable glimpses of how religion could inspire men and women see John of Forde, *The Life of Wulfric of Haselbury, Anchorite,* trans. Pauline Matarasso (Cistercian Publications, Collegeville, 2011) and the autobiographical *Book of Margery Kempe,* ed. B. A. Windeatt (London, 2004).

PART FOUR
LANDSCAPES

Nancy Edwards (ed.), *Landscape and Settlement in Medieval Wales* (Oxford, 1997)
R. Jones and M. Page, *Medieval Villages in an English Landscape* (Macclesfield, 2006)
S. A. Mileson, *Parks in Medieval England* (Oxford, 2009)
Oliver Rackham, *Trees and Woodland in the British Landscape* (London, 2001)
Oliver Rackham, *The Illustrated History Of The Countryside* (London, 2003)
Stephen Rippon, *Beyond the Medieval Village: the diversification of landscape character in southern Britain* (Oxford, 2008)
Tom Williamson, *Shaping Medieval Landscapes: settlement, society, environment* (Macclesfield, 2003)

ANATOMY AND ARCHAEOLOGY

T. B. Barry, *The Archaeology of Medieval Ireland* (London, 1987)
Martin Biddle (ed.), *King Arthur's Round Table: An archaeological investigation* (Woodbridge, 2000)
Roberta Gilchrist, *Medieval Life. Archaeology and the Life Course* (Woodbridge, 2012)

David A. Hinton, *Archaeology, Economy and Society England from the Fifth to the Fifteenth century* (London, 1990)

David A. Hinton, *Gold & Gilt, Pots & Pins: possessions and people in medieval Britain* (Oxford, 2005)

Kieran Denis O'Conor, *The Archaeology of Medieval Rural Settlement in Ireland* (Dublin, 1998)

Carole Rawcliffe, *Leprosy in Medieval England* (Woodbridge, 2009)

Charlotte Roberts and Margaret Cox, *Health and Disease in Britain: from prehistory to the present day* (Stroud, 2003)

Tom Williamson, *Rabbits, Warrens and Archaeology* (Stroud, 2007)

INFRASTRUCTURE AND TECHNOLOGY

John Blair and Nigel Ramsay (eds.), *English Medieval Industries: craftsmen, techniques, products* (London, 1991)

John Blair (ed.), *Waterways and Canal-Building in Medieval England* (Oxford, 2007)

David Harrison, *The Bridges of Medieval England Transport and Society 400–1800* (Oxford, 2004)

John Langdon, *Horses, Oxen and Technological Innovation, 1066–1500* (Cambridge, 2002)

John Langdon, *Mills in the Medieval Economy: England 1300–1540* (Oxford, 2004)

ENGLISH ECONOMIC DEVELOPMENT

Richard H. Britnell, *The Commercialization of English Society 1000–1500* (second edn., Manchester, 1996)

Christopher Dyer, *Standards of Living in the Later Middle Ages* (second edn., Cambridge, 1998)

Christopher Dyer, *Making a Living in the Middle Ages. The People of Britain 850–1520* (New Haven, 2002)

John Hatcher and Mark Bailey, *Modelling the Middle Ages. The History and Theory of England's Economic Development* (Oxford, 2001)

RURAL SOCIETY AND ECONOMY

Mark Bailey, *The English Manor c.1200–c.1500* (Manchester, 2002). Sources in translation.

Mark Bailey, *The Decline of Serfdom in Late Medieval England* (Woodbridge, 2014)

Bruce M. S. Campbell, *English Seigniorial Agriculture 1250–1450* (Cambridge, 2005)

Christopher Dyer and Richard Jones (eds.), *Deserted Villages Revisited* (Hatfield, 2010)

David Hall, *The Open Fields of England* (Oxford, 2014)

David A. E. Pelteret, *Slavery in Early Medieval England* (Woodbridge, 1995)

Philipp R. Schofield, *Peasant and Community in Medieval England 1200–1500* (Basingstoke, 2003)

C. M. Woolgar, D. Serjeantson, T. Waldron (eds.), *Food in Medieval England* (Oxford, 2006)

MONEY, MARKETS, TOWNS

Martin Allen, *Mints and Money in Medieval England* (Cambridge, 2012)

Maurice Beresford, *New Towns of the Middle Ages* (Gloucester, 1988)

J. L. Bolton, *Money in the Medieval English Economy: 973–1489* (Manchester, 2012)

Ben Dodds and Christian D Liddy (eds.), *Commercial Activity, Markets and Entrepreneurs in the Middle Ages* (Woodbridge, 2011)

Pamela Nightingale, *A Medieval Mercantile Community* (New Haven and London, 1995)

D. M. Palliser (ed.), *The Cambridge Urban History of Britain, Volume 1, 600–1540* (Cambridge, 2000)

D. M. Palliser, *Medieval York* (Oxford, 2014)

Carole Rawcliffe, *Urban Bodies: communal health in late medieval English towns and cities* (Woodbridge, 2013)

Heather Swanson, *Medieval British Towns* (Basingstoke, 1999)

BLACK DEATH

John Hatcher, *The Black Death The Story of a Village, 1345–1350* (London, 2008)

Ole J. Benedictow, *The Black Death 1346–1353* (Woodbridge, 2004)

Mark Bailey and Stephen Rigby (eds.), *Town and Countryside in the Age of the Black Death* (Turnhout, 2012)

Rosemary Horrox, *The Black Death* (Manchester, 1994). Sources in translation.

DOMESDAY BOOK

Elizabeth Hallam and David Bates, *Domesday Book* (Stroud, 2001)

Sally Harvey, *Domesday. Book of Judgement* (Oxford, 2014)

F. W. Maitland, *Domesday Book and Beyond* (Cambridge, 1897, repr. 1997)

David Roffe, *Decoding Domesday* (Woodbridge, 2007)

Ann Williams and G. H. Martin (eds.), *Domesday Book: a complete translation* (London, 2002)

NORMAN CONQUEST

Marjorie Chibnall, *The Debate on the Norman Conquest* (Manchester, 1999)

Brian Golding, *Conquest and Colonisation: the Normans in Britain, 1066–1100* (second edn., New York and London, 2013)

George Garnett, *The Norman Conquest: a very short introduction* (Oxford, 2009)

Wolfgang Grape, *The Bayeux Tapestry* (Munich and New York, 1994)

Marc Morris, *The Norman Conquest* (London, 2012)

Elizabeth Pastan and Stephen White, *The Bayeux Tapestry and its Contents: a reassessment* (Woodbridge, 2014)

Hugh M. Thomas, *The Norman Conquest* (Lanham, 2008)

Ann Williams, *The English and the Norman Conquest* (Woodbridge, 1995)

ANGLO-NORMAN REALM AND ANGEVIN EMPIRE

William M. Aird, *Robert Curthose* (Woodbridge, 2008)

Martin Aurell, *The Plantagenet Empire 1154–1224* (Harlow, 2007)

David Bates, *The Normans and Empire* (Oxford, 2013)

J. A. Everard and J. C. Holt, *Jersey 1204: the forging of an island community* (London, 2004)

John Gillingham, *The Angevin Empire* (second edn., London, 2001)

Donald Matthew, *Britain and the Continent 1000–1300: the impact of the Norman Conquest* (London, 2005)

Eljas Oksanen, *Flanders and the Anglo-Norman World 1066–1216* (Cambridge, 2012)

Daniel Power, *The Norman Frontier in the Twelfth and Thirteenth Centuries* (Cambridge, 2004)

MAGNA CARTA AND REBELLION

Juliet Barker, *England Arise: the people, the King and the Great Revolt of 1381* (London, 2014)

Richard Barrie Dobson, *The Peasants' Revolt of 1381* (London, 1983). Sources in translation.

Christine Carpenter, *The Wars of the Roses* (Cambridge, 1997)

David Carpenter, *Magna Carta* (Oxford, 2015)

Helen Castor, *Blood and Roses: The Paston Family and the Wars of the Roses* (London, 2003)

Stephen Church, *The Household Knights of King John* (Cambridge, 1999)

Danny Danziger and John Gillingham, *1215 The Year of Magna Carta* (London, 2004)

John Gillingham, *The Wars of the Roses: peace and conflict in fifteenth-century England* (London, 2001)

R. H. Hilton (with an introduction by Christopher Dyer), *Bond Men Made Free:*

medieval peasant movements and the English rising of 1381 (London, 2003)

J. C. Holt, *The Northerners* (second edn., Oxford, 1992)

J. C. Holt, *Magna Carta* (second edn., Cambridge, 1992)

Dan Jones, *Summer of Blood: The Peasants' Revolt of 1381* (London, 2009)

Dan Jones, *The Hollow Crown: The Wars of the Roses and the Rise of the Tudors* (London, 2014)

Janet Loengard (ed.), *Magna Carta and the England of King John* (Woodbridge, 2010)

John R. Maddicott, *Simon de Montfort* (Cambridge, 1994)

A. J. Pollard, *The Wars of the Roses* (London, 2013)

Ralph V. Turner, *Magna Carta: through the ages* (Harlow, 2003)

Nicholas Vincent, *Magna Carta: a very short introduction* (Oxford, 2012)

Claire Valente, *The Theory and Practice of Revolt in Medieval England* (Aldershot, 2003)

Björn Weiler, *Kingship, Rebellion and Political Culture. England and Germany c.1215–c.1250* (New York and London, 2007)

KINGSHIP AND GOVERNMENT

To set the European scene:

Susan Reynolds, *Kingdoms and Communities in Western Europe 900–1300* (second edn., Oxford, 1997)

John Watts, *The Making of Polities: Europe 1300–1500* (Cambridge, 2009)

In England:

Alan Cooper, *Bridges, Law and Power in Medieval England 700–1400* (Woodbridge, 2006)

David Crouch, *The Normans: the history of a dynasty* (London, 2002)

George Garnett, *Conquered England: kingship, succession and tenure 1066–1166* (Oxford, 2007)

Dan Jones, *The Plantagenets. The Kings who Made England* (London, 2012).

Max Lieberman, *The Medieval March of Wales: the creation and perception of a frontier, 1066–1283* (Cambridge, 2010)

Jenni Nuttall, *The Creation of Lancastrian Kingship: literature, language and politics in late medieval England* (Cambridge, 2007)

Nigel Saul, *The Three Richards: Richard I, Richard II, Richard III* (London, 2005)

In Scotland:

G. W. S. Barrow (ed.), *The Declaration of Arbroath: history, significance, setting* (Edinburgh, 2003)

David Ditchburn, *Scotland and Europe: the medieval kingdom and its contacts with Christendom c.1215–1545* (East Linton, 2001)

A. A. M. Ducan, *The Kingship of the Scots, 842–1292: succession and independence* (Edinburgh, 2002)

R. Andrew MacDonald, *The Kingdom of the Isles: Scotland's western seaboard, c.1100–c.1336* (East Linton, 1997)

John Marsden, *Somerled and the Emergence of Gaelic Scotland* (East Linton, 2000)

In Wales:

J. Beverley Smith, *Llywelyn ap Gruffudd, Prince of Wales* (Cardiff, 1998)

R. R. Davies, *The Revolt of Owain Glyn Dŵr* (Oxford, 1995)

Kari Maund, *The Welsh Kings: warriors, warlords and princes* (Stroud, 2006)

R. Turvey, *The Welsh Princes 1063–1283* (London, 2002)

In Ireland:

Peter Crooks (ed.), *Government, War and Society in Medieval Ireland* (Dublin, 2009)

Benjamin Hudson, *Irish Sea Studies 900–1200* (Dublin, 2006)

Katharine Simms, *From Kings to Warlords. The Changing Political Structure of Gaelic Ireland in the Later Middle Ages* (Woodbridge, 1987)

Brendan Smith, *Colonisation and Conquest in Medieval Ireland: the English in Louth, 1170–1330* (Cambridge, 1999)

Brendan Smith, *Crisis and Survival in Late Medieval Ireland: the English of Louth and their neighbours, 1330–1450* (Oxford, 2013)

KINGS OF ENGLAND

(The number of books under this, and the next two sub-headings, suggests that in the twenty-first century biographical studies of rulers remains a flourishing form).

Mark Hagger, *William King and Conqueror* (London and New York, 2012)

David Bates, *William the Conqueror* (Stroud, 2001)

Emma Mason, *William II: Rufus, the Red King* (Stroud, 2005)

Frank Barlow, *William Rufus* (New Haven, 1983)

Judith A. Green, *Henry I: King of England and Duke of Normandy* (Cambridge, 2006)

Donald Matthew, *King Stephen* (London and New York, 2002)

David Crouch, *The Reign of King Stephen 1135–1154* (Harlow, 2000)

Edmund King, *King Stephen* (New Haven, 2010)

W. L. Warren, *Henry II* (New Haven and London, 1973, with a new introduction, 2000)

Christopher Harper-Bill and Nicholas Vincent (eds.) *Henry II: new interpretations* (Woodbridge, 2007)

John Gillingham, *Richard I* (New Haven and London, 2002)

Ralph V. Turner, *King John* (London, 1994)

Stephen Church (ed.), *King John: new interpretations* (Woodbridge, 1999)

Marc Morris, *A Great and Terrible King: Edward I and the forging of Britain* (London, 2008)

Seymour Phillips, *Edward II* (New Haven and London, 2010)

W. Mark Ormrod, *Edward III* (New Haven and London, 2011)

Nigel Saul, *Richard II* (New Haven and London, 1997)

Ian Mortimer, *The Fears of Henry IV* (London, 2007)

Christopher Allmand, *Henry V* (second edn., New Haven and London, 1997)

Gwilym Dodd (ed.), *Henry V: new interpretations* (Woodbridge, 2013)

Bertram Wolffe, *Henry VI* (New Haven and London, 2001)

John Watts, *Henry VI and the Politics of Kingship* (Cambridge, 1999)

Michael Hicks, *Edward IV* (London, 2004)

Michael Hicks, *Edward V The Prince in the Tower* (Stroud, 2003)

A. J. Pollard, *Richard III and the Princes in the Tower* (London, 1993)

KINGS OF SCOTLAND

Richard Oram, *David I: the king who made Scotland* (Stroud, 2004)

D. D. R. Owen, *William the Lion 1143–1214: kingship and culture* (East Linton, 1997)

Richard Oram, *Alexander II King of Scots 1214–1249* (Edinburgh, 2012)

Marion Campbell, *Alexander III: King of Scots* (Edinburgh, 1999)

Michael Penman, *Robert the Bruce: King of the Scots* (New Haven and London, 2014)

G. W. S. Barrow, *Robert the Bruce and the Community of the Realm of Scotland* (fourth edn., Edinburgh, 2005)

Michael Penman, *David II, 1329–1371* (East Linton, 2004)

Stephen Boardman, *The Early Stuart Kings: Robert II and Robert III 1371–1406* (East Linton, 1996)

Michael Brown, *James I* (East Linton, 2000)

Christine McGladdery, *James II* (Edinburgh, 1997)

Norman McDougall, *James III: A political study* (second edn., Edinburgh, 2009)

QUEENS

Pauline Stafford, *Queen Emma and Queen Edith* (Oxford, 1997)

Marjorie Chibnall, *The Empress Matilda* (Oxford, 1991)

Lois L. Huneycutt, *Matilda of Scotland. A Study in medieval queenship* (Woodbridge, 2003).

Catherine Keene, *Saint Margaret, Queen of Scots: a life in perspective* (Basingstoke, 2013)

Ralph V. Turner, *Eleanor of Aquitaine* (New Haven and London, 2009)

Fiona Downie, *She is But a Woman: Queenship in Scotland, 1424–1463* (Edinburgh, 2006)

Margaret Howell, *Eleanor of Provence. Queenship in Thirteenth-Century England* (Oxford, 1998)

Helen Castor, *She-Wolves: the women who ruled England before Elizabeth* (London, 2011)

J. L. Laynesmith, *The Last Medieval Queens: English Queenship 1445–1503* (Oxford, 2004)

POWER AND ARISTOCRACY

Amanda Beam, *The Balliol Dynasty, 1210–1364* (Edinburgh, 2008)

Ruth M. Blakely, *The Brus Family in England and Scotland, 1100–1295* (Woodbridge, 2005)

Stephen Boardman, *The Campbells, 1250–1513* (Edinburgh, 2006)

J. S. Bothwell, *Falling from Grace: reversal of fortune and the English nobility 1087–1455* (Manchester, 2008)

David Crouch, *The English Aristocracy 1070–1272* (New Haven, 2011)

Alistair Dunn, *The Politics of Magnate Power: England and Wales, 1389–1413* (Oxford, 2003)

Ralph A. Griffiths and Roger S. Thomas, *The Making of the Tudor Dynasty* (second edn., Stroud, 2005)

Mark S. Hagger, *The Fortunes of a Norman Family. The De Verduns in England, Ireland and Wales, 1066–1316* (Dublin, 2001)

E. Hamilton, *Mighty Subjects: the Dunbar Earls in Scotland, c.1072–1289* (Edinburgh, 2010)

Michael Hicks, *Warwick the Kingmaker* (Oxford, 1998)

Brock Holden, *Lords of the Central Marches: English aristocracy and frontier society, 1087–1265* (Oxford, 2008)

K. B. MacFarlane, *The Nobility of Later Medieval England* (Oxford, 1973)

Marc Morris, *The Bigod Earls of Norfolk in the Thirteenth Century* (Woodbridge, 2005)

C. M. Woolgar, *The Great Household in Late Medieval England* (New Haven, 1999)

WOMEN

Cordelia Beattie, *Medieval Single Women: the politics of social classification in late medieval England* (Oxford, 2007)

Peter R. Coss, *The Lady in Medieval England, 1100–1500* (Stroud, 1998)

P. J. P. Goldberg, *Women in England 1275–1525* (Manchester, 2002). Sources in translation.

Susan M. Johns, *Noblewomen, Aristocracy and Power in the Twelfth-Century Anglo-Norman Realm* (Manchester, 2003)

Ruth Mazo Karras, *Common Women: Prostitution and Sexuality in Medieval England* (Oxford, 1996)

Kim M. Phillips, *Medieval Maidens: young women and gender in England, 1270–1540* (Manchester, 2003)

Jennifer Ward, *Women in England in the Middle Ages* (London, 2006)

Louise J. Wilkinson, *Women in Thirteenth-Century Lincolnshire* (Woodbridge, 2007)

Louise J. Wilkinson, *Eleanor de Montfort: a rebel countess in medieval England* (London, 2012)

PARLIAMENTS

Keith M. Brown and Alan R. MacDonald (eds.), *The History of the Scottish Parliament: parliament in context* (Edinburgh, 2010)

P. R. Cavill, *The English Parliaments of Henry VII 1485–1504* (Oxford, 2009)

Matthew Giancarlo, *Parliament and Literature in Late Medieval England* (Cambridge, 2010)

Clyve Jones (ed.), *A Short History of Parliament* (Woodbridge, 2009)

J. R. Maddicott, *The Origins of the English Parliament* (Oxford, 2010)

LAW

J. G. Bellamy, *The Criminal Trial in Later Medieval England* (Stroud, 1998)

Paul Brand, *The Origins of the English Legal Profession* (Oxford, 1992)

John Hudson, *The Formation of the English Common Law* (Harlow, 1996)

John Hudson, *The Oxford History of the Laws of England Volume II 871–1216* (Oxford, 2012)

Paul Hyams, *Rancor and Reconciliation in Medieval England* (Ithaca, 2003)

Fergus Kelly, *A Guide to Early Irish Law* (Dublin, 1995)

Conor McCarthy, *Marriage in Medieval England: law, literature and practice* (Woodbridge, 2004)

Cynthia J. Neville, *Land, Law and People in Medieval Scotland* (Edinburgh, 2010)

Bruce R. O'Brien, *God's Peace and King's Peace: the laws of Edward the Confessor* (Philadelphia, 1999)

F. Pollock and F. W. Maitland, *The History of English Law* (2 vols., Cambridge, 1898)

Alice Taylor, *The Shape of the State in Medieval Scotland, 1124–1290* (forthcoming)

CHURCHES AND RELIGION

John H. Arnold and Katherine J. Lewis (eds.) *A Companion to the Book of Margery Kempe* (Woodbridge, 2004)

Frank Barlow, *The English Church 1066–1154* (London, 1979)

Robert Bartlett, *The Hanged Man* (Princeton, 2004)

G. W. Bernard, *The Late Medieval English Church: vitality and vulnerability before the break with Rome* (New Haven, 2012)

D. Bracken and D. Ó Riain-Raedel (eds.), *Ireland and Europe in the Twelfth Century: reform and renewal* (Dublin, 2006)

Andrew Brown, *Church and Society in England, 1000–1500* (Basingstoke, 2003)

H. E. J. Cowdrey, *Lanfranc: scholar, monk and archbishop* (Oxford, 2003)

Paul Dalton, Charles Insley and Louise J. Wilkinson, *Cathedrals, Communities and Conflict in the Anglo-Norman World* (Woodbrdge, 2011)

Virginia Davis, *William Wykeham: a life* (London, 2007)

Eamon Duffy, *The Stripping of the Altars* (New Haven, 1992)

Eamon Duffy, *Marking the Hours. English People and their Prayers* (New Haven, 2006)

Anne Duggan, *Thomas Becket* (London, 2004)

Marie Therese Flanagan, *The Transformation of the Irish Church in the Twelfth Century* (Woodbridge, 2010)

R. H. Helmholz, *The Canon Law and Ecclesiastical Jurisdiction from 597 to the 1640s: the Oxford history of the laws of England, volume I* (Oxford, 2004)

Tom Licence, *Hermits and Recluses in English Society 950–1200* (Oxford, 2011)

Henry Mayr-Harting, *Religion, Politics and Society in Britain 1066–1272* (Harlow, 2011)

Joel T. Rosenthal, *Margaret Paston's Piety* (Basingstoke, 2010)

John Shinners and William J. Dohar (eds.), *Pastors and the Care of Souls in Medieval England* (Notre Dame, 1998)

R. W. Southern, *Saint Anselm: a portrait in a landscape* (Cambridge, 1990)

Michael Staunton, *Thomas Becket and his Biographers* (Woodbridge, 2006)

R. N. Swanson, *Catholic England: faith, religion and observance before the Reformation* (Manchester, 1993). Sources in translation.

Hugh M. Thomas, *The Secular Clergy in England, 1066–1216* (Oxford, 2014)

Sally N. Vaughn, *Archbishop Anselm 1093–1109* (Farnham, 2012)

D. E. R. Watt, *Medieval Church Councils in Scotland* (Edinburgh, 2000)

J. A. Watt, *The Church in Medieval Ireland* (second edn., Dublin, 1998)

Diana Webb, *Pilgrimage in Medieval England* (London, 2000)

Glanmor Williams, *The Welsh Church from Conquest to Reformation* (Cardiff, 1962)

Simon Yarrow, *Saints and their Communities: miracle stories in twelfth-century England* (Oxford, 2006)

MONASTERIES

Janet Burton, *The Monastic and Religious Orders in England c.1000–1300* (Cambridge, 1994)

Janet Burton, *The Monastic Order in Yorkshire, 1069–1215* (Cambridge, 1999)

Janet Burton and Karen Stöber (eds.), *The Regular Canons in the Medieval British Isles* (Turnhout, 2011)

Barbara Harvey, *Living and Dying in England, 1100–1540: the monastic experience* (Oxford, 1993)

Julie Kerr, *Monastic Hospitality: the Benedictines in England c.1070–c.1250* (Woodbridge, 2007)

Julie Kerr, *Life in the Medieval Cloister* (London, 2009)

David Robinson (ed.), *The Cistercian Abbeys of Britain* (London, 2002)

Karen Stöber, *Late Medieval Monasteries and their Patrons: England and Wales c.1300–1540* (Woodbridge, 2007)

JEWS

Sarah Rees Jones and Sethina Watson (eds.), *Christians and Jews in Angevin England. The York Massacre of 1190, Narratives and Contexts* (Woodbridge, 2013)

Robert R. Mundill, *England's Jewish Solution, 1262–1290: experiment and expulsion* (Cambridge, 1998)

Patricia Skinner (ed.), *Jews in Medieval Britain* (Woodbridge, 2003)

EDUCATION AND CULTURE

Laura Ashe, *Fiction and History in England, 1066–1200* (Cambridge, 2007)

Robert Bartlett, *Gerald of Wales, 1145–1223* (Oxford, 1982)

M. T. Clanchy, *From Memory to Written Record. England 1066–1377* (third edn., Oxford, 2013)

A. B. Cobban, *The Medieval Universities* (London, 1975)

G. R. Evans, *The University of Oxford: A New History* (Oxford, 2010), chapter two

Elizabeth Freeman, *Narratives of a New Order: Cistercian Historical Writing in England, 1150–1220* (Turnhout, 2002)

Chris Given-Wilson, *Chronicles: the writing of history in medieval England* (London, 2004)

Karen Jankulak, *Geoffrey of Monmouth* (Cardiff, 2010)

Maurice Keen, *The Outlaws of Medieval Legend* (second edn., London, 2000)

Ruth Kennedy and Simon Meecham-Jones (eds.), *Writers of the Reign of Henry II* (Basingstoke, 2006)

James McEvoy, *Robert Grosseteste* (Oxford, 2000)

Cary J. Nederman, *John of Salisbury* (Tempe, 2005)

John North, *God's Clockmaker: Richard of Wallingford and the invention of time* (London, 2005)

Nicholas Orme, *Medieval Schools: from Roman Britain to the Renaissance* (London, 2006)

Sophie Page (ed.), *The Unorthodox Imagination in Late Medieval Britain* (London, 2010)

A. J. Pollard, *Imagining Robin Hood: the late-medieval stories in historical context* (London, 2004)

Amanda Power, *Roger Bacon and the Defence of Christendom* (Cambridge, 2013)

Huw Pryce (ed.), *Literacy in Medieval Celtic Societies* (Cambridge, 2006)

Rodney M. Thomson, *William of Malmesbury* (revised edn., Woodbridge, 2003)

Rodney M. Thomson, *Books and Learning in Twelfth-Century England* (Walkern, 2006)

Jocelyn Wogan-Browne (ed.), *Language and Culture in Medieval Britain. The French of England c.1100–c.1500* (Woodbridge, 2013)

COURTESY AND CHIVALRY

David Burnley, *Courtliness and Literature in Medieval England* (London, 1998)

Hugh Collins, *The Order of the Garter 1348–1461* (Oxford, 2000)

David Crouch, *William Marshal: knighthood, war and chivalry, 1149–1219* (second edn., London, 2002)

Mark Duffy, *Royal Tombs of Medieval England* (Stroud, 2003)

Maurice Keen, *Origins of the English Gentleman: Heraldry, Chivalry and Gentility in Medieval England, c.1300–c.1500* (Stroud, 2002)

Colin Richmond, *John Hopton: a fifteenth-century Suffolk gentleman* (Cambridge, 2005)

Nigel Saul, *Death, Art and Memory in Medieval England: the Cobham family and their monuments 1300–1500* (Oxford, 2001)

Nigel Saul, *For Honour and Fame. Chivalry in England 1066–1500* (London, 2011)

Alexandra Sinclair (ed.), *The Beauchamp Pageant* (Donington, 2003)

Katie Stevenson, *Knighthood and Chivalry in Scotland 1424–1513* (Woodbridge, 2006)

WARFARE

Michael Brown, *Bannockburn: the Scottish war and the British Isles, 1307–1323* (Edinburgh, 2008)

Juliet Barker, *Conquest: the English Kingdom of France 1417–1450* (London, 2009)

David Cornell, *Bannockburn: the triumph of Robert the Bruce* (New Haven, 2009)

Anne Curry, *Agincourt: a new history* (Stroud, 2005)

Sean Davies, *Welsh Military Institutions, 633–1283* (Cardiff, 2004)

Seán Duffy (ed.), *The World of the Galloglass: kings, warlords and warriors in Ireland and Scotland 1200–1600* (Dublin, 2007)

Sean McGlynn, *Blood Cries Afar: the forgotten invasion of England 1216* (Stroud, 2013)

Frank McLynn, *Lionheart and Lackland: King Richard, King John and the wars of conquest* (London, 2006)

Colin McNamee, *The Wars of the Bruces: Scotland, England and Ireland 1306–1328* (East Linton, 1997)

David Moore, *The Welsh Wars of Independence* (Stroud, 2005)

John Norris, *Welsh Castles at War* (Stroud, 2004)

Michael Prestwich, *Armies and Warfare in the Middle Ages. The English Experience* (New Haven, 1996)

J. O. Prestwich, *The Place of War in English History, 1066–1214*, ed. Michael Prestwich (Woodbridge, 2004)

Clifford J. Rogers, *War Cruel and Sharp. English Strategy under Edward III, 1327–1360* (Woodbridge, 2014)

N. A. M. Rodger, *The Safeguard of the Sea: A naval history of Britain, 660–1649* (London, 1997)

Matthew Strickland, *War and Chivalry: the conduct and perception of war in England and Normandy 1066–1217* (Cambridge, 1996)

Matthew Strickland and Robert Hardy, *The Great Warbow: from Hastings to the Mary Rose* (Stroud, 2005)

Jonathan Sumption, *The Hundred Years War I: trial by battle* (London, 1990)

Jonathan Sumption, *The Hundred Years War II: trial by fire* (London, 1999)

Jonathan Sumption, *Divided Houses: the Hundred Years War III* (London, 2009)

BIG BUILDINGS

Paul Binki, *Becket's Crown: art and imagination in Gothic England 1170–1300* (New Haven, 2004)

Eric Fernie, *The Architecture of Norman England* (Oxford, 2000)

John Goodall, *The English Castle 1066–1650* (New Haven, 2011)

T. McNeill, *Castles in Ireland* (London, 1997)

Marc Morris, *Castle. A History of the Buildings that Shaped Medieval Britain* (London, 2003)

David Sweetman, *The Medieval Castles of Ireland* (Woodbridge, 2000)

C. J. Tabraham, *Castles of Scotland* (Edinburgh, 2005)

Tim Tatton-Brown, *English Cathedrals* (London, 2002)

IDENTITIES

John Gillingham, *The English in the Twelfth Century: imperialism, national identity and political values* (Woodbridge, 2000)

Kathy Lavezzo, *Angels on the Edge of the World: geography, literature and the English community, 1000–1534* (Ithaca, 2006)

Huw Pryce and John Watts (eds.), *Power and Identity in the Middle Ages. Essays in Memory of Rees Davies* (Oxford, 2007)

Hugh M. Thomas, *The English and the Normans: ethnic hostility, assimilation and identity 1066–c.1220* (Oxford, 2003)

Hirokazu Tsurushima (ed.), *Nations in Medieval Britain* (Donington, 2010)

Thorlac Turville-Petre, *England the Nation: language, literature and national identity, 1290–1340* (Oxford, 1996)

Bruce Webster, *Medieval Scotland: the making of an identity* (London, 1997)

Subject Index

Index of People and Places

www.vintage-books.co.uk